MAKING THE MOST OF ACCREDITATION

About NAAC

The National Assessment and Accreditation Council (NAAC) is an autonomous organization, established by the University Grants Commission (UGC) in 1994, with its headquarters at Bangalore. The main function of NAAC is to assess and accredit institutions of higher education. The process of assessment and accreditation involves preparation of a Self-Study Report of the institution and validation of the same by the on-site visit of a team of assessors. The outcome of assessment and accreditation will be a grade which is valid up to 5 years. As of June 2003, more than five hundred institutions of higher education have been assessed by NAAC and there is an overall appreciation for the intrinsic benefits of quality assessment in the country.

Website: www.naac-india.com

About the Authors

Dr. Antony Stella is the Adviser of the National Assessment and Accreditation Council (NAAC). As one of the founding team of officers of NAAC, she has been a part of all its developmental activities for the past seven years. With a Ph.D. in educational technology, she has more than 75 papers and eight books – four on Assessment and Accreditation and the rest on education – to her credit. She has authored a Report for UNESCO about external quality assurance in India and co-edited two books on international perspectives and developments in quality assurance. She is the recipient of Shastri Indo-Canadian Faculty Research Award and Fulbright Post-doctoral Fellowship. She has visited many countries to share the country experience on quality assurance. As a Fulbright Scholar at the Center for Quality Assurance in International Education and the George Washington University, she has analysed the US experience of Quality Assurance in Higher Education. She has been consulted by many quality assurance agencies on various issues of quality assessment. She is a member of the International Reference Group of the Higher Education Quality Committee of South Africa.

Prof. A Gnanam has been a leading Plant Molecular Biologist-Biotechnologist before turning to be an educational administrator in early eighties. As a Fulbright Scholar he completed his graduate studies in Biochemistry from the State University at Raleigh. He taught Plant Sciences at Cornell University before he returned to continue his research in India. He established the now well-known School of Biological Sciences and the Centre for Plant Molecular Biology at Madurai Kamaraj University. He had guided many graduate students for their doctoral degree and published 140 scientific papers. He is a fellow and its senior Vice-President of Indian National Science Academy, New Delhi and the Indian Academy of Sciences. He is a recipient of many recognitions and awards. He turned to educational administration as the Vice-Chancellor of Bharathidasan, Madras and Pondicherry Universities successively. He became the Chairman of the National Assessment and Accreditation Council in India in 1995 and served as the Chairman of its Executive Committee till mid 2003. With additional responsibilities of the Director of NAAC during mid 1998- mid 2001, he has been instrumental to its growth. He is currently a member of the UNESCO Global Forum and the co-ordinator of the Asia-Pacific sub network of quality assurance agencies. He has published more than 30 articles and co-authored four books on higher education.

MAKING THE MOST OF ACCREDITATION

Balancing the National and International Developments in Higher Education

ANTONY STELLA

A. GNANAM

CONCEPT PUBLISHING COMPANY, NEW DELHI-110059

To a large extent, this book is based on the experiences of the authors with NAAC.But the opinions expressed and the inferences drawn on the issues taken up for discussion in this book are solely of the authors and they are not necessarily the official stand of NAAC.

ISBN 81-8069-069-5

First Published 2003

Published and Printed by
Ashok Kumar Mittal
Concept Publishing Company
A/15-16, Commercial Block, Mohan Garden
New Delhi-110059 (INDIA)

Phones : 25351460, 25351794
Fax : 091-11-25357103
E-mail : publishing@conceptpub.com

Preface

Quality Assurance in higher education is still an evolving mechanism. There are no set priorities and standards to follow. Every system of higher education has to evolve its own model of quality assurance taking into consideration both national and international developments. In different national contexts and with consequent variance in their procedures, quality assurance agencies are working towards the same purpose, namely, Quality Improvement. Thus, the evolution of quality assurance is marked by unity in diversity.

Consequently, there is a growing fund of knowledge based on the experiences in various issues of quality and quality assurance. However, at present this knowledge is highly fragmented; it is well developed only in a few countries, highly contextualised to their nations. However fragmented they are, the lessons of experience are always useful to broaden the horizons of thinking and for evolving a system of our own. Likewise, the Indian experience and its contribution to the various quality-related issues will be of advantage to others.

With the second largest system of higher education in the world—298 universities and more than 13,000 colleges—that caters to 8 million direct and full-time students with 0.4 million teachers, the Indian experience has made its mark. For such a large and diverse system, conceptualizing a national quality assurance mechanism and operationalizing the processes have been formidable tasks. Since its inception in 1994, the National Assessment and Accreditation Council (NAAC) had spent 3–4 years in evolving its policies, principles and instruments. During the same period, it also had strived hard to convince the academia of the merits of quality assurance. It has achieved reasonable success in its efforts. Today, quality assurance has moved from the initial stage of rejection by higher education institutions to the stage of appreciation.

As the Indian system of quality assurance evolves, it consolidates its strengths and expands its scope to be in tune with the international developments. Along with expansion and consolidation, more issues of fine-tuning surface, new challenges emerge and the system explores uncharted dimensions at the national as well as international levels. This book is an attempt to share those developmental issues and the international experiences with the hope that this would be useful to those interested in quality assurance of both national and transnational education.

Dr. Antony Stella
and
Prof. A. Gnanam

Acknowledgements

The authors wish to thank the academic community from all over the world for the encouragement and support extended to their earlier three publications in the general area of quality assurance in higher education. This has given them the courage to venture on this book, elaborating on the challenges ahead and the fine-tuning needed for quality assurance agencies like NAAC, in the context of national and international developments.

The first author is much beholden to a large number of international experts with whom she has had the opportunity of interacting in different fora. The first author is particularly grateful to the United States Educational Foundation of India (USEFI) for the award of the Fulbright postdoctoral fellowship which gave her the opportunity to analyse the Indo-US developments in quality assurance and to interact with many US experts and leading officials of the national and regional accrediting agencies.

Particular mention should be made of the valuable support extended by Dr. Marjorie Peace Lenn, Executive Director, Center for Quality Assurance in International Education (CQAIE), Washington DC. Thanks are also due to Dr. James Williams, George Washington University and the staff of the library of the American Council on Education (ACE). The up-to-date resource collection of the ACE library has enhanced the quality of the review of related literature needed for this book.

Lessons of Experience of NAAC (Chapter 4) is the modified version of the paper accepted for presentation in the INQAAHE-2003 conference. *Quality Assurance of Distance Education* (Chapter 7) has been published in the *Journal of Higher*

Education by Kluwer Academic Publishers, Netherlands and has been included in this book with their approval. Policies on conflict of interst and substantive changes (Chapter 5) and *Challenging the Post-Accreditation Complacency* (Chapter 8) have been published in the *University News* and have been included in this book with approval from the Association of Indian Universities. Chapters 9-12 are the modified version of the paper *Quality Assurance across National Boundaries: National Context and International Developments* published in University News and has been included in this book with approval from the Association of Indian Universities. *The Asia-Pacific Regional Cooperation in Quality Assurance* (Chapter 13) is the paper presented by the co-author in the UNESCO meet held in Lisbon in April 2001.

Last but not the least, thanks are due to a large number of experts associated with NAAC. The authors are thankful to all the authorities and officers of NAAC who have collectively contributed to its policies and procedures and subsequently to the success of external quality assurance in India.

Bangalore

Dr. Antony Stella
and
Prof. A. Gnanam

Contents

Abbreviations

AAUP	American Association of University Professors
AB	Accreditation Board, *(India)*
ABET	Accreditation Board for Engineering and Technology, *(USA)*
ACEJMC	Accrediting Council for Education, Journalism and Mass Communication, *(USA)*
AICTE	All India Council for Technical Education
AIU	Association of Indian Universities
APQN	Asia-Pacific Quality Network
ASEAN	Association of South East Asian Nations
AUAP	Association of Universities of Asia Pacific
AUN	ASEAN Universities Network
BITS	Birla Institute of Technology and Science, *(India)*
CEEC	Commission for Evaluation of College Education, *(Canada)*
CHEA	Council on Higher Education Accreditation, *(USA)*
CINDA	Centro Interuniversitario De Desarrollo, *(Chile)*
COPA	Council on Post-secondary Accreditation, *(USA)*
CORPA	Commission on Recognition of Post-secondary Accreditation, *(USA)*
DAAD	Deutscher Akademischer Austauschdienst (German Academic Exchange Service)
DCE	Directorate of Collegiate Education, *(India)*
DCI	Dental Council of India
DEC	Distance Education Council, *(India)*
DEI	Distance Education Institution
DETC	Distance Education and Training Council, *(USA)*
DST	Department of Science and Technology, *(India)*
EC	Executive Committee, *(NAAC, India)*
EQA	External Quality Assurance
GATE	Global Alliance for Transnational Education
GC	General Council, *(NAAC, India)*
GNP	Gross National Product

HE	Higher Education
HEFCE	Higher Education Funding Council of England
HEI	Higher Education Institution
HEQC	Higher Education Quality Council, *(England)*
HEQC	Higher Education Quality Committee, *(South Africa)*
IAUP	International Association of University Presidents
ICAR	Indian Council of Agricultural Research
ICT	Information and Communication Technology
IGNOU	Indira Gandhi National Open University, *(India)*
IIM	Indian Institute of Management
IIQ	International Institute for Quality
IISc	Indian Institute of Science
IIT	Indian Institute of Technology
ILT	Institute for Learning and Teaching, *(UK)*
INQAAHE	International Network of Quality Assurance Agencies in Higher Education
IQAC	Internal Quality Assurance Cell, *(India)*
IQRP	Internationalisation of Quality Review Project
ISO	International Organisation for Standardisation
MCI	Medical Council of India
MHRD	Ministry of Human Resources Development, *(India)*
MoA	Memorandum of Association
MoU	Memorandum of Understanding
MR	Mutual Recognition
MSA	Middle States Association, *(USA)*
NAAC	National Assessment and Accreditation Council, *(India)*
NABHE	National Accreditation Board for Higher Education
NBA	National Board of Accreditation, *(India)*
NCACS	North Central Association of Colleges and Schools, *(USA)*
NCTE	National Council for Teacher Education, *(India)*
NET	National Eligibility Testing
NIEPA	National Institute for Educational Planning and Administration, *(India)*
NPE	National Policy on Education
NQF	National Qualifications Framework
OCGS	Ontario Council for Graduate Studies, *(Canada)*
OECD	Organisation for Economic Cooperation and Development
OU	Open University
PB	Professional Body
PHE	Private Higher Education

PI	Performance Indicator
PoA	Programme of Action
QA	Quality Assurance
QAA	Quality Assurance Agency
QAI	Quality Assurance International
QCI	Quality Council of India
R&D	Research and Development
RAE	Research Assessment Exercise, *(UK)*
S&T	Science and Technology
SC	Speciality Council
SEAMEO	South East Asian Ministers of Education Organization
SEAMEO-RIHED	SEAMEO Regional Institute for Higher Education
SLET	State Level Eligibility Test
SOU	State Open University
TANSCHE	Tamil Nadu State Council for Higher Education
TQA	Teaching Quality Assessment, *(UK)*
UCTS	UMAP Credit Transfer Scheme
UGC	University Grants Commission, (*India*)
UHE	Universalization of Higher Education
UMAP	University Mobility in Asia and the Pacific
UNESCO	United Nations Educational, Scientific and Cultural Organization
UNESCO-PROAP	UNESCO Principal Office for Asia-Pacific
WGU	Western Governor's University, *(USA)*
WQR	World Quality Register
WTO	World Trade Organization
GATS	General Agreement on Trade in Services

Part I
The National Scenario

The higher education system is undergoing far-reaching transformations in the wake of rapid socio-economic changes the world over; India is no exception. Significant among the changes is the emergence of a quality assurance mechanism with national standards. With the second largest system of higher education with 8 million direct and full-time students and 0.4 million teachers, in more than 13,0C0 universities and colleges well spread out in 35 states, the Indian effort to evolve a viable national quality assurance mechanism over and above the national regulatory framework and its impact on the system in enhancing the overall quality of educational offerings carries a wealth of information for others. The chapters in this part highlight those developments and experiences.

1. New Paradigms in Higher Education

Higher education institutions of today face challenges that they have not faced before—the need for expansion coupled with the demand for diversity, the need to integrate with the rest of the world coupled with the competition at the international level and the like. They face now, not a paradigm shift, but a landslide of changing trends. The pressures of globalisation like the restructuring of the economic system and the consequent increase in the real and virtual mobility of people have made our traditional academic provisions out of place. Further, the erosion of the nation-state and its capacity to master the economic and political transformations, complex cultural changes like increasing homogenisation and multicultural realities, worldwide hegemony of the English language as the universal lingua franca and the spread of commercial culture demand new adjustment strategies. They have far-reaching impact on the citadels of higher learning the world over. To cope with the challenges of the new paradigms, a pragmatic approach, rather than any dogmatism is called for and that is the focus of this chapter.

Higher Education Institutions (HEIs) of today are expected to reorient their structure, retool their function, assure the quality of their products and remain accountable. They are to focus on international competitiveness of the national system of higher education and develop competencies along with knowledge of a new order. Application orientation, transdisciplinarity and heterogeneity in the skills needed for its mastery characterise knowledge of the new order. In addition, the HEIs have to be versatile in the increased use of the new forms of educational delivery systems that are based on Information and Communication Technologies (ICT), particularly the Internet. Resorting to these new sources and methods of learning has become crucial as they facilitate not only the students and the teachers in flexible educational transactions but also lifelong learning. More than anything else, the universities have to respond now to fast changing paradigms *faster* than ever. Analysing these demands on education and their implications, evaluating the options available and identifying the workable strategies are the need of the hour.

Characteristics of the New Paradigms

The new paradigms are characterised by the following major changes:

- Shift in the objective of higher education from transmission of knowledge to skill and competency building
- Change in the curricular transaction from a teacher-centered approach to a student-oriented approach
- Moving away from rigid curricula to a flexible curricular structure
- Growth in the non-traditional modes of educational provisions
- Introduction of new forms of educational delivery
- Replacing the traditional academic skills by computer-fortified skills

- Moving away from career specific qualifications towards more general training
- Increasing leaning towards private providers and private sources of funding
- Change in the general perception of education as public good to education as a tradable service
- Shift from a non-competitive ambience of higher education to a competitive environment
- Shift from national focus to international orientation

Most of these changes are necessitated by the demand for value-added human resources in a variety of settings that have proliferated due to the impact of science and technology. The higher education systems in different regions have been responding to this changing context differently. The different strategies to be adopted to meet the new paradigms, though they come under different domains in the educational structure, are not mutually exclusive. The successful implementation of these strategies requires coordination among the different functionaries of the education system as a whole. The teachers, institutions and the governments have to share the responsibility of bringing the intended changes. The major tasks to be done to cope with the new paradigms may be broadly grouped into five levels under the following familiar academic structural domains.

a) At the *curricular design level,* where there is a shift from 'knowledge intensive curricula' to 'skills intensive curricula'.
b) At the *curricular transaction level,* where the emergence of new forms of education requires teachers of higher education to become facilitators of learning through both conventional and new forms of education. The teachers require appropriate training and retraining to be effective in their roles.
c) At the *educational management and institutional governance level,* where the educational leaders like

principals of colleges and heads of university departments are the key players in managing the educational experiences of the students. The educational leaders too need to be equipped with appropriate management strategies.

d) At the *system level* of dispensing higher education, where there should be a shift from the present approach of 'inspection' to 'academic leadership'.

e) At the *national level,* where there is a need to create a *consistent higher education dimension* compatible with the region and competitive at the international level. This requires a balance between national priorities and international developments.

These five major tasks are elaborated in the following pages.

a) Curricular Design

In the institutionalised mass education system, the curriculum is the core around which the entire educational edifice is built. The curricular design outlines what is to be taught and what the students would acquire in totality during their period of study at the institution and the level of achievement they can hope to gain. Curriculum also determines the extent of resources to be mobilised, the infrastructure needed and the coordination to be ensured among the institutional managers and providers. Although the academic community has to ultimately build the curriculum, the increasing role of educational providers and employers is evident in the changing context.

To respond to the changing context, the curricular development needs to be built around the specific purpose for which the provisions are made. It should spell out explicitly the intended outcomes and be designed with appropriate strategies to achieve the intended outcomes. It should also contain, besides other details, a set of standard benchmarks to indicate the level of achievement a student can aspire to reach. Evolving subject benchmark statements, offering modular credit-based courses, and ensuring attainment of adequate level of skills and competencies are a few of the strategies towards this objective.

Subject Benchmark Statements

The subject benchmark statements provide a means to describe the nature and characteristics of the programmes in a specific subject leading to a qualification. They also represent general expectations about the standards of the qualification at a given level and outline the attributes and capabilities that those possessing such qualifications should be able to demonstrate. Such benchmark statements should accompany any programme leading to an award of degree or a diploma. (In the following discussion, the term 'programme' refers to the combination of courses of study leading to the award of a degree. The term 'course' refers to modules or units that constitute the programme.)

Modular Credit-Based Courses

Academic mobility is one of the key aspects of education in the new global context. Students demand flexibility in pursuing their studies to match their interest and talent. Modular credit-based courses have the potential to provide both flexibility and mobility in learning. It would enable students to have vertical as well as horizontal mobility without losing any time or credits gained as they progress in their studies. It would give them the advantage of transferring the credits gained from other institutions and other sources like fieldwork, industrial training and non-higher education avenues.

The integration of the semester system with choice-based credit courses would be more beneficial to students. The organisation and credit allotment of the modular courses should conform to the national standards indicating clearly the level of learning intended and should fall under the nationally consistent framework. It should also be emphasised that the modular curriculum is the best option to evolve a number of interdisciplinary and multidisciplinary programmes of varying hues to match the specific demands of expertise required for the highly diversified technology-intensive and skill-specific job market.

Skill and Competencies

The prime place given to knowledge in education appears to demand rethinking. It looks as though the era of acquiring knowledge for knowledge sake is over. With information storage and retrieval made easy by the computer and the internet revolution, to retain the transfer of knowledge as the only function of education seems to be out of place.

The curricula at the undergraduate and postgraduate levels require to be restructured to generate graduates with higher levels of general and cognitive skills and competencies. The present practice of preparing the syllabus for a degree course with the list of subject knowledge units related to the discipline has to be replaced. The shift from the 'knowledge-intensive curricula' to 'competency building of the learners' has to be clearly reflected in the curriculum.

The ability to read and use texts and other materials both critically and empathetically, appreciation of the complexity and diversity of situations and mentalities, and respect for other viewpoints are some of the basic skills and qualities of mind that have a premium in the contemporary employment market. The generic skills such as self-discipline, self direction, independence of mind, initiative, ability to work with others, ability to process information, capacity to solve problems, intellectual integrity and maturity are the other attributes that need to be integrated in the curricula of any subject of study. In addition, computational skills relating to the subject information are becoming essential. The other attributes that have a premium in the employment market are transferable skills such as communication, numeracy, interpersonal relationship skills, time management and self-learning, which are also generally subject neutral.

While selecting the content of the courses that make up the programme, due attention should be paid to ensure scope for developing each one of the skills and attributes mentioned above. A typical example is an assignment that allows the student to formulate, execute and complete an independent extended piece of written work with appropriate supervision. Likewise, the identified skills and competencies—subject-specific and subject-neutral—should form the core rubric around which the contents of the courses may be chosen and woven into. Modular courses increase the scope of integrating the skill and competency components with subject-based knowledge. If for some reason this is found difficult to do so, a stand-alone modular unit may be designed to train for these skills and attributes. They can complement the other academic courses and thus form part of the overall curriculum.

b) Curricular Transaction

Curricular transaction is the core function of educational institutions at all levels of education. Even with the best of curricular design, unless curricular transactions are effective and facilitative, the learning outcome of any programme will not be at the desired level. It is a multi-factorial transaction involving the teachers, students, learning resources, training centers, institutional links and academic management. The key factors of effective curricular transactions that require a reorientation in the changing context are highlighted below.

Professional Training of the Teachers

Academics in higher education are rarely 'trained' teachers. In the main they learn 'on the job'. As such they tend to perpetuate traditional methods in education and are often ill-equipped to facilitate learning and much less in training for the skills. Unfortunately, at the level of higher education, the stringent requirement of extensive training before practicing is not insisted upon for reasons that do not have a sound base. In the words of an educationist who sums up perfectly the challenge facing a lecturer, an untrained teacher at the tertiary education level, "the lecturer must guide the collection of individuals through territory the students are unfamiliar with, towards a meeting point, but without knowing where they are starting from, how much baggage they are carrying, and what kind of vehicle they are using."

In the present context, we need a professional approach for the development of academics as facilitators of learning and training of new knowledge and a range of skills and abilities. Today, the teachers in the tertiary level of education are required not only to engage in teaching the already existing body of knowledge but are also expected to create new knowledge. The aim of teaching then for a tertiary education teacher is not only to produce knowledgeable students, but also to develop students as 'critical thinkers' which is so essential for their success either at their work or at home or, if they choose to generate new knowledge through career in research (Harvey, 1997).

Teaching through the new forms of education such as distance education and online delivery requires skills of a different order. Just as much a classroom teacher need not be a good textbook writer, traditional teachers without specific training might not be effective in teaching through the emerging educational modes of delivery. A lesson writer or a contact teacher for the virtual university needs an in-depth understanding of the course-related knowledge, the knowledge-related skills, fluency in computer applications, information technology, and above all knowledge about the mind set and potential of the mature learners. There is an emerging need for a different class of teachers with different and/or additional skills in the non-traditional modes of learning environment.

Although no formal training is insisted upon for the tertiary level teachers in the Western world, there are ample opportunities for professional development in a non-formal way. Membership in professional societies, annual conventions and information exchange through high quality professional journals on pedagogy in higher education facilitate the tertiary level teachers to keep abreast with the current trends in the teaching profession. In the UK, the Institute for Learning and Teaching in Higher Education (ILT) is the professional body for all who teach and support learning in higher education in the UK. It exists to enhance the status of teaching, improve the experience of learning and support innovation. It also develops and maintains professional standards of practice. It is becoming the main source of professional recognition and professional development for all staff engaged in teaching and support of learning in higher education.

The importance of quality in teaching at the higher education level has been well recognised in developed countries. The quality audit of Australia in 1994 was based upon teaching and learning processes within higher education institutions. As a result many institutions started focusing on their teaching and learning processes, with an emphasis on improving the quality of these. A further indication of increasing efforts to improve the quality of teaching is the establishment of the Committee for the Advancement of University Teaching in 1993. This committee operates in a way similar to the Australian Research Council but provides liberal grants to develop improved methods/techniques for teaching.

The Australian Universities place importance on individual staff members' commitment to teaching quality.

In the eighties, commitment to high quality research in universities had meant that, academic staff could be appointed and promoted on the merit of their research alone, even though they were also expected to be involved in teaching. But now, staff members being considered for appointment and or promotion have to demonstrate commitment to quality teaching. One of the essential criteria to be assessed by selection panels is concerned with demonstrated commitment to quality of teaching. To assist further in enhancing quality teaching, many universities have established institution-wide arrangements similar to the longstanding institution-wide Research Committees.

In the UK, the teaching quality assessment exercises are mandatory for institutions of higher education to get public funding. The Learning and Teaching Support Network (LTSN) of ILT is a development that deserves a mention here. It is a network of 24 subject centers based in HEIs throughout the UK. The generic center of LTSN builds links between the subject centers and offers generic expertise on learning and teaching issues that cross subject boundaries.

Even in the USA, the institutional accreditation by the regional accrediting agencies has a primary focus on teaching/learning. Many other accrediting agencies explicitly declare in the guidelines that the primary focus is to assure quality of teaching. This indicates the importance the international community attaches to the quality and relevance of teaching/learning at the higher education level.

While these are the good models of the developed countries, the developing countries, unfortunately have very little of these activities for the benefit of the practicing teaching community and the Western model of professional improvement on the job is also not effective in the context of the developing countries. The alternative arrangement made available for the young collegiate teachers in India through the so-called Academic Staff Colleges, needs a mention. It is an ad hoc interim measure in which all that the teacher needs to know is condensed into a 21-day crash programme called "Orientation Course". However, it is not designed for the purpose of infusing professionalism of the order that is required now. There are not many professional trainers involved in those programmes to impart the professional skills required for the emerging forms of education. A formal training through a yearlong education programme like in the case of the teachers in the other levels is the best option for developing countries.

Viewed against this background, it is reasonable to expect that like any other profession, teaching also should be licensed formally after an appropriate level of training. For such training of the college and university teachers, detailed curricula should be evolved and the training structure should be firmed up. The content of such a programme should be relevant to the level of educational provisions and the age group of the students. Appropriate courses in educational psychology, general philosophy and principles of education, history of higher education systems and educational technology commonly required at this level will have to be developed. They need to be culled out from the available information as well as through appropriate research.

Evaluation

In many countries, the present system of examining student learning focuses only on the knowledge component without looking at the other objectives such as abilities and skills. Wherever large numbers of students are involved in examinations, the evaluation process has been reduced to the random sampling and testing of bits of subject based knowledge and finally reduced to testing of rote memory. Even the external examiner system seems to have been evolved as a result of the mistrust of the class teachers. Although effective in absolving the teacher concerned, it does not help either the evaluation per se or the quality enhancement of education. In fact, in most of the systems with a common examination body like the Indian system of an affiliating university with affiliated colleges, the affiliating functions of the parent university have been reduced to the routine of conducting university examinations annually as a ritual rather than for evaluating the real learning outcomes in all its dimensions.

In India, examination reforms have been attempted during the past 50 years without significantly improving what is being practiced. There are no standard settings for achievements and consequently, the interuniversity grades are not comparable. Consequently, there is a realisation that the system requires a continuous evaluation by the teachers/ field supervisors based on the levels of standards indicated in the curriculum. In fact, having the modular credit-based courses that constitute the programme with the involvement of a large number of teachers in an undergraduate programme of 3 or 4 years should remove any subjectivity or favouritism suspected in grading of the students. The final grade should reflect the level of achievement of students in acquiring knowledge and skills and abilities. To achieve this, the existing evaluation practice may need a reorientation in many systems.

In some of the Western countries, though the external examination is still continued, it is of a different type and serves a different purpose. In the UK, for example, the term 'external examiners' does not refer to the bunch of teachers belonging to other institutions evaluating every one of the answer scripts either at a central place or at their homes as is being practiced in India now. They use a team of experts trained to evaluate the educational outcome of the institutions, drawn from a national panel of examiners. They—generally a few of them—randomly choose about 10-15 per cent of the answer scripts already evaluated by the teachers concerned and assess whether the grades given are comparable nationally. They also evaluate the content of the curriculum and teaching effectiveness, and give an overall report on the performance of the students of a particular year in a particular subject. This report to the head of the institution is generally used as a feedback for further improving the quality of the offering and for various corrective measures. Their 'external evaluation' does not determine the grade of the students. In an indirect way it also promotes the objectivity of the internal examiners as their valuation is evaluated by a group of externals at least through a random sampling. In fact, the national quality assurance agency in that country uses the reports of the external examiners for their assessment exercise.

The feasibility of adopting this model may be tested in other systems through well-designed pilot projects using the willing HEIs. If it works well, it would be a major examination reform.

Shift from Teacher-Centered Education to Student-Oriented Learning Resources

In today's information-enriched world, the teacher is not the only source of knowledge and information and the classroom cannot be the only place of learning. In such an educational process, the skills of learning to learn, self-learning and lifelong-learning gain significance. Unless adequate and diverse learning resources in the campus are ensured there is very little scope for the students to acquire the self-learning skill. This requires the institutions to strengthen the other learning resources and build a variety of learning resources besides the traditional libraries. Internet surfing centers, audio-video centers with electronic forms of relevant learning materials, other avenues like debating clubs, laboratories, campus academic societies, field trips and institution linked work places are equally important learning resources for both academic and general skills. Further, learning materials should be structured for self-learning. Learning to learn will become one of the attributes expected of students to be successful in their career and life. Teacher availability for discussions and guidance, as a part of their duty will have to be ensured.

c) Educational Management and Institutional Governance

In any mass education system where thousands of students seek opportunities to pursue higher education and training, educational management and institutional governance become very important. Development of academic programmes that are relevant to the society, identifying targets for the short term, developing a long-term strategic plan, and many other functions are emerging as prerequisites for sound educational management. These require dynamic leadership and a facilitating governance structure.

Leadership

Educational institutions are expected to ensure that traditional goals are respected and at the same time accomplish future-oriented tasks in a climate of radical change. Pressure, change, restructuring and accountability—these are the words that reflect the harsh realities of our times and spell out the challenges the leaders of the education community have to face. To manage these changes, the head of the institution should have a blend of *experience* and *innovation.* Therefore careful attention in the choice and training of academic leaders as institutional heads should be exercised. The various roles they have to play and the challenges they have to face have made experts attempt to answer the question "What skills do administrators need to possess?"

The management experts talk about three kinds of skills for administrators—Technical Skills, Human Skills, Conceptual Skills. To these, one more could be added—the ability to design solutions. One of the recent studies has identified a high correlation between the excellence of institutions and the above-mentioned skills of the head. Yet another study has established the close relationship between the success of the institution and the head's ability to be centralised as well as decentralised depending on the appropriateness of the situation.

In India, the National Institute of Educational Planning and Administration (NIEPA) has done pioneering work in this field and one of the studies supported by NIEPA has listed as many as 53 skills required for the educational administrator to be successful. A few of the skills identified by NIEPA are given below as illustrative examples:

1. Curriculum Planning and Management
2. Management of Examination and Evaluation
3. Staff Appraisal
4. Staff Development including Recruitment
5. Budgeting
6. Mobilisation of Resources
7. Management of Student Information System
8. Guidance and Counselling Services
9. Inventory Control and Management
10. Organisational Diagnosis and Need Assessment
11. Project Formulation and Management
12. Conflict Management.

From the range of skills and attributes one expects from educational administrators, it becomes clear that we need *educational administrators of a new order* and the conventional mode of choosing the heads of the institutions by seniority may not be adequate or even appropriate for the new context. While experience matters a lot, leadership calls for many more abilities and appropriate training. There is a realisation now that the system of education might not pull on longer with the luxury of going by seniority alone.

Use of Technology

Technology has improved the overall standard of living in many ways. While we appreciate the advantages these modern tools have brought in, we have to think of the corresponding changes that these new things have ushered into our way of 'managing' and 'administering' the institutions. When we look for the impact of technological advancement on educational transactions—both academic and administrative—we find that our system of education is still uncomfortable with new technology. At a time when our educational institutions are expected to do more with less input, one should make use of the technological innovations that are readily available. Conscious effort to invest on hardware and to train the teaching and non-teaching staff suitably to remove the initial reluctance in using anything new and gadget-oriented is needed.

Academic Linkages

Today institutions of higher education are expected to work in partnership with industry and commerce for mutual benefit. The linkages with the major sectors of economic activities would provide practical training to students. The faculty and staff may have to proactively interact with the leaders of industry and commerce, consciously to develop expertise that would be of help to them. In fact such engagement with society and its activities is considered as an added function of the universities, besides teaching and research. Though this may not be an entirely new idea, the relevance and importance of an increased intensity and volume of such interactions require new academic management skills. Integrating the field experiences with academic programmes such as assigning credits for the field experience for the students, involving the leaders of commerce and industry in evaluating the student performance while at work would be a major task. Coordinating the placement and related activities and providing academic supervision at factories or shops will be a new experience even for the experienced teachers and it will need a different type of acumen for academic management.

Universities have always had linkages with national and foreign universities for research all along which now should be expanded to teaching as well. In an era of knowledge explosion and growth of multidisciplinary subjects, interactions with other institutions through formal linkages have become necessary. Further, the emergence of new forms of educational delivery systems with a large number of private providers has also put pressure on traditional institutions to diversify and establish linkages with other institutions. All formal education centers—universities and colleges—should expand their activities to non-formal educational provisions either as a part of continuing education or as a supplement to the formal programmes of studies.

The link between the formal and non-formal education provisions is also emerging as an issue of concern. For example, in India, all the 64-odd distance education centers are part of the diversification initiatives of the traditional universities. But, the formal and non-formal educational offerings are kept apart as distinct units even within the same university and no academic linkages have been formulated except perhaps for a few universities like the Pondicherry University. In the Pondicherry University, the students have the option to accrue credits through other delivery systems. The Indira Gandhi National Open University as well as the Community College and the Directorate of Distance Education of the Pondicherry University are recognised for earning credits. But such efforts are yet to be initiated in other universities.

Likewise most of the open university programmes in India are not linked with the formal educational provisions of the universities. To begin with, a formal link between the formal courses and the distance education provisions of the same university should be established. Such linkages can be fostered between the open universities of the country and the regular universities. Adoption of curricular materials, sharing faculty time, besides twinning arrangements for educational offerings are on the increase, but they should now be formalised to enhance the range of academic offerings particularly, for the use of 'copyrighted' online learning materials from other sources.

Institutional Governance

The changing context warrants the resetting of the institutional governance structure, organisational pattern, management strategy and functional tradition. The HEIs that draw public support have a similar common democratic governing structure the world over as most of them are patterned after the late medieval European models. The authorities and officers of HEIs are responsible for the design and delivery of the academic programmes and other social obligations. In Indian Universities, the Executive Committee (Syndicate or Board of Management), with a set of representatives from the various stakeholders provides the collective leadership and executes the academic and administrative functions through a full-time officer. The university may also have a senate/court or a larger body having its members drawn from a wider spectrum of stakeholders, providers and people from different walks of society, mainly to formulate general policies, amend them now and then to meet changing demands, monitor the progress annually and approve the budget. The other major authority is the Academic bodies with members drawn from the academia to advise on all matters of academic interest and the related guidelines in the form of academic ordinances and regulations. In addition, these authorities may have a few other minor ceremonial functions like convocation.

The above-mentioned structure would indicate that the basic organisational structure of any university does not differ much from that of a major corporate organisation or an industrial house. The institutions of higher learning are self-governing and enjoy academic freedom within the overall limits of the revenue budget of which the government grant is the major source. Corporate organisations and industrial houses also have similar freedom but have to function within the limits of their resources. In both the groups—universities and industrial houses—one can see both the extremes of good and bad levels of functional efficiency. It is not uncommon that big multinational companies fare poorly and fold up because of bad management. Apparently the trouble lies elsewhere; possibly the way in which these authorities are constituted needs a reorientation.

For example, in India, the university governance structure consists of three major authorities with functions well defined by the acts and statutes, the basic ground rules of any educational institution. The identities of these functions are however, based on 19th century expectations. Some factors that weaken the traditional but good governance structure of the universities in India could possibly be attributed to the following:

1. The nature and size of each one of the authorities as prescribed in the acts and statutes. In most of the institutions, there are too many members in these bodies, making it difficult to transact any reasonable agenda.
2. Membership to some of these bodies is gained through 'election', resulting in the members being more loyal to their constituency rather than making objective decisions.
3. Lack of coordination between these authorities while responding to changing contexts. None is responsible for the failure.
4. Exposure to internal and external pressures including those from bureaucratic, political and other groups.
5. Absence of basic management principles in the governance like principles of participation, decentralisation, autonomy for the smaller functional groups and accountability.
6. Not so clearly defined relationship of the government and funding agencies with the universities. In fact, all of them are anxious to regulate rather than

facilitate. The conflict of interest between the state and central agencies are often the source of hindrance rather than support.

7. Lack of sufficient resources to retrain the academic and administrative staff in modern methods of teaching and training, record keeping, accounting and other governance protocols using education technology, computers and communication networks.

(Source: *Report of the UGC Committee Towards New Educational Management, 1990*)

The recent trend seen in most of the states of India, more so in the southern part of the nation, to bring in a comprehensive and uniform act for their state universities is to be considered as an opportunity to restructure some of the archaic governance structures. So long as the basic structure is restricted to three or four authorities, most of the problems related to governance procedures may not get complicated and time-consuming. On the other hand, they would facilitate the effective functioning of these bodies. This would also be an occasion to introduce a few more reforms, as many would hesitate to amend the acts frequently. Instead of tinkering with the minor details as to who will select the vice-chancellor and how, and the tenure and terms of the vice-chancellor, this opportunity could be well used to bring in the long-pending corrective measures. They include improvements such as revising the size and composition of the various authorities. The 200-year-old University of London Act that formed the basis for all Indian universities cannot possibly meet the current demands of student and staff mobility across national boundaries, employability in the global job market and competitiveness/ attractiveness of our education to the students of other countries. Unless appropriate changes are made in the overall governance, the universities cannot be dynamic and be responsive to the changing expectations.

These weakening factors can be corrected without many financial inputs, provided there is a political will and concern for quality education. If one can make a conscious effort to clarify the roles and functions of the various university authorities and reduce their overlapping functions, most of the delays in decision-making at the institutional level can be reduced. Likewise, introduction of decentralised or self-management at different levels linked with accountability can help in avoiding the undue delays.

d) Systemic Changes

The changes at this level have more relevance to the Indian subcontinent, where the medieval practice of dispensing higher education through what is known as the affiliating system is prevalent. In this arrangement, the university provides the academic programmes and plays a regulatory role to ensure the satisfactory standards of education provided by the number of colleges 'affiliated' to it; neither the university nor the colleges have any choice on whether and with whom the affiliating relationship could be established. In essence, the parent university provides the curriculum and conducts the common examination and awards the degrees to all the successful students of the affiliated colleges. The university also regulates the functioning of the colleges in a number of ways including as to what academic programmes the colleges can run, the number of days in a year the colleges should work, and the like. The colleges admit students and teach the curriculum prescribed by the university and prepare the students for the common university examinations to be held at the end of each semester or academic year. As the universities do not fund the affiliated colleges, there is no direct financial obligation between them. This kind of relationship between the university and the colleges is maintained through legal provisions by the government, no other option being generally available. The universities generally confine themselves to postgraduate teaching and research leaving the bulk of the undergraduate studies to the colleges though there may be minor exceptions. This system worked well when the parent university had only 20 to 30 colleges to take care of. With the expansion of the system and with hundreds of colleges affiliated to them, over the years, the envisioned role of academic leadership of the universities has deteriorated except perhaps for the conduct of common examinations and the award of degrees to successful candidates. Consequently, neither the university nor the college is responsible for the quality of education. In the ultimate analysis, this kind of ambiguity has led to the deterioration of quality and standards of the qualifications and also in the substantial wastage in the educational efforts as seen from the percentage of failure in the examinations conducted by the university.

This affiliating model in which one provides the academic contents, another teaches and a third party (government) provides the funds is not suitable for a prompt response to the changing needs of society. An alternative system has to be found at the earliest. Declaring each one of the institutions as 'autonomous' with the provision to confer degrees in their name and thus own the responsibility of providing quality education and being accountable is the best option. In a small country—at least population-wise—like Japan there are 687 universities including 99 national universities, a figure which is comparable to the number of universities and colleges put together in any of the average-sized states like Tamil Nadu or Karnataka. Even if all the colleges in a state are declared as universities and made responsible for the quality of their academic provisions, the number may not exceed the number of universities even in the same-sized countries of the West. However, it needs preparation at the national level and HEIs should get ready to manage their affairs well without looking for props from elsewhere.

e) State and National Initiatives

In the global scenario, where the mobility of students and workforce across national boundaries is increasing, the national character of education should be built on comparability and competitiveness rather than being totally oriented to local conditions. Ensuring compatibility is only one of the many responsibilities of both the national and state governments to promote international mobility of graduates. There are other issues like foreign currency regulations, visa regulations and quality assurance modalities that cannot possibly be tackled by educational institutions. Only appropriate policy formulations, legislative facilitation and support by the national government can promote and sustain international mobility of the faculty and students, which will become crucial in the years to come.

Although it is very difficult to generalise at the level of national initiatives to be taken, the developing countries have a lot in common with the situation in India. In the context of the Indian system of higher education, there are three areas where concrete measures have to be taken—National Qualifications Framework, Firm policy on private initiatives in higher education, National Quality Assurance mechanism; areas requiring action in most of the developing countries.

National Qualifications Framework (NQF)

In the changing context at the global level, educational provisions should be designed to promote mobility of graduates both within and across national boundaries. The prerequisite for mobility is the recognition of the qualifications gained in one country by others. In order to achieve this, the qualifications framework in a given country should broadly conform to the trend seen internationally with sufficient and precise description of the purpose, content, duration and level of each one of the qualifications offered in the country in a general way.

The qualifications framework is considered as one of a number of measures to promote public understanding and confidence in academic standards. Besides, when the higher education system has to move from the sellers pedestal to the buyers market, objectives and usefulness of all the qualifications offered should be made clear to help stakeholders make meaningful choices. Therefore, the qualifications framework should be designed to provide:

- A structure of clear demarcation points by which one can distinguish the character level and the intended outcomes of qualifications
- A basis for a consistent use of qualification titles within the higher education system.

Such a national qualifications framework should encompass all of the existing qualifications, irrespective of their mode and structure of offerings such as annual or semester pattern, credit-based or otherwise and formal or non-formal mode of delivery. Precise, well-articulated descriptors should be brought out for each level of qualifications and for the sub-levels that spell out the learning outcomes at each stage.

Fortunately, because of the British legacy, the Indian system of higher education falls well within the general pattern prevailing in the UK and consequently in the Commonwealth and other Anglophonic countries of the world. However, there are variations in the structure and duration of academic programmes among the 35 states in the country. The overall pattern of 10+2+3 that was recommended a few decades back is yet to be implemented in some of the states. A few follow the 10+1+1+3 pattern with pre-university or junior colleges teaching the programme before the collegiate studies after 10 or 11 years of schooling. A few other states still linger with undergraduate 'Honours' programmes in addition to 'pass' courses, while most of the states have dispensed with this special category of undergraduate provisions. Many of the certificate and diploma programmes offered for varying duration ranging from three months to three years have not been properly slotted yet to be integrated with the various levels of qualifications offered normally. Consequently, the due credits for these diplomas are not counted for either credit transfer or for credit accumulation for a specific degree. The countries of the European Union, with diverse and non-comparable qualification structures and duration, have now agreed to have their higher education programmes uniformly structured into two main cycles of three years of undergraduate and two years of postgraduate studies. The qualifications framework of each of the awards now contains all details like purpose, content and plans along with what they now call diploma supplements. The credit structures of the various diplomas are also being streamlined to integrate them with the post-secondary education appropriately. A similar effort is taking place in the other regions of the world including India.

National Quality Assurance (NQA) Mechanism

The advent of a complex mass higher education system has led to the need to assure quality of the educational provisions. Having been the major provider of higher education all along, it is important that the national and state governments arrange for quality assurance mechanisms as a part of the higher education system in the country. Since the 1980s, with the increasing intake of students in higher education institutions and with a tendency to allow more autonomy to the often centrally steered higher education, establishment of structured quality assurance agencies has become a common phenomenon worldwide. Such national quality assurance agencies have either been established by the national governments or by the higher education institutions themselves.

In India, as most of the Indian higher education institutions were public institutions until recently, the Government of India took the initiative to establish the national quality assurance agency known as National

Assessment and Accreditation Council (NAAC). It was established with the twin objectives of fostering quality enhancement and accountability of these public-funded educational institutions. In addition there are two more accrediting bodies functioning, one for technical and engineering education and the other for agriculture education, established as in-house agencies of the national councils catering to those two professional sectors. The specialty councils like Medical Council of India and Dental Council of India are envisaging their own accrediting bodies.

Although the assessment and accreditation by NAAC is gaining general acceptance among the academia, it has to conform to certain international criteria for worldwide recognition of its accreditation outcome. It can be achieved only with the backing of both the national and state governments by making NAAC reasonably autonomous and helping it to assess and accredit all the national institutions of higher learning as early as possible. This can be achieved by linking the outcomes of assessment to certain monetary or non-monetary incentives. The University Grants Commission of India has given a momentum to NAAC's process by linking a part of its funding with accreditation status. Such linkages are in place in countries like Japan and UK. In Japan, by law all universities are made to undergo self-analysis and self-evaluation. It is also mandatory for them to seek external evaluation by the approved national agencies. In Japan, there are two major national accreditation agencies which are supported by the member universities but are fairly independent. Of the 687 universities including 99 national universities in Japan, 281 universities including 42 national ones are full members of the Japan University Accreditation Association (JUAA). Most of the traditional universities are covered either by the National Institute for Academic Degrees (NIAD) or JUAA. One should understand that neither NIAD nor JUAA are strictly national but due to the government's insistence that HEIs should be accredited by one of the approved accrediting bodies, they have acquired the status of national Quality Assurance (QA) systems.

Similar trends can be seen in many other countries as well. Moving away from the traditional inspection oriented and centralised regulation of higher education by the government or its agencies and increasing reliance on the outcomes of national quality assurance bodies will integrate quality assurance with the higher education system. There has been an increasing awareness that only such externalised quality evaluating mechanisms can help in gaining worldwide recognition of qualifications that is essential for the mobility of students globally.

Promotion of Private Higher Education

It has been the experience of both the developed and developing countries that the government cannot provide free higher education to all in the relevant age group and to the adult learners who have to constantly refresh their knowledge and training related to their careers. India, being one of the largest countries of the world with a population of a billion, cannot possibly hope to spend more than what it has been spending all along. In fact, anticipating this reality of financial crunch for any massive expansion, both the national and state governments stopped establishing public institutions about 20 years ago and have been encouraging private initiatives. Now in many states, particularly in the southern part of India, there are more private colleges than the public ones, though they cater only to about 30 per cent of the total student enrollment in higher education.

This move towards private participation in education is reversal to pre-independence practice, when private institutions were predominant at all levels. Only after the national government was established in 1947, all the private institutions were nationalised and funded by the government as a policy towards national development. As the government now finds it difficult to sustain its support to the existing institutions and has no funds to establish more institutions, the private providers are allowed to come to the field. However, though the inevitability of resorting to private participation is understood well, there is some reluctance in trusting their *bona fides* and their ability to provide quality education. Although the private initiatives are not supposed to have the "for profit only" approach, the private institutions are suspected for their possible exploitative tendency and their lack of commitment in ensuring equity. Nonetheless, the private institutions have come up in large numbers. They should now be brought into the mainstream with appropriate policies and helped to establish themselves with some support. Providing 10 to 20 per cent of their expenses as grants, allocating lands for these institutions on a long lease, extending generous scholarship schemes and loans to students of these institutions to match the high fee structure of these institutions etc., are ways in which the government can help the private institutions. In fact, in the USA and some of the developed nations, the difference between the private and public institutions is only in the marginal difference in the public support given to them. While the public institutions get about 50 per cent of the budget as government grants, the private ones are provided with about 25 per cent.

Another issue of equal importance in India is whether or not to have private universities. The private university bill introduced some years ago is still pending before the parliament for approval for want of political will. The reluctance on the part of the elected parliamentarians to pass this bill is largely due to their concern about equity. If private colleges can function, it should be possible to allow private universities also to function. One can hope, if the private university bill is passed, that major corporate groups with substantial finances can enter and provide a healthy competitive environment for the public universities to function. A beginning has been made in this direction by allowing private deemed universities to be established.

Besides the issues discussed above, there are many more concerns that need the attention of the governments at the policy level in the context of globalisation. The implication is that they have to be tackled appropriately and collectively by all the stakeholders, taking action at different levels of the system's functioning. For example, the institutions individually or collectively cannot possibly undertake any policy-based reformative measures, which may involve the interplay of various ministries. With the advent of private providers including the transnational ones, a national framework that would need a dialogue between more than one ministry is necessary. The ministries have to take a fresh look at the role of the national quality assurance agencies in these dialogues. Likewise promoting regional or global collaboration in education can be achieved only through a dialogue between the education ministers of the participating countries. The Bologna declaration is a typical example of such ministerial level commitments. Similarly, with the advent of borderless education through electronic media, national infrastructure like communication and computer facilities have to be developed with enormous inputs and these can be achieved only with the political will of the nation. These and the related issues are elaborated in the later chapters, with a specific focus on quality assurance in higher education.

2. The Accreditation System in India

In India, improving the quality of higher education has always been the focus of various higher education reforms. However, the explicit focus on quality assurance through accreditation is relatively new. The national context, the built-in quality controls and the way the accreditation bodies evolved during the last decade have valuable lessons for emerging quality assurance systems. The sharing of information and experiences is always useful to broaden the horizons and helps in analysis and evaluation. However, the experiences of one country may not offer a perfect solution to the problems under consideration of another country, since any strategy has to necessarily take cognizance of the contextual conditions. The Indian scenario should be viewed with this understanding.

The accreditation experience of India may seem to be just a few years old; but it should be seen against the backdrop of the quality controls the Indian higher education system had for the past 150 years, most of them being a British legacy. Various regulatory stipulations on minimum requirements for the establishment and expansion of institutions of higher education have been well in place for more than fifty years. The annual inspections and audits by the state governments, affiliating function of the universities to monitor the colleges, performance appraisal of universities by the University Grants Commission and review by the funding agencies all have contributed to ensuring 'satisfactory functioning'. Inspection and certification by professional bodies, which is primarily a recognition or approval process and for licensure to practice the profession, has been in place for a long time. If these built-in regulatory mechanisms can also be counted as quality assurance mechanisms, the Indian system of quality assurance may be said to be more than a century old. However, accreditation as an "explicit national external quality assurance mechanism" made its presence felt only during the 1990s.

The term 'accreditation' is used to denote different things in different countries. In the USA, which is the pioneer in accreditation, the process of accreditation is "equivalent of other countries' ministerial recognition of institutions belonging to the national system" (www.ed.gov). But the national accreditation in India is a process over and above the regulatory or recognition mechanisms. Consequently, the objective for such a mechanism is different from that of the existing systems of regulation in the country. It aims to lead institutions of higher education towards maximising their potential for quality education, contrary to the minimum standards ensured by the regulatory mechanisms.

The International Network for Quality Assurance Agencies in Higher Education (INQAAHE) defines accreditation by using the generic term 'Quality Assurance'. The INQAAHE definition of Quality Assurance is as follows: "...quality assurance may relate to a programme, an institution or a whole higher education system. In each case, quality assurance is all of those attitudes, objects, actions, and procedures, which, through their existence and use, and together with the quality control activities, ensure that appropriate academic standards are being maintained and enhanced in and by each programme. Quality assurance extends to making the process and standards known to the educational community and the public at large." In the light of this definition, the built-in regulatory mechanisms of the Indian system can be equated with the quality assurance mechanisms that serve similar purposes elsewhere. However, accreditation as the national external quality assurance mechanism was initiated only in 1994. This makes the Indian system of accreditation unique in many ways and from the initial stages there was a consensus that such a mechanism should focus on excellence in standards rather than satisfactory functioning. In fact, revamping the existing regulatory mechanisms would do well to ensure minimal functioning but the goal of Indian higher education today is to move towards "excellence" rather than "adequacy". A note on the existing checks and schemes follows.

Checks and Schemes that Already Exist

University Grants Commission

When the University Grants Commission (UGC) was established in 1956, it was given the mandate to be responsible for the determination and maintenance of standards of higher education. Section 12 of the UGC Act of 1956 states: "*It shall be the general duty of the Commission to take, in consultation with the Universities or other bodies concerned, all such steps as it may think fit for the promotion and coordination of University education and for the determination and maintenance of standards of teaching, examination and research in Universities...*" (UGC Act 1956, p.10). Towards fulfilling this mandate, UGC has evolved various strategies, mostly guidelines, such as the "Minimum Standards of Instruction for the Grant of the First Degree through Formal Education" and "Regulations for the Non-formal/Distance Education Mode". The other efforts include the introduction of the *National Eligibility Test,* commonly known by its acronym NET, to establish higher standards of teaching. It is a nationwide test conducted in different subjects based on syllabi prescribed by UGC, to certify the minimum capability of those who aspire to become teachers in higher education. NET is being conducted by UGC and CSIR since 1989 for eligibility for lectureship and research fellowship. Around 50,000 students appear for the test every year. The pass percentage is around 5 per cent. Eight State-level Tests known as SLETs have been accredited at par with NET. Only those who clear NET or its equivalent at the state level are eligible for teaching positions in higher education institutions. Institutions that do not comply with these guidelines are not eligible to get financial support from UGC.

UGC also initiates special schemes to enrich the quality of higher education. The inter-university centers are noteworthy efforts towards providing the best facilities in chosen subject areas. These centers were set up as autonomous bodies to provide common facilities, since heavy investment in infrastructure is beyond the reach of the individual university. In addition to the Inter-University Centers, UGC has set up other national facilities. The inter-university centers and the national facilities provide service to the universities in research, library networking, audio-visual communication, information resources, etc. to improve the quality of learning, teaching and research. *Academic Staff Colleges* are another effort of UGC to reorient the in-service teachers through orientation and refresher courses. Curriculum Development Centers, UGC Panels on Subject Areas in 27 subjects, Examination reforms and Question banks are other areas through which UGC is trying to enhance the quality of higher education. In addition, financial assistance is available under various schemes like special assistance for research, automation of libraries, electronic networking of libraries, and audio-visual research centers.

Universities and their Affiliating Functions

In the case of colleges, the affiliating functions of the universities take care of some of the essential infrastructural and other facilities to be fulfilled by the colleges. India follows the erstwhile London University Model where the colleges are attached to a parent university in accordance with the predetermined geographical jurisdiction of the university. Only the universities and university level institutions have the power to award degrees. The affiliating university legislates on courses of study and holds examinations centrally on common syllabi for its affiliates. It has the power to inspect the colleges and scrutinise their financial and academic records. In many universities the university also nominates the experts on the selection committees for the teachers and the principals. Most Indian universities are of the affiliating type with the larger ones like the Osmania University in the state of Andhra Pradesh and Bangalore University in the state of Karnataka having more than 400 affiliated colleges. This system was effective when a parent university had around 30-40 affiliates. But the growth in the number of affiliates has reduced the role of academic leadership of universities to a mere monitoring of minimum requirements.

The States and the Center

The state governments, which are the major providers of the state universities and colleges of the respective states, have their annual audit and review mechanisms. The center also has similar mechanisms. The coordination and cooperation between the Union and the States is brought about in the field of education through the Central Advisory Board of Education (CABE). However, all that these providers do is to oversee the monitoring mechanisms through financial and academic audit and satisfy themselves that minimal performance has taken place. The major concern of the governments has been to increase access to higher education and quality is entrusted to the affiliating functions.

The Professional Bodies

Apart from the review committees, inspections and internal regulatory mechanisms in the UGC-University-Colleges chain, the professional bodies play a significant role in licensing and ensuring quality in professional areas such as medicine, engineering, law, education and agriculture. While UGC is responsible for coordination, determination and maintenance of overall standards, the professional bodies are responsible for certification of the professional programmes and authorising the candidates to practice their profession. Some of them are authorised to release grants under specific heads and make policy recommendations on funding. There are more than 30 such bodies of which the following are statutory in India for various considerations:

- All India Council for Technical Education (AICTE)
- Distance Education Council (DEC)
- Indian Council for Agriculture Research (ICAR)
- National Council for Teacher Education (NCTE)
- Medical Council of India (MCI)
- Pharmacy Council of India
- Indian Nursing Council
- Dental Council of India
- Central Council of Homeopathy
- Rehabilitation Council of India
- Central Council of Indian Medicine
- Bar Council of India

The All India Council for Technical Education (AICTE) was established in 1987 by an Act of Parliament as a statutory body for planning and coordinating the growth of technical education in the country. It also has the responsibility to assure the quality of technical education imparted by the institutions in the country. The approval of AICTE for establishing new institutions or for starting new programmes is based on the credibility of the institution, assurance of compliance to AICTE norms, prior approval by the state government and parent university and Market sensitivity to the programme output.

Distance Education Council (DEC) was established in 1985 by IGNOU and it has the mandate for promotion and maintenance of standards in distance education. The policies and programmes of DEC are accordingly designed to effect improvement in the teaching–learning process of distance education

The Indian Council of Agricultural Research (ICAR) is an autonomous apex national organisation registered as a society which plans, conducts and promotes research, education, training and transfer of technology for advancement of agriculture and allied sciences. It was set up as early as 1929 by the British on the recommendations of the Royal Commission on Agriculture. It was re-organised in 1965, and again in 1973. Over the years it has developed a huge research and training infrastructure to work on production and other emerging problems in agriculture. It operates through 46 Central Research Institutes, 4 National Bureaus, 10 Project Directorates, 27 National Research Centres, 261 Krishi Vigyan Kendras and 8 Trainers Training Centres.

The National Council for Teacher Education (NCTE) was established by an Act of Parliament and is responsible for planned and coordinated development for the teacher education system throughout the country. The council regulates and maintains norms and standards in teacher education and gives recognition to institutions offering courses or training in teacher education.

Medical Council of India (MCI) was established as a statutory body with the aim of maintaining uniform standards of medical education in the country at the undergraduate and postgraduate levels. It is mandatory for a doctor to register himself with the council after gathering necessary medical qualifications. Another important function of the council is to establish reciprocity with foreign countries in the matter of mutual recognition of medical qualifications. The council also maintains the Indian Medical Register containing information about all the medical practitioners in the country.

Pharmacy Council of India prescribes, regulates and maintains minimum educational standards for the training of pharmacists. It prescribes the syllabus, norms, etc. for the institutions and regulations for the diploma course in pharmacy. It registers pharmacists.

Indian Nursing Council is responsible for regulation and maintenance of a uniform standard of training for nurses, midwives, auxiliary nurse-midwives and health visitors. It prescribes the syllabus and regulations for various nursing courses. It inspects nursing schools and examination centers to maintain uniformity and the requisite standard of nursing education.

Dental Council of India's main objective is to regulate dental education, the dental profession and dental ethics in the country. It recommends to the Government of India to accord permission to start a dental college, start a higher course and increase the seats.

Rehabilitation Council of India (RCI) regulates the training policies and programmes in the field of rehabilitation and standardises training courses for paramedics engaged in rehabilitation of people with disabilities. Like MCI it also establishes reciprocity with foreign universities/institutes in the matter of mutual recognition of qualifications awarded in the field of rehabilitation. It also maintains the Central Rehabilitation Register of persons possessing the recognised rehabilitation qualification.

Central Council of Homeopathy is a statutory body responsible for laying down the minimum standards of education in homeopathy and recognising or derecognising medical qualifications. It advises the central government in matters connected with the study and practice of homeopathy. The council also maintains a Central Register of Homoeopathy containing details of homoeopath practitioners.

Central Council of Indian Medicine is responsible for laying down and maintaining uniform standards of education in the fields of ayurveda, siddha and unani and regulating practice in these systems. The council prescribes the curriculum and syllabus for undergraduate and postgraduate education in these systems and amends them from time to time as per requirement. It also advises the central government in matters relating to recognition of medical qualifications of Indian Medicine. The council also maintains a Central Register of Indian Medicine containing details of practitioners of these systems.

The Bar Council of India is empowered to make rules to discharge its functions under the Advocates Act, 1961. An important rule-making power is with reference to laying down guidelines for the standards of professional conduct and etiquette to be observed by advocates. The Bar Council of India may prescribe rules for a class or category of persons entitled to be enrolled as advocates. The Bar Council of India can also specify the conditions subject to which an advocate must have the right to practice and the circumstances under which a person must be deemed to practise as an advocate in a court.

It should be noted that these professional bodies are not to be equated with quality assurance agencies though they may have quality assurance as one of their objectives. Some of the professional bodies have established separate mechanisms for accreditation and a few others are contemplating to do the same. The initiatives of AICTE, ICAR and DEC to monitor the quality of engineering-related, agriculture-related and distance education provisions respectively are discussed in detail in a later part of this chapter.

A multi-faculty university with faculties of studies in all the above-mentioned areas may have to undergo the on-site visit and assessment by each one of these professional bodies. These bodies are regulatory in nature to look into the minimal requirements. For example, Medical Council of India, Dental Council and National Council of Teacher Education have the overseeing function to ensure that institutions have the optimal facilities and potential to run programmes satisfactorily.

Need for a New Initiative

In spite of the built-in regulatory mechanisms mentioned above, there is increasing criticism that the country has permitted the mushrooming of institutions of higher education with substandard facilities. It was felt that many of the preconditions which ensured educational quality while granting affiliation to colleges, have been either ignored or soft-pedaled, with the result that many substandard institutions have come into existence, with the possibility of many more getting created. This has led to the dilution of standards of the higher education system that was already deficient in some respects (Nair, S., 1990). To address the issues of deterioration in quality, the National Policy on Education-1986 (NPE-1986) noted a few major steps that include the following:

- *Excellence in performance of institutions and individuals will be recognised and rewarded. The emergence of substandard institutions will be checked. A climate conducive to excellence and innovation will be promoted with full involvement of the faculty.*
- *Select institutions will be awarded academic, administrative and financial autonomy of varying degrees, building in safeguards with respect to accountability.*

Again, under the section 'To make the system work', the policy document identified that the strategy would consist of creation of a system of performance appraisals of institutions according to standards and norms set at the national or state levels. To translate the recommendations of the policy document into action, the Programme of Action (PoA) was evolved which spelt out the strategies to achieve the objectives. Both the policy document and the PoA-1986 *inter alia* recommended the establishment of a national accreditation body. In 1992 the revised policy document and programme of action were approved by the Parliament. The revised policy document (1992) also laid stress on the need to take urgent steps to protect the system from degradation. Due to the policy recommendations, the accreditation movement in India was given a significant momentum.

Today, there are three bodies performing accreditation in Indian Higher Education — the National Assessment and Accreditation Council (NAAC) established by UGC as an autonomous body, the National Board of Accreditation (NBA) established by AICTE and the Accreditation Board (AB) of the ICAR. While NBA and AB function as units of their respective parent body, NAAC has been established as an autonomous body and hence truly qualifies to be a national external quality assurance agency. A brief account of the quality assurance efforts of these three agencies follows.

Quality Assurance of Engineering Education

AICTE set up the National Board of Accreditation (NBA) in September 1994 as an in-house unit to assess the qualitative aspects of educational programmes offered by the engineering institutions in the country. NBA accredits programmes from the diploma level to the postgraduate level, rather than institutions. So far NBA has accredited about 400 programmes in engineering and management. It is voluntary on the part of the institutions to get their programmes accredited by NBA.

NBA documents define accreditation as "a process of quality assurance, giving credit where it is due for some clearly visible and demonstrable strategies of academic activities and objectives of the institutions, known to be honestly pursued and efficiently achieved by the resources currently available with a potential for continuous improvement in quality for effective growth". An institution with the programme approved by the AICTE is eligible to apply for NBA accreditation if at least two batches of students have passed out of the programme. Under the provisions of the AICTE Act of 1987, all diploma, degree and postgraduate programmes that come under the following disciplines are eligible to apply for NBA accreditation:

- Engineering and Technology
- Management
- Architecture
- Pharmacy
- Hotel Management and Catering Technology
- Town and Country Planning
- Applied Arts and Crafts

The standard methodology of self-study and peer review is followed for accreditation. The visiting team assesses the programme for the following criteria and with the weightages listed below.

For undergraduate programmes

Human Resources: Faculty	200
Students	100
Finance and Physical Resources	100
Mission, Goals	100

Research and Development	030
Industry-Institute Interaction	070
Supplementary Process	050
Teaching-Learning Processes	350

For postgraduate programmes

Human Resource: Faculty	200
Students	100
Finance and Physical Resource	080
Mission, Goals	070
Research and Development	150
Industry-Institute Interaction	100
Supplementary Process	050
Teaching-Learning Processes	250

The visiting team consists of a chairperson and two programme experts, one of them chosen from the industry or end-user organisation. The team members are either senior academics or engineers, who are selected on the basis of their standing in the profession. The visiting team also assesses parameters like academic ambience and institutional morale, which are not obvious from quantitative data. The visiting team provides scores on the basis of its assessment and the programmes are finally accorded Quality Grading. Team recommendations are presented to the Sectoral Committee. NBA considers the recommendations of the Sectoral Committee and takes a final decision. The results are placed in the Executive Committee of AICTE for information. The results are notified and published in the *Directory of Accredited Programmes*.

NBA has revised the grading pattern since January 2003 to a two-part grading system *i.e.* Accredited and Not accredited. Those programmes which score more than 650 marks will be considered as Accredited whereas those who score less than 650 will be Not Accredited. In order to differentiate between the programmes getting more than 650 marks, the programmes which score between 650-750 will be Accredited for a period of 3 years, whereas those institutions which score more than 750 will be Accredited for a period of 5 years.

Institutional Accreditation by NAAC

According to Section 12 CCC of the UGC Act, UGC may establish *"institutions for providing common facilities, services and programmes for a group of universities or for the universities in general and maintain such institutions or provide for their maintenance by allocating and disbursing out of the Fund of the Commission such grants as the Commission may deem necessary"* (UGC Act 1956, p.11). The National Assessment and Accreditation Council (NAAC) was established under this provision by UGC in 1994 as an autonomous body with the mandate to assess and accredit institutions of higher education or the units thereof in the country. In line with the international trend, NAAC follows a three-stage process for accrediting a unit of assessment:

- Preparation and submission of self-study report by the unit of assessment
- On-site visit of the peer team for validation of the report and for recommending the assessment outcome to NAAC
- Final decision by the Executive Council of NAAC.

Accreditation by NAAC is voluntary and the outcome is valid for a period of 5 years. As of June, 2003, around 500 institutions have been accredited by NAAC. During the first phase of assessment, NAAC consciously promoted institutional accreditation. Although there are many reasons for promoting institutional accreditation, NAAC has recognised that the institutional assessment and department/

programme assessment are not alternatives and that there is no institutional review without assessing the constituent departments of studies. NAAC has the provision and a separate process to assess and accredit departments if the institution prefers.

The Academic Advisory Committee (AAC) of NAAC advises NAAC on such issues. It is a statutory body "*created for the purpose of monitoring and promoting the activities of NAAC with reference to various publication, selection and shaping of instruments of Assessment and Accreditation, modalities of operation in charge, the rules, regulation and guidelines*" (MoA of NAAC). Based on the AAC's recommendations, the criteria for assessment, grading pattern and the methodology of self-study with peer review have been kept the same for both institutional and departmental accreditation, but with a difference in focus. While institutional accreditation is open to both universities and colleges, departmental accreditation is open only to university departments. However, NAAC is yet to carry out any departmental accreditation.

In practice, an institution that wishes to volunteer for assessment sends a letter of intent to NAAC with the basic details of its eligibility. Only the universities that are recognised by UGC and institutions that offer programmes approved and recognised by either a parent university or by a statutory professional council are eligible to volunteer. Further, the institution should have been in existence for at least five years or at least two batches of students should have passed out of the institution. At present, the seven criteria, namely, Curricular Aspects; Teaching-learning and Evaluation; Research, Consultancy and Extension; Infrastructure and Learning Resources; Student Support and Progression; Organisation and Management, and Healthy Practices, form the basis for assessment. The self-study report is expected to cover these areas.

The validation of the self-study report and the

subsequent assessment lead to an overall institutional grade and a detailed report, which begins with the team agreeing on the criterion-wise scores. Taking cognizance of the variance in types of institutions, different criteria have been allotted differential weightages. The weightages marked below are used for calculating the institutional score.

Criteria	*University*	*Affiliated/ Constituent Colleges*	*Autonomous Colleges*
Curricular Aspects	15	10	15
Teaching-learning and Evaluation	25	40	30
Research, Consultancy and Extension	15	05	10
Infrastructure and Learning Resources	15	15	15
Student Support and Progression	10	10	10
Organisation and Management	10	10	10
Healthy Practices	10	10	10

The peer team's job ends with assigning criterion scores, calculating the weighted average (which is also the institutional score) and writing a detailed assessment report. NAAC assigns the institutional grade on a nine-point scale based on the institutional score. Till 14 March 2002 NAAC was following a five-point grading system. Around 240 institutions had been assessed under this pattern. As a result of the recommendations of the UGC Committee on NAAC's Policy and Procedures (2001) and consequent deliberations, NAAC has adopted the nine-point scale with effect from 15 March, 2002.

In the new grading system, if the overall score is equal to or more than 55 per cent, the institution gets the "Accredited status" and any score less than that will lead to "Not Accredited" status. The accredited institutions are graded on a nine-point scale with the following scale values:

New Grading System

Grade	*Institutional score (upper limit exclusive)*
A++	95-100
A+	90-95
A	85-90
B++	80-85
B+	75-80
B	70-75
C++	65-70
C+	60-65
C	55-60

The grade will also be supplemented by a qualitative report by the team that would highlight the strengths and weaknesses of the institution under various criteria. Institutions, which do not attain the minimum 55 per cent points for accreditation, would also be intimated and notified indicating that the institution is "Assessed And Found Not Qualified For Accreditation".

Quality Assurance of Agriculture Education

ICAR established its Accreditation Board (AB) in 1996 to set, enforce and monitor compliance with norms and standards for agricultural education in India. The Board is assisted by three Sectoral Committees: a) Accreditation Norms and New Institutions/Programmes, b) Curricula and Equivalence, and c) Governance and Personnel and Financial Policies. The Director-General of the ICAR is the ex-officio Chairperson of the Board, which has membership from agricultural universities, national accrediting agencies and eminent persons from agriculture, industry, etc.

According to AB, "accreditation is a process of assuring acceptable institutional quality and a tool for improving educational standards." Institutions are assessed with reference to the following criteria:

- The institution has clear and publicly stated objectives consistent with its mission.
- The institution has organised effectively human, financial and physical resources, necessary to accomplish its objectives.
- The institution is accomplishing its educational objectives.
- The institution can continue to accomplish its objectives and improve its quality of educational programmes and effectiveness.

AB has also identified the General Institutional Requirements that include areas such as authorisation, governance, mission, academic programmes, faculty, students welfare, library and learning centres, physical facilities, financial resources, research and extension education, public information system, etc. As of now, AB covers only the public-funded institutions. It has not extended its process to the private institutions that offer agricultural programmes covering 30–35 per cent of the undergraduates and 5–7 per cent of the postgraduates of the country. Thus AB functions as an in-house unit of ICAR and restricts its activities only to those institutions that are established and/or funded by ICAR.

The first assessment visit can be held once the institution successfully sends out one batch of students. The process of accreditation is the same as the one followed by other agencies like NAAC and NBA—self-study and peer review. The evaluation team records one of the three recommendations—accreditation, provisional accreditation, no accreditation—with substantive reasons. The self-study report of the institution and the report of the evaluation team are reviewed by the Education Division and the recommendations are submitted to the Accreditation Board. The Board takes the final decision. The accreditation status is valid for a period of five to ten years. Based on the suggestions of the evaluation team, the Board may ask an institution to overcome any deficiency within a specified time schedule. The implementation of the recommendations are monitored by the Education Division and reported to the Accreditation Board annually. In case AB is not satisfied with the efforts and progress made in overcoming the deficiencies, the funding may be reduced/stopped, till the situation improves. ICAR being the funding body also for the agricultural institutions covered by AB, no accreditation fee is charged. The first accreditation visit was organised by AB during November 1998 and the result was announced in August 1999. As of mid-2002, AB has accredited four agricultural universities along with their thirty-two out of thirty-five constituent colleges. It is proposed to complete the accreditation process by the year 2004 for all 35 Agricultural Universities with their 200 constituent colleges. Around 20 agricultural universities with more than 100 constituent colleges are at various stages of the accreditation process.

Quality Assurance of Distance Education

Of the 298 university level institutions in India, 64 have established their distance education units. At present, there are ten open universities—IGNOU (1985) as the National Open University and nine State Open Universities (SOUs). While there is an increase in the number of distance education providers and takers, the purpose of some of the distance education initiatives and their effectiveness are debatable. In most of the initiatives of even public-funded universities, the purpose of distance education provision is for profit. The profit generated is often diverted to meet other expenses of the traditional programmes. As a result, the mode of delivery predominantly remains printed study material. While some of the providers have mechanisms in place to standardise the study material, many others are yet to give serious thought to the recent developments in distance education. One is not sure whether the developments in distance education in India are keeping pace with the international trend in assuring quality. The Distance Education Council (DEC) monitors these issues and the notable efforts of the DEC are as below:

- DEC provides some marginal development grants for improvement in infrastructure.
- DEC extends financial support to research and faculty development in the distance education units.
- It has evolved guidelines that indicate the minimum infrastructure requirement for offering quality programmes. In a number of disciplines DEC has prepared norms and guidelines for programmes and teachers in distance education. DEC provides financial assistance for satisfying the norms.
- DEC has taken initiatives to evolve procedures, norms and guidelines for approval of courses related to management studies and teacher education offered through distance mode by entering into MoUs with All India Council of Technical Education and National Council of Teacher Education respectively.

Since DEC is an adjunct body of IGNOU that itself offers programmes through distance mode, the DEC initiatives for promoting the quality of distance education are equivalent to internal quality enhancement mechanisms. To be in line with the international trend, quality assurance of distance education has to be done by an external agency. This has brought NAAC and DEC together to develop the tools and methodology for quality assurance in distance education and DEC has entered into an agreement with NAAC for accreditation of the distance education providers in the country.

NAAC-DEC deliberations have resulted an agreement that the same criteria used for traditional institutions will serve as the basis of the assessment procedures for the distance education and open education providers. With due consideration to the distinctive aspects of distance education, the same three-stage process for the traditional institutions for accreditation is to be followed. The operational definitions of open and distance learning and the assessment procedures are given in the chapter *Quality Assurance of Distance Education.*

Quality Assurance of Teacher Education

For a planned and coordinated development of teacher education in the country the establishment of the National Council for Teacher Education (NCTE) as a statutory body was passed by an Act of Parliament in 1993 and the body was established on 17 August 1995. The Council regulates and maintains norms and standards in teacher education and gives recognition to institutions offering courses or training in teacher education. Since inception, NCTE has framed regulations from time to time to carry out the functions assigned to it in the Act. The regulations that have been issued broadly cover qualifications for appointment of teachers for different stages of school education, the norms and standards for professional development of teachers and teacher educators through teacher education programmes, the procedures for grant of recognition to institutions by the Regional Committees for conducting teacher education programmes, through face-to-face and distance-education modes, fixation of fees for teacher education programmes, etc. The Act 12 k of NCTE also notes that NCTE will *evolve suitable performance appraisal systems, norms and mechanisms for enforcing accountability on recognised institutions*. In fulfillment of this mandate, in addition to its regulatory function, NCTE has initiated a quality assurance mechanism in collaboration with NAAC. The MoU has been signed in August 2002 and NCTE has instructed all the teacher education institutions to undergo the collaborative assessment shortly.

The methodology is the same as in the case of collaborative assessment with DEC. The criteria have been slightly modified, without losing sight of the key aspects of functioning, to suit the context of the teacher education institutions and they are as follows:

- Curriculum Design and Planning
- Curriculum Transaction and Evaluation
- Research, Development and Extension
- Infrastructure and Learning Resources
- Student Support and Progression
- Organisation and Management.

Accreditation by Other Agencies

Some of the other professional bodies are attempting to establish their own accreditation bodies. The Dental Council of India and the Medical Council of India are contemplating evolving their own accreditation procedures. There are also certification bodies for industrial quality that have extended their scope to include education. But they have not received much attention from the higher education sector. There are very rare cases of one or two higher education institutions that have gone to these agencies for certification of their quality.

The Quality Council of India (QCI) registered as a non-profit, autonomous society was formed by the joint initiative of Indian Industry and the Government of India. Its main objective is to promote, coordinate, guide and implement a national quality initiative for building confidence in Indian products and services and for improving the competitiveness of the Indian Industry. Although it is primarily concerned with industry, institutions that offer strong industry-based programmes like the engineering institutions have shown interest in the QCI certification. However, QCI is contemplating on considering only those educational institutions that have been accredited by the national accreditation agencies. A define pattern is yet to emerge.

Link between Programme Accreditation and Institutional Accreditation

It is well understood that every system of higher education has mechanisms for the review of whole institutions as well as of individual subjects. The balance between the two depends on the objectives for which quality assurance mechanisms have been initiated, how much of quality assurance a system cab absorb and how much resources a country can spend on quality assurance. Especially in developing countries where resources for sustenance of higher education itself is limited, how much resources could be allocated to quality assurance and at what levels? Moreover, in many developing countries, due to limited resources most of the facilities that are essential for quality education are centralised and for such systems institutional assessment would be appropriate. Maybe for mutual recognition of qualifications, programme assessment will be of greater value. The problem gets compounded in India due to the size of the higher education system. Assessing hundreds of general education programmes in 14,000 institutions of higher education is not a feasible task. Due to these considerations, prioritising institutional accreditation for general education institutions has been the acceptable strategy.

However, programme accreditation works well for professional areas due to their limited student enrolment. Around 85 per cent of the student population is under the umbrella of general higher education. The major professional courses absorb only a small proportion of the student population, remaining the 15 per cent. In the order of enrolment, these are law, engineering, medicine, agriculture, and veterinary science, followed by other minor ones. Most of the professional institutions that were established after the 1980s are self-financing. The implication is that a few hundred professional institutions established before the 1980s to cater to a few thousand students get more funding than the general education institutions that cater to more than 7 million students. It is reasonable to expect that such professional areas that are of national priority need to be assessed more rigorously at the programme level.

As of now, the question of linkage between programme accreditation and institutional accreditation does not arise since NAAC is the only national external quality assurance agency and it has consciously promoted institutional accreditation in the first phase. It is now ready with the methodology and instrument for departmental accreditation for universities but not programme accreditation. Since departmental accreditation is yet to take off, the linkage between the two types of accreditation has not emerged as a burning problem. The situation is similar in the case of the institutions that offer only agriculture programmes and are under the purview of ICAR. The Accreditation Board of ICAR evaluates only institutions and discussions are going on for the accreditation of programmes. In any event, both the processes will be with AB and would not pose any problem. The same can be said about the specialised institutions that offer programmes in areas that come under AICTE since NBA does only programme accreditation. There are many specialised institutions in engineering and management that have undergone the institutional accreditation by NAAC and some of them have gone to NBA for programme accreditation and vice versa. Since the unit of accreditation and the purposes they serve are different, the linkage between the two has not been raised as an issue by the HEIs.

The issue becomes different in the case of multi-faculty institutions. A multi-faculty university may have programmes in engineering, medicine, agriculture and a whole lot of other areas along with the liberal arts and sciences. It has to face the regulatory visits of all those specialty councils. The institutional accreditation by NAAC possibly cannot replace the assessment by specialty councils which is meant for licensing the graduates to practice professions like medicine and law. The regulatory recognition processes by the professional bodies will have to continue. But, the emerging trend to establish accreditation bodies for every professional area of study by the respective professional bodies needs attention. If the agencies work together with NAAC, it should be possible to combine the accreditation efforts of both the groups and reduce the burden of too many visits, especially for the multi-faculty institutions. NAAC is working to bring in collaboration in these processes for joint visits as practiced in the USA. One should also remember that so far institutions have not complained about having to meet too many visits. In fact there are not too many institutions in the country that offer both general education and professional education programmes and therefore it is not a burning problem. Further, apart from NAAC only ICAR and AICTE have a separate accreditation mechanism in addition to the approval/recognition mechanisms. But in future, if more accreditation mechanisms are initiated by the professional bodies, assessment overload will become a problem and collaborative assessment needs consideration.

Collaborative Assessment

Collaborative assessment may be defined as a cooperative accreditation review process conducted jointly by two or more quality assurance bodies. The purposes of each of those bodies may be different but through an appropriate collaboration it may be possible to plan for an integrated assessment and an outcome that will serve the concerned agencies. NAAC took the lead to combine its resources and experiences with the specialised knowledge of the Professional Bodies (PBs)/Specialty Councils (SCs). At the instance of the Ministry of Human Resources Development (Department of Education), NAAC organised the meeting of various Heads of the other Councils in 1996 to deliberate on this issue. It was agreed that each institution of higher education must be free to decide for itself whether or not to seek collaborative assessment. Participants of the meeting endorsed the following:

- The standard process – self-study and peer review – may be followed for collaborative assessment.
- NAAC may undertake preparation of self-study manuals for professional subjects in collaboration with the respective agencies.
- Accreditation of professional institutions should be a joint endeavour of NAAC and the concerned councils.

However, no concrete understanding to have joint visits could be arrived at in the next few years. The efforts towards collaboration became fruitful with the Distance Education Council and the National Council on Teacher Education in 2001 and 2002 respectively. The distance education units and teacher education institutions will be assessed jointly by NAAC and the concerned council. It is also important to remember that these collaborative assessments are not to be equated with the recognition processes of these councils.

Accreditation Framework and Quality Enhancement

In line with international practice, the accreditation agencies have identified the aspects that have a direct bearing on the quality of education and adopted them as "criteria for assessment". Although the objective is the same, the way the framework has been evolved to guide the self-study process varies. While the criteria of NAAC has the "major aspects of functioning" as the basis similar to the UK model of Teaching Quality Assessment, the Accreditation Board of ICAR follows a different model. It has statements on standards and General Institutional Requirements following the US models. NBA's model is similar to NAAC's approach. Despite the differences, the data on these criteria would give a picture about the quality of the institution/programme. In the case of other professional bodies, due to the difference in focus, norms and guidelines may check only the minimum requirement. However, all agencies – accrediting agencies as well as the professional bodies—have norms, indicators and guidelines, evolved through national level consultations and expert meets, to streamline their assessment/approval processes.

Except AICTE and ICAR, the other agencies function with a small core staff with a simple budget. Most of them run on the fees paid by the member institutions and the registrants who apply for licensure. The resource persons involved in the quality assurance activities are not full-time members of these bodies and they come from the field on invitation. This makes the agencies cost effective. Even the relatively big agencies like AICTE and ICAR maintain only a core staff structure at both administrative and support staff levels. There have not been any systematic studies to analyse the cost effectiveness of these arrangements. But it is obvious that for the dozens or hundreds of assessment/ recognition visits an agency has to handle, it is not cost effective to have those assessors/inspectors as full-time staff. In practice, it has been found to be working well. The action that could be taken by the quality assurance agencies based on the report of the assessment visit is a powerful factor that enables the small core group to uphold the effectiveness of its processes. In most cases denial of accreditation can have serious implications for the institutions.

In the case of NBA, AB and the other professional bodies, if the institutions are given recommendations or warnings or conditions for further action, they are expected to report back on the action taken. With varying period of validity, the institutions are also expected to send reports to the concerned bodies. This ensures that the recommendations of the assessment team and the norms laid down by the professional body or quality assurance agency are taken seriously and contribute to the quality improvement of the programmes.

NAAC has a different approach and rationale for its follow-up mechanism. Its process does not provide a continuous supervision or review. It is, rather, an assessment of an institution at a given time, resulting in a grade and a report about the quality of education offered in that institution at that time and about its potential of maintaining that quality. As of now, the follow-up is left to the institutions themselves. Although there are discussions about the monitoring of institutions for their potential to sustain the accredited status and the exercise of authority to withdraw the accredited status in the event of malpractices, the policies are yet to take a definite shape. These issues are discussed in detail in Chapter VI.

The emphasis placed by NAAC on strengthening the internal quality assurance mechanism in the institutions has also contributed to quality enhancement. The concept of Internal Quality Assurance Cell to integrate the self-analysis as an ongoing institutional mechanism has been received well by the institutions. The other agencies like NBA and AB do not seem to emphasise this aspect.

Tensions in the System and the Lessons of Experience

To a large extent, the present scenario of quality assurance in India seems to be simple and productive. The regulatory bodies take care of the minimum functioning and the accreditation bodies take care of a higher level of quality. Being clear about the scope of the different quality assurance mechanisms is fundamental to their effectiveness.

The implications of the "accreditation/assessment outcome" have been firmed up keeping in mind the national context. In India, regulation is linked to recognition and basic funding whereas accreditation is linked to development grants and incentives. There is a consensus that in a developing country like India which has a long way to go in increasing access to higher education, linking assessment with basic funding may not be appropriate. But at the same time the expectations of institutions on incentives for good performance cannot be ignored. UGC has announced that it would sanction "development grants" only to the accredited institutions. ICAR and AICTE have incentive schemes to support quality initiatives and infrastructure development. NAAC also has evolved a plan to support the quality enhancement activities of accredited institutions in a minor way. But we should bear in mind that NAAC is not a funding agency and it is accountable to UGC for the financial support it gets from UGC. Hence any incentive scheme by NAAC could only be a token to encourage quality initiatives.

The voluntary versus mandatory nature of the accreditation process remains a debatable issue. The fact that accreditation is voluntary eased out a lot of unnecessary tensions in the beginning. Anything that is imposed on the system is sure to be resisted strongly. The voluntary nature of the accreditation process made institutions analyse the benefits with an open mind. At the same time, the stakeholders' decision to use the accreditation outcome has served as a catalyst. UGC's decision that part of the development grant will be released only when an institution gets accredited is an example. The state government of Tamil Nadu has made accreditation a prerequisite for application for autonomy or deemed university status. Following the state of Tamil Nadu, many other states have announced schemes linked to accreditation.

Although NAAC started its process as a voluntary mechanism, at present there is some ambiguity about its voluntary nature, as more and more stakeholders are making institutional accreditation a prerequisite. The major factor that contributed to this situation is the UGC circular that was sent to all universities fixing a deadline for getting themselves accredited. It has given the process a flavour of mandated accreditation. Other than losing a part of the development grant in the tenth plan period, what the consequences would be of not getting accredited is yet to be known. But it has given a clear signal that more decision-making—financial and otherwise—will be based on accreditation in the years to come.

The national scenario also indicates that there will be more tensions in the system, if each professional body tries to establish its own accreditation board. It may do good if the other specialty councils enter into MoUs with NAAC as in the case of DEC and NCTE, instead of establishing their own accreditation bodies. However, collaboration will lead to tensions if it is not understood properly. If it is perceived as the effort of an agency trying to gain control over the accreditation process, it will lead to unhealthy territorial issues. To some extent this has already happened. From the beginning it has to be made clear that NAAC is not going to replace the recognition or approval procedures of the professional bodies. But what is aimed at is a collaboration in the accreditation efforts which is more than the process of ensuring minimum requirements. While retaining their rightful place in regulating the professional programmes and institutions, for quality assurance, these bodies should come forward to collaborate with NAAC and there is no need for duplicating the quality assurance efforts.

In this context, the relationship between the national quality assurance agency and the specialty councils is an issue that could cause a lot of confusion. For example, NAAC cannot interpret the intentions of the government and declare itself to be the umbrella agency. It is an area where MHRD should take the lead, conduct national deliberations and make a policy decision. The US approach to collaborative assessment where two or more willing quality assurance bodies enter into a partnership will not be feasible in the Indian context.

Even if MHRD takes a policy decision to have one umbrella body for quality assurance, whether it would be a good option is a debatable issue. Will that umbrella body be able to withstand the pressure of such a huge system of higher education? As mentioned earlier, when "too many visits" is not a burning problem in India, the umbrella body concept might actually create unnecessary complications.

From the policy perspective, although established and

funded by national apex bodies like UGC, AICTE and ICAR, it is to be seen how far the advice of the accreditation agencies will have a direct bearing on educational policy making. NAAC has initiated the state-wise analysis of the assessment reports so that the outcome could feed into the decision-making of the stakeholders—institutions, government and funding agencies. The outcome of this effort will throw more light on the usage of assessment outcome for decision-making.

Very often even the quality assurance agencies get locked into routine visits and do not get into exploring the emerging challenges. NAAC has been careful about not falling into this trap. One cannot be sure of this in the case of the many other professional bodies that have an important role in the quality assurance scenario of the country. In general, it can be said that the quality assurance agencies of the country have to strengthen their national, regional and international dialogue with one another and the research on quality-related issues. The quality assurance systems can be productive only when the national network of quality assurance agencies develops into a cohesive system with a clear understanding of their scope, responsibilities and interdependence. With encouraging dialogue going on among only a few agencies like NAAC, NCTE and DEC, this is a substantial task to achieve. However, the significant impact NAAC has made on the system of higher education within a short span of eight years indicates that success in taking forward the positive developments like collaborative assessment is within the reach of NAAC.

3. Transformative Impact of Institutional Accreditation

The Impact Analysis done by NAAC indicates that there have been expected transformative changes in areas like articulating mission statements, institutionalising hitherto informal activities like collecting student feedback on their educational experience, strengthening extension activities, grievance redressal and initiating quality management procedures. Today most of the accredited institutions have Internal Quality Assurance Cells in place. Inter-institutional exchange of information on healthy practices and implementation of the relevant ones have transformed the attitude and functioning of HEIs. At the same time, the impact made by accreditation on policy making and funding decisions is evolving—it is very positive in some states and is yet to be noticed in the other states. This chapter is an expression of satisfaction about the aspects that have really been transformed among HEIs due to quality assurance by NAAC and the policy level issues that are still emerging.

The Backdrop

For a long time India did not have any organised way of educating its people. The *Gurukula* system was prevalent in the country in the past, which made access to education very difficult for the common man. The shift in the middle of the 19th century from the *Gurukula* system to an organised system of education is a British legacy, although some contributions from the Moghuls is evident from the 16th century. The shift towards a more organised system of dispensing higher education was followed by the quantitative expansion progressively in the early part of the 20th century. At the time of independence, in 1947, there were 21 universities and 500 colleges in the country. A cursory look at the following table indicates the quantitative expansion that took place during the post-independence era.

Table 1: Growth in Institutions of Higher Education

Year	*Number of Universities*	*Number of Colleges*	*Student Enrolment (in millions)*
1947	21	500	0.20
1950-51	30	750	0.26
1960-61	49	1,537	0.65
1970-71	93	3,604	1.95
1980-81	123	4,722	2.75
1990-91	177	7,346	4.43
2000-01	259	10,750	7.40
2002	298	12,600	8.00

(www.education.nic.in, *Universities Handbook*, 28th edition)

The increase in student enrolment seems to be impressive in India but it is not different from the experience of other nations. Worldwide, there has been a near seven-fold expansion in the number of students from 13 million in 1960 to 82 million in 1985 (UNESCO, 1998), and 85 million at the turn of the century. In absolute terms India has succeeded to a great extent in providing increased access as the number of students in higher education has registered a phenomenal 40-fold increase from about .02 million in 1947 to about 8 million in 2002. However, its impact becomes nullified due to the growing population here, as compared to other countries.

A World Bank-UNESCO Task Force on Higher Education and Society in its report (World Bank, 2000; Bloom and Rosovsky, 2001) has drawn attention to the fact that while India's tertiary enrolment rate of 613 per 10,000 population compares favourably with that of many sub-Saharan African countries, it is well below the averages of other developing regions such as Latin America (1,638) and the Middle East and North Africa (1,465) and extremely low in comparison with Europe and Central Asia (2,436) and the United States (5,339). The quantitative expansion, though well below the desirable level, has resulted in a many-fold increase in expenditure on higher education.

Table 2: Expenditure on Higher Education (1951–52 to 1993–94)

Year	*Expenditure (in '000 Rs)*	*Per Student Expenditure in Rs*
1951-52	72,319	416
1961-62	3,44,931	639
1971-72	8,35,982	428
1981-82	9,55,309	1,800
1991-92	2,44,27,774	5,522
1993-94	2,91,55,611	4,537

The expenditure on higher education has registered a considerable increase from Rs. 7.23 crores in 1951–52 to Rs. 2915.56 crores in 1993. Despite the increase by 11 times in per student expenditure, the students have not benefited much due to inflation. In terms of the relative proportion of the national income, the percentage has increased from 0.2 to 0.5 during this period. In spite of such a steep increase in student enrolment, number of institutions and consequent expenditure on higher education, the Indian higher education system still caters only to 6 per cent of the relevant age group of 17 to 23 years. This is abysmally low in comparison to the over 50 per cent in the OECD countries, and the 20 per cent considered essential for sustained economic development (Powar, 2000a). Even the South East Asian neighbours of India show much higher enrolment such as in the Philippines (27.8%), Thailand (19.0%) and Malaysia (10.1%) (Joshi, M.M., 1998).

The changing perception on the subsidisation of higher education by the government also needs a mention here. The government has been the major source of funding higher education. Since independence, the government contribution to higher education in absolute terms has been increasing while the funding from other sources has been on the decline. Data also reveals that the share of the higher education sector in the total outlay for education in the five-year plans remained between 11 per cent and 13 per cent during 1951–52 to 1991–92. It was only in 1981–82 that higher education received 15 per cent. Even this percentage is much lower than that of many developed countries. The expenditure on higher education, as a percentage of GNP, has fallen from 0.98 per cent in 1980–81 to 0.35 per cent in 1994–95 (Powar, 2002). Table 3 gives the details of the declining share of higher education in the total educational budget.

In the First Five Year Plan, the allocation for higher education was only 9 per cent. The allocations were almost doubled in the Second Five Year Plan and declined slightly in the Third Five Year Plan. The allocations in the Fourth, Fifth and Sixth Plans were relatively high, but declined slightly in the subsequent Five Year Plans and reached 8 per cent in the Eighth Five Year Plan. This is the lowest so far, less than the allocation made in the First Five Year Plan. Even adult education gets a higher allocation than higher education. In fact, in the eighth plan, school and adult education put together get 74 per cent while higher education gets a meager 8 per cent. In sum, higher education in India

Table 3: Plan Expenditure on Different Sectors of Education (in per cent)

Sector	*I Plan 1951-56*	*II Plan 1956-61*	*III Plan 1961-66*	*Plan Holiday 1966-69*	*IV Plan 1969-74*	*V Plan 1974-79*	*VI Plan 1980-85*	*VII Plan 1985-90*	*Plan Holiday*	*VIII Plan 1992-97*
Elementary Education	56	35	34	24	30	35	33	37	37	47
Secondary Education	13	19	18	16	18	17	21	24	22	18
Adult Education	—	—	—	—	—	—	9	6	9	9
Higher Education	9	18	15	24	25	22	22	16	12	8
Technical Education	13	18	21	25	13	12	11	14	17	14
Others	9	10	12	11	14	14	4	3	2	4
Total	100	100	100	100	100	100	100	100	100	100

Source: *Govt. of India (1995), Budgetary resources for education (1951-52–1993-94): MHRD*

is in deep financial crisis, with escalating costs and increasing needs, on the one hand, and shrinking budgetary resources, on the other. Thus although higher education in India is characterised by massive public investment, this investment is still regarded as much below the optimum (Joshi, M.M., 1998).

Due to these changing perceptions and policies, higher education is faced with a resource crunch. Due to the decreasing government support, there is a need to augment the resources for the higher education system by encouraging private initiatives. With the experience of the flawed and ineffective public enterprises in many sectors, privatisation is also viewed as a strategy to facilitate competitive efficiency. The policy of the government is to encourage private initiatives without giving room for commercialisation of educational services. While such private initiatives are encouraged at the college level, there has been reluctance in establishing private universities by successive governments, both at the center and in the states. There are various reasons for this; the chief among them being the objection raised by many that the public would be exploited.

In additions to the resource crunch coupled with the need to increase access to higher education, by 1980, criticisms on the inadequacy of the then existing regulatory mechanisms to ensure quality and relevance mounted.

Inadequacy of Existing Mechanisms

The Indian higher education system inherited many regulatory mechanisms from the British legacy of higher education. While the regulatory mechanisms have ensured satisfactory functioning of the system, with unprecedented quantitative expansion, raising the standards of higher education could not be achieved well. The size of the higher education system may look impressive in terms of numbers—298 universities, more than 13,000 colleges, 0.4 million teachers and 8 million students—but it covers only 6 per cent of the relevant age group. Ensuring the quality of education provided to this small percentage is vital to the success of the nation.

The situation gets further complicated with colleges taking a lead in undergraduate education, with 88 per cent of the student enrolment in undergraduate education in the affiliating system that loosely connects the colleges and universities. Most Indian universities are of the affiliating type where the affiliating university legislates on courses of study, holds examinations centrally on common syllabi for its affiliates and awards the degree to successful candidates. With the larger affiliating universities having more than 400 affiliated colleges, the academic leadership provided to affiliates has come under severe criticism. Many of the conditions which ensured educational quality while granting affiliation to colleges, have now been either ignored or soft-pedaled, with the result that many substandard institutions have come into existence, with the possibility of many more getting created.

The growth of private initiatives has also increased the concern for quality. To increase access to education India has encouraged private initiatives. The government-run colleges are few and privately managed trusts or societies have founded the greater number of colleges—about 70 per cent of the total. Most of the private colleges established before the 1980s get more than 95 per cent of their financial support from the state government and they are called grant-in-aid colleges. With limited resources, the government could not extend financial support to the private initiatives established after the 1980s. These colleges run on student fees and they are known as self-financing colleges. Though self-financing, they have to comply with the rules of the government and the affiliating university. The growth in the number of self-financing colleges adds to the pressure on the affiliating universities. The direct public expenditure on the public-funded institutions, the high fee structure of the self-financing colleges and the substandard facilities available in some of these institutions have raised the question of "value for money"; hence the need for an effective mechanism for Quality Assurance. Accreditation by an autonomous body was seen as an appropriate strategy for quality assurance and hence National Assessment and Accreditation Council (NAAC) was established in 1994.

Recently, NAAC conducted a study to analyse the impact of accreditation on the institutions of higher education. The Impact Analysis indicates that external quality assurance as promoted by NAAC has made an impact on all the stakeholders. However, how significant the impact is and whether it has been strong enough to transform the policies, procedures and practices of the system of higher education are issues to be probed further.

The Transformative Impact

Since NAAC's process is voluntary, (although UGC has set a deadline for HEIs to undergo accreditation), it is not possible to expect a transformation in the whole system within such a short span of eight years. It is true that the institutions that have undergone the process have experienced a major impact. But, out of the 13,000 HEIs, only a small fraction have experienced the process. As of June, 2003, NAAC has accredited 512 HEIs — less than 4 per cent of the total number of HEIs in the country. However, in terms of the universities and their affiliating functions the analysis is interesting; around 70 per cent of the traditional affiliating universities have been accredited. It is reasonable to assume that the benefits percolate to the colleges as well through the academic leadership of the affiliating universities. Even after making corrections for the unitary universities that do not have any affiliating functions, the inference is that around 50 per cent of the affiliated colleges have experienced the benefit of accreditation indirectly.

The picture with respect to the autonomous colleges is also noteworthy. The autonomous colleges are the ones that have been given the privilege of innovating in curriculum and examination due to their ability to manage those affairs on their own, adhering to broad guidelines laid down by the university and the UGC. These are the colleges that have come forward to use academic freedom. It is heartening to note that more than 50 per cent of these colleges have been accredited. The impact analysis by NAAC also reveals that these colleges have been successful in acting on the assessment report leading to significant changes in their practices.

In the order of hierarchy with reference to academic freedom the HEIs enjoy, universities come first followed by the autonomous colleges. In both these cases, more than 50 per cent of the institutions have been accredited. The HEIs that have the academic freedom have been truly influenced by accreditation. Since the affiliated colleges are under the academic leadership of the universities, it can be assumed that through the affiliating function of the accredited universities, the affiliates have also been influenced. In sum, it is reasonable to say that 50 per cent of all HEIs in the country have been influenced by accreditation, either directly or indirectly.

As mentioned above, with reference to the direct benefits, the accredited institutions are the primary beneficiaries. NAAC's process aims to promote self-improvement by institutions and at the same time facilitates the other beneficiaries in their decision-making. This is achieved well by grading institutions under nine categories for the quality of education and giving them a detailed assessment report. When the grades are made known, institutions understand as to where they stand in the quality continuum. The assessment report that highlights the strengths and weaknesses enables the institutions to plan further quality enhancement strategies. There is also the public disclosure of the assessment report, by including the full report in the NAAC website, thus facilitating the other beneficiaries to use the assessment outcome. Many institutions have shared with NAAC that this process has resulted in bringing about many desirable changes in their functioning. To understand these changes well, recently, NAAC conducted a study to analyse the impact of accreditation on the institutions. The analysis revealed that the impact of accreditation has been felt by institutions in all aspects of their functioning—pedagogical, managerial and administrative; only the significant ones among them are mentioned below.

Ownership on Quality Matters

NAAC's process has made institutions realise that quality is the responsibility of the institutions themselves. This realisation has made the institutions take up initiatives beyond the mandatory requirements of the affiliating system. Quality management procedures were introduced in some institutions. Management was often able to bring in major changes on the grounds that it would demonstrate a commitment to quality. For example, institutions introduced peer appraisal and student evaluation of teachers, issues that still continue to be the bone of contention in many institutions.

Impact on Curricular Aspects and Research

The introduction of need-based programmes, increasing the programme options, was observed in most of the institutions. Many institutions started their own skill-oriented certificate and diploma programmes to fulfill the growing demand from students. The autonomous institutions—universities and autonomous colleges—that had the freedom to innovate in curriculum restructured the curriculum. Institutions also understood effective ways of doing it, such as involving employers and peers.

Research initiatives and supporting efforts to publish have improved. Some institutions have established research centers with liberal seed money from their governing bodies. Community-oriented activities, extending expertise to the development of the immediate neighbourhood, initiating research that would solve the problems of the neighbourhood, students and faculty participation in those activities, etc. have increased.

Improved Learning Resources and Support Services

The attention of the institutions has been focused on the support services within their reach, which they had never thought of before. Student support like open access and extended working hours of the library, getting the latest books and quality journals, establishing inter-library linkages, centralised computer center with easy access to it, placement cell, campus interviews, on-the-job training, guidance and counselling and financial assistance were greatly improved.

Although the use of information technology was spreading in all institutions, NAAC's process made its need felt by all the sections of the institutions instead of confining the benefits to a few sections like the computer science department and the administrative office. Institutional efforts for its appropriate use and preparing its members for optimum use greatly improved. That led to the use of information technology as a learning resource in the real sense by more faculty members.

Computerisation helped in improved documentation also. Although some mentioned that the process of preparing the self-study report and getting ready for the assessment visit involved a lot of unnecessary documentation, most thought that it was a promising tool for improvement of their documentation, especially for teacher appraisal, student progression, alumni profiles and placement services.

The Synergy

Small differences were forgotten and the faculty and the management became united. Departments that were functioning like islands within the bigger system started sharing their experiences and expertise, which developed inter-departmental initiatives, intimacy and a new synergy.

Quality assessment triggered new healthy practices. Things taken for granted were rediscovered. Interaction with employers to strengthen the industry linkage to capitalise on strengths was observed. Collecting feedback from parents, alumni and students for improving the educational experiences and consultations with peers to overcome the weak links were initiated. In short, initiatives that require confidence, self-reliance, team spirit and potential bloomed.

Change in the Policies and Practices of the Management

There is a change in the management on issues of faculty workload, supporting research culture and encouraging faculty development. The relations between the management and the other units of the institutions improved. There was a change towards a more transparent style of management, involving the other units in decision-making. Training of the staff in new communication technologies, faculty development programmes, and student activities gained a new thrust. They were seen as useful investments for the development of the human resources of the institution.

Recognising Stakeholder Expectations and their Greater Involvement

The expectations of the employers, students and parents formed a substantial basis for many new initiatives of the institutions. Opinions from students and parents were sought on the educational experiences provided in the institution.

Alumni involvement and parent involvement in improving the institution became explicit. Institutions also realised the importance of projecting their strengths and unique features to the stakeholders to get good resources—funds, students and teachers.

Greater Value of Accreditation

Institutions started thinking beyond routine teaching-learning and chalked out future plans. Even institutions that volunteered for the process with apprehension have understood the great value of assessment after undergoing the process. Initially some institutions volunteered just because the neighbouring institutions had done so or the accreditation of NAAC was seen as a marketing strategy. But later, they realised that the process of assessment had done a lot to revive and stimulate the quality culture of the institution.

Impact on the Employers, Students and Parents

Employers are not active information seekers from the assessment reports and that is understandable. In general the most important criteria that guide their recruitment choices are the personal qualities of the candidate like aptitude for team work, creativity, capacity to solve problems, openness to further learning and communication skills—qualities that are assessed through interviews or other instruments. Information on the quality of the HEI that trains the students for the world of work tends to become secondary, even though general institutional prestige is often acknowledged and taken into account. The study conducted in Chile about the information needs of the stakeholders is worth noting here. The study revealed that the recruiting agencies show a low level of interest in the existence of a public information system on higher education. Although a systematic study at the national level has not been attempted in India, local surveys and informal discussions with a few groups indicate that the findings of the Chilean study hold good in India as well. This is the case in a few other countries also.

A study carried out in 1999 by the Higher Education Funding Council of England (HEFCE) found out that there was a low level of awareness of quality-related information and even where there was awareness, the process and outputs were not fully understood by some important groups (Maria Jose, 2001). In fact quality assurance agency of the UK prints the assessment reports and makes them available on the website. It had undertaken extensive mailing of reports to various groups of stakeholders. A telephone survey conducted by the Council on Higher Education Accreditation (CHEA) in 1999 among the public found out that the majority of the respondents did not know who performed accreditation in USA. The next largest group said that it was by the government. Only a minority (12 per cent) knew that private organisations were responsible for accreditation.

The studies mentioned above indicate a lesson of experience for NAAC. The "appropriate use of assessment outcome" has to go hand in hand with "informing the stakeholders". The implication is that NAAC has yet another responsibility to shoulder. In addition to creating awareness about quality-related issues among the academia, it has to work on educating the potential users of the assessment reports about identifying necessary information.

The impact on the students and parents in India could be seen in the change in the enrolment pattern in accredited and yet-to-be-accredited colleges. It is true that the choice of the institution in the case of the majority of the student community depends on factors other than quality rating. For example, affordability of the family to spend on education, location of the institution and societal prestige attached to professional courses, etc. determine the choice of the institution. The Chilean study found out that quality and standards are not the main criteria for the applicants nor for their parents, and general institutional reputation and prestige seemed to be enough for their choices. The CHEA survey revealed that a good number of respondents did not have a clear idea about accreditation and were ready to take educational decisions not based on the accreditation status. This is true to a large extent in India. However, within the framework dictated by the other conditions, the accredited institutions are able to attract talented students. A student may not decide to go all the way to a highly rated institution situated a few hundred miles away from his/her place of stay (while it is done in the case of getting admission into professional courses), but once the place of study is selected to suit the economic conditions of the family, a student's choice is always for an accredited institution.

Among the accredited institutions, the institutional grade has made significant impact on student choice of the institution. Within the same city, colleges that enjoyed the same social status but receiving different institutional grades in NAAC's assessment have experienced major changes in the enrolment pattern, with more demand for the HEI with a higher rating. This is becoming more visible as the public comes to know more and more about QA efforts of NAAC. To build on this positive trend, NAAC disseminates the QA developments through popular media like newspapers, magazines and TV. Meeting groups of parents and alumni during the on-site visit has helped in this awareness building to some extent. As the college gets accredited, the message spreads to the parents who take interest in the institutional affairs of their wards. In some colleges, the Parent Teacher Associations have taken the initiative to make the colleges volunteer for accreditation and paid for all or part of the accreditation expenses. They are exceptions and in general there is a need to strengthen the efforts to reach out to the public about the assessment outcome and about the benefits of making informed educational decisions.

Impact on the Peers

Hundreds of peers, who were involved in the various activities of NAAC—assessment exercise, awareness programmes and workshops—became convinced of the merits of quality assessment. They became the change agents in their own institutions. They were able to clear the unfounded fears of their colleagues. In many institutions, they became the nucleus of the assessment initiative and were invited to chair the steering committees to prepare the self-study reports. The neighbouring institutions approached them for consultation. Since NAAC has the policy not to invite peers from the same state where the institution is located, the impact of the peers spread across the country very quickly. Peers have also played an important role in the dissemination of healthy practices and innovative strategies among institutions. What they observe in an institution often triggers new developments in their parent institutions.

Impact on Providers

The UGC has already taken a decision to use the assessment outcome for funding decisions for certain grants without affecting the basic funding to the institutions. The outcome of assessment has been used for other decision-making as well. Recently, the state government of Tamil Nadu with the aid of the State Council for Higher Education resolved to recommend for either autonomous or *deemed university* status, only those colleges that are accredited and rated high—a special status with more autonomy given to institutions of proven potential. Similar moves are on in a few other states like Karnataka, Maharashtra, Punjab and Haryana.

NAAC has promoted its partnership with the states by developing action plans for them to meet the UGC deadline of 2003 to get the colleges accredited. In Karnataka, Kerala and Maharashtra the efforts of NAAC have already resulted in drafting a comprehensive action plan for the states. The action plan includes an analysis of the assessment reports to identify the strengths and weaknesses of the institutions in the state and suggesting ways to remedy the weaknesses. State level Coordination Committees have been constituted in those states for overseeing the process of accreditation. The increasing involvement of the state governments is becoming more pronounced.

Parent universities like the University of Pune and Punjab University insist that their affiliates get themselves accredited and they also provide guidance to the affiliates in preparing the self-study report. In Haryana, the Commissioner of Higher Education fixed a deadline for all its HEIs to submit the self-study report to NAAC. States like Nagaland have approached NAAC to get an insight into the status of their higher education system.

Concerns and Challenges

The impact could be seen in ways that were not very pleasant also. In spite of emphasising that institutional uniqueness will be taken care of, institutions have started copying the top-bracket institutions; this may lead to decrease in diversity among institutions. Some institutions had spent much time preparing documents and plans that would impress the peer team. In some instances the assessment report seems to be used for purposes which may not be appropriate to the intended outcomes.

While the impact of NAAC on HEIs and students has been very significant, the policy decisions of the government and the funding agencies on using assessment outcome are still emerging. While UGC's announcement that it would sanction 'development grants' only to the accredited institutions is a positive development, the extent of its impact needs attention. UGC is a major provider only to the Central Universities which number 18, colleges affiliated to Delhi and Banaras Hindu Universities and some of the institutions accorded the status of 'Deemed-to-be Universities'. State Universities and colleges receive UGC support (less than 5 per cent of their budget in most cases) only for certain development schemes. Their major providers, the state governments, are yet to take note of the assessment outcome of NAAC in a major way except in Tamil Nadu, Punjab, Haryana, Karnataka and Maharashtra. To give a momentum to this development, NAAC initiated a focused dialogue with all the states and by January 2002 eight states had evolved an action plan to get all their HEIs accredited. To further promote the accredited colleges, suggestions have been given to the states that around 2 per cent of the higher education budget should be allotted for quality improvement schemes and incentives. By the time this information reaches the readers, the situation may be more encouraging, since all the states have accepted in principle to promote quality assurance by NAAC.

In sum, the course of development is significant, indicative of major changes in institutional perspectives, in the case of institutions that have participated in the process. However, the policy-related transformations are still evolving. For a governmental initiative like this – NAAC being an outcome of the National Policy of Education 1986 – it should not be difficult to bring in policy-related changes. For the kind of national level consultations and deliberations that have led to what NAAC is today, the transition in policy perspectives should be very smooth to achieve, without any lobbying. Nonetheless, the developments are encouraging and there cannot be two opinions on the positive impact of assessment on the Indian higher education system. It is reasonable to hope that it will continue to be so.

4. Lessons of Experience of NAAC

India has the second largest system of higher education in the world—298 universities and more than 13,000 colleges—that caters to 8 million direct and full-time students with 0.4 million teachers. For such a large and diverse system, conceptualising a national quality assurance mechanism and operationalising the processes have been a formidable task. Since its inception in 1994, the National Assessment and Accreditation Council (NAAC) had spent 3-4 years for evolving its policies, principles and instruments. Since 1998, about 500 institutions have been assessed. Hopefully, the first cycle of assessing and grading all the universities that offer liberal arts and science general education (around 150) will be completed by the end of the year 2003. The number of institutions assessed so far constitutes only a fraction of the target. But, the experience gained in evolving an acceptable methodology of External Quality Assurance (EQA) for such a complex system and the field experience could be of relevance to nations aspiring to evolve their own quality assurance mechanisms. This chapter is an attempt to share those lessons of experience.

External quality assessment worldwide has a dual purpose, namely, assessment for accountability and for improvement. The emphasis on either one of the two varies between different countries, depending on the degree of accountability required by various authorities. NAAC has consciously decided to adopt assessment for improvement as its main objective and evolved its instruments accordingly. Accountability concerns were addressed unobtrusively as an incidental outcome. This conscious decision was based on the fact that in the London model of higher education prevalent in the country, there are adequate checks and balances built in to ensure accountability of institutions, as mentioned in the earlier chapters. Moreover, India has to go a long way to ensure access and equity to a larger percentage of the population and an overemphasis on accountability may become counter-productive. In spite of the huge network of higher education, only 6 per cent of the relevant age group are enrolled in higher education. With this in the background, the lessons learnt by NAAC are given briefly in the following pages.

Learning from Others

While evolving the instrument and methodology, NAAC has followed the following cardinal principles, for which the experiences of other countries interpreted in the light of the distinct characteristics of the Indian context formed the basis.

1. Assessment and accreditation need not be an answer to all the quality concerns in higher education.
2. Quality assessment is a complex issue and hence should be used to address issues of high priority.
3. Assessment should be built on the existing data.
4. The process should be acceptable to the clientele.
5. Quality assessment to a large extent depends on peer judgment and not just on quantitative indicators.

6. Despite differences in national contexts, the critical elements of quality assessment are bound to be the same.

In a developing country, the factors that affect the quality of education are many, ranging from financial constraints to sociological contexts. The EQA mechanism cannot possibly address all the factors and cannot provide the answers to all the problems related to the quality of higher education. Quality assessment is valuable for providing an outcome to be used in the prioritisation and decision-making processes of institutions and other stakeholders. At the same time one should realise that quality assessment is a complex issue in itself—it is much more than merely applying predetermined criteria to arrive at simple and straightforward solutions.

EQA can help to clarify issues, but is an extravagant way of confirming that "below average performance is still below average". Many issues can be resolved simply by giving them attention. There are enough mandatory mechanisms already built in the Indian system like annual inspection and reviews to take care of most of the routine issues. The experiences of other countries indicated that quality assessment as conceived by NAAC is a substantial task and would require a lot of resources and commitment. Such a mechanism should have clear priorities of a high order.

Another important assumption NAAC made was that assessment should be built on existing data as much as possible. Higher education has all along used a lot of data, being traditionally awash in data on aspects like finance, staffing, and student enrolment. Generally, these data have been used to justify budgets or obtain more funding. Obviously, little has been used to improve the quality of higher education. The traditional data such as annual endowment growth, educational and general operating expenditures per student, research income generated, class size, student–faculty ratio, library holdings, student success rate and rate of employment of students may not address the issue of quality directly and explicitly. However, they may be useful indicators and hence quality assessment should use these existing data without too much emphasis on documentation and generation of newer data to begin with. Too much of emphasis on new ways of documentation will become an intimidating factor. It may raise doubts whether the benefits would match such additional efforts. The best way is to induce improved documentation as the process progresses with the realisation that it cannot be achieved overnight.

An important requirement for the success of evaluation of institutions is to ensure the acceptability of the process. The academic community knows only too well that anything that is imposed on the system will be resisted, if not rejected. If quality assessment has to lead to self-improvement, and if it has to remain an enabling and ameliorative mechanism, it is necessary to convince the system of the merits of the mechanism and allow the institutions to take their own time to get ready for it. The US system of accreditation was seen as an example of how influential the voluntary mechanism could be if implemented well. In the USA, the state and federal governments rely heavily on accreditation to allocate student aid funds. Many other federal funds and billions of dollars in state funds are allocated, based on the accredited status. State certification of professionals is heavily dependent on whether or not students have completed accredited programmes. Decisions by well-informed students about where to attend college and determinations by the enlightened public about whether an institution is considered "quality" depends on the accredited status. All this is happening in spite of accreditation being "non-governmental voluntary self-regulation". Therefore, the concept paper on accreditation for the Indian system stated that assessment would be voluntary and that the stakeholders would be encouraged to use the assessment outcome for their decision-making.

The world over, EQA agencies have not found a better alternative to peer assessment; performance indicators and procedural safeguards are in use, largely, to guide peer assessment. In the Indian context too, it was well understood that quality assessment would have to largely rely on peer assessment. While external quality assessment itself is a new culture that is slowly being nurtured in the higher education system, overemphasis on performance indicators will defeat the very purpose of assessment. Allowing variance for institutional differences, performance indicators can be used for inter-institutional comparison in certain areas, and that too for purposes of internal management and improvement. Anything more than that such as teaching output, research income, student progression, etc. should be balanced with peer judgment, and this became clear in all the consultations NAAC had on quantifying quality.

While it is essential to evolve the methodology to suit the national context, it is equally essential to ensure that it is in line with international trends. An analysis of the current practices of the national accrediting agencies of various countries reveals a great deal of diversity. They vary in structure and function. Variations can also be seen in their methodology, nature of the process (mandatory or voluntary), unit of assessment (institution or programme), outcome and policy on disclosure of the outcome (confidential or public). In spite of the variance, the process of external quality assurance has the following critical common elements:

- Independent nature of the accrediting body
- Assessment based on pre-determined criteria
- Combination of self-study and peer review
- Safeguards and protocols to guide peer assessment
- Public disclosure of the outcome (The extent of public disclosure varies from disclosure of only the final outcome to disclosure of the full assessment report)

- Period of validity of the assessment outcome, varying from 3 to 10 years

In line with this trend, NAAC adopted the following three-stage process, the outcome of which would be valid for a period of five years and be made public:

- Preparation and submission of self-study report by the unit of assessment
- On-site visit of the peer team for validation of the report and for recommending the assessment outcome to NAAC
- Final decision by the Executive Council of NAAC and public disclosure of the assessment outcome.

With these major conceptual clarifications, a lot more emerged at the practical level when the assessment efforts proceeded.

Lessons of Field Experience

Defining the Boundary

For any strategy to be successful, it is necessary to identify the "if and only if" conditions and the degrees of freedom the system can afford—aspects where deviation must be avoided and areas where changes can be introduced which may lead to improvement. Once those issues are agreed upon, there may be no turning back for quite some time. The field experience may lead to further fine-tuning, but the consistency in the strategy would have to be maintained. Lack of clarity on those major aspects would eventually lead to a situation where the assessment mechanism may be expected to achieve conflicting objectives. The rationale with which NAAC firmed up some of those decisions and the contentious issues may still be debated but they gave a strong foundation to the developments of NAAC. NAAC was aware that two major issues that had to be clarified at the start were the "unit of assessment" and "reporting the assessment outcome".

Unit of Assessment

The rationale that the unit of assessment chosen should be appropriate to the objectives of assessment, viable, feasible and practical in the national context was well understood. If the purpose is to see whether an institution has the potential to offer a programme of study as in the case of the Ontario Council for Graduate Studies (OCGS) of Canada, focussing on programmes is necessary. Further, OCGS could do it due to its optimum size—seventeen universities. The Commission on Evaluation of College Education (CEEC) of Quebec with 120 institutions within its jurisdiction has adopted a combination of institutional evaluation and specific aspects that are common to all institutions like the general education component, the computer education component, etc. It is the case with the UK and many other systems that have mechanisms for department/programme assessment. However, in the Indian context, in view of the large number of institutions that are small in size, where the total student strength in an average institution may be around 1,500, it was agreed that NAAC would promote institutional accreditation with provision for departmental accreditation. Although there are many reasons for promoting institutional accreditation, as discussed in Chapter 2, NAAC has recognised that institutional assessment and department/ programme assessment are not separate alternatives. There should be a place for review of whole institutions as well as of individual subjects and the balance between the two must be handled carefully. To prioritise the assessment efforts, institutional assessment has been promoted in the first cycle and discussions are going on about departmental accreditation.

Reporting Strategy

The reporting strategy of NAAC is an overall institutional grade supplemented with a detailed assessment report, which is made public. The reporting strategy is expected to promote self-improvement by institutions. This is achieved well by classifying or grading institutions under nine categories and giving them a detailed assessment report. When the grades are made known, institutions understand where they stand in the quality continuum. The assessment report highlights their strengths and weaknesses, which enables the institutions to plan further quality enhancement strategies. Even the ones that get a higher rating plan on sustaining it through coordinated and conscious efforts.

The public disclosure of the assessment report, by putting it in the NAAC website, helps other beneficiaries to use the assessment outcome for making a choice among institutions. NAAC was aware that "confidentiality vs public disclosure" of the assessment report is a bone of contention in many countries, and that both the viewpoints have valid arguments. In fact, within the same country different approaches can be seen. In Canada, while CEEC makes the reports public, OCGS reports are confidential. In the USA, while most of the accrediting agencies support confidentiality, the Accrediting Council on Education in Journalism and Mass Communications (ACEJMC) makes the reports public. Although it is argued that confidentiality encourages a more honest and critical self-evaluation, there is a growing acceptance that openness is essential. In countries like Denmark, France, Finland, Netherlands (VSNU and HBO-raad), Sweden and the UK (QAA), and in the Flemish speaking community of Belgium, the assessment reports are made public. Even in countries where assessment reports are confidential as in Korea, Canada and the USA, there is a growing demand for more public information. With QA systems evolving more towards public disclosure, NAAC consciously opted for the public disclosure of assessment reports.

As mentioned earlier, the assessment report is included in the website of NAAC. While this is seen as one of the strengths of NAAC, there are varying opinions about what part of the report should be made public. NAAC consciously decided that the full report would be made public after ensuring through appropriate safeguards that the report qualifies to be a NAAC document. It should be mentioned that these major decisions were not just recommendations of a few committees but the considered view/favoured opinion/collective decision of a cross-section of our academia, evolved through a large number of national level consultations and focused workshops.

Reporting the assessment in line with the prime tasks of the council and at the same time making it useful to all the stakeholders is a very critical responsibility. To be specific, the expectations of the students, parents and society may be relatively simple and the information in the website, the directory of accredited institutions and the assessment reports may serve their purpose well. However, the report that may be useful to the government and the fund-giving agencies may not be that simple. What kind of report will benefit the various stakeholders? What information should be for public disclosure? What information should have privileged access? These questions need to be clearly answered. NAAC firmed up these decisions in the beginning itself and it was made clear that in the first cycle of assessment, the primary stakeholder would be the institutions. Accordingly the reporting strategy was firmed up. However, the expectations of the stakeholders were taken into consideration while fine-tuning the reporting strategy.

Role of the Council in Steering Assessment

Some agencies (as in Finland and the USA) keep their role in assessment per se minimal and only coordinate the assessment visits. In the process of CEEC of Quebec and

QAA of the UK, the agency's role is more evaluative. In CEEC, every team has one of the commissioners of CEEC. In QAA, the agency representatives at times lead the assessment teams. NAAC started its assessment visits with the assumption that the staff of the agency need not be directly involved in assessment per se. At the same time the need to ensure inter-team variance was a substantial task. As noted by Thune, the strength of this approach is dependent to a very large extent on the professionalism of the experts, especially of the chairperson and on how well the expert team functions as a group. This has been ensured to a large extent through training of the assessors. However, to further ensure the consistency and credibility of the assessment process, NAAC plays a major role in planning the evaluation framework, in developing the instruments and methodology, and in fine-tuning the implementation and ensuring the objectivity of the process before the outcome is made public. Thus, NAAC does not stop as a mere coordinating agency but strikes a balance between the coordinating functions and steering the assessment processes—a stand that has been found to be appropriate.

Multi-pronged Approach

While working towards the support of the academia, NAAC was aware that it would not be possible to expect 100 per cent acceptance of all its efforts. Whatever be the strategy followed, there may always be a minority group to criticise it. The criticism need not be based on ignorance or lack of conceptual clarity or skepticism but may be due to genuine concerns. Keeping this in mind, NAAC followed a multi-pronged approach targeting the various stakeholders for information dissemination on the assessment philosophy and principles.

In fact, during the first three years of NAAC's existence the founder Director's major commitment was to implement multi-pronged strategies at various levels—awareness programmes to reach out to the academic community, publication programmes for dissemination of information, debates on critical issues, workshops on development of instruments, training experts for assessment, discussions with administrators to rope in government support and so on.

Reaching Out

Hundreds of seminars and academic interactions were organised with various groups of academia at the national level, familiarising them with the concept of assessment and accreditation. A wide range of promotional materials was prepared and distributed to thousands of teachers of higher education. The materials included a few booklets that would answer most of the queries and apprehensions of the academia. The *NAAC News*, the quarterly newsletter of NAAC, also added to the efforts to reach out to more number of institutions. Numerous awareness activities were conducted involving various universities, colleges, state councils of higher education, state governments, directorates of collegiate education and other forums like the All India Association of Christian Higher Education and the Association of College Principals. It helped NAAC to reach out to thousands of faculty and administrators.

Ensuring Wider Participation

In the initial stages of the development of the instrument and methodology, NAAC agreed on rigorous in-house efforts coupled with wider national consultations. In spite of external quality assessment through accreditation being a new initiative, there was enough expertise outside NAAC. As mentioned earlier the system has seen many initiatives towards improving quality over and above the existing regulatory mechanisms. Many experts had contributed to those developments. It was agreed that the in-depth groundwork should be done by NAAC, which was to be enhanced, by the appropriate combination of focus group workshops and national level seminars. While the focus groups led to micro-level discussions, the national level consultations broadened the horizons of thinking.

Bringing in people from various backgrounds and interests also helped to enhance the insights of the group process. During all discussions, NAAC was cautious not to impose its ideas on the working group to allow new and open-minded suggestions to come up. In fact it even helped in avoiding counter-productive effects. It allowed the consensus to evolve from the group and that strengthened the feeling of ownership of the process among the institutions.

Careful Development of Instruments

Through a series of consultative interactions with a large body of academia, NAAC evolved the norms, methods and a series of instruments for assessment. Among the norms, it was decided that NAAC would concentrate on institutions as the unit of assessment, with a provision for assessing individual departments also, and that accreditation should continue to be a voluntary process, the outcome of which would be valid for a period of five years. Detailed manuals and guidelines to facilitate institutional preparation were published to cater to the different segments of the Indian higher education system. Presently NAAC is working on developing the manual for departmental accreditation for which a series of national level workshops has been initiated. A National Consultative Committee for Sciences has been formed and the first meeting of the committee was held in June 2001. Soon similar meetings will be organised for the humanities and social sciences. The large number of academia involved in these activities became the nucleus for clearing the apprehensions of colleagues in their institutions.

Assuring Transparency

The transparency in all efforts has instilled confidence among the academia. Every stage of the assessment process is transparent and carried out in consultation with the institution. NAAC is careful to ensure that the accreditation process is seen as an exercise in partnership and not as something imposed from above. Preparation of the self-study report, checking for conflict of interest in constituting the panel, fixing the dates for the visit, firming up the visit schedule, agreeing on the agenda for interactions, sharing the assessment report with the institution before it is submitted to NAAC, etc. are some of the events where the institutions experience the transparency of the process.

Of all the events mentioned above, checking for any conflict of interest of the peers and sharing the assessment report with the institution have had a significant impact on the acceptability of NAAC's process. In fact, this transparency has served the purpose of enhancing the professionalism of assessment. NAAC takes care to see that the right kind of experts are invited for the right responsibility and the peers take care that the evaluative statements of the assessment report are based on clear evidence.

Ensuring Objectivity

The objectivity of peer assessment was a major issue of concern. It was addressed appropriately by evolving safeguards. Pointers of quality were developed based on national statistics. The development of the pointers of quality was based on the logic that the existing situation in reasonably good and representative institutions may be taken as an indicator of mid-level achievement and any institution that exceeds that level deserves to be credited. For every key aspect of the seven criteria, if we take the existing situation in most of the good institutions as the base standard, a standard higher than the base would give a higher level of classification, and a standard lower than the base would give another category. Data were collected from a representative sample of around 40 good institutions and averages were calculated for the quantitative aspects. For some aspects it was possible to fix a three-level classification, and for others a two-point scale was fixed. After a thorough discussion with a group of experts, the pointers of quality were piloted on a few institutions. It became clear that for initial focus on aspects of importance, the credits were useful as the referral point. Guiding peer assessment through these pointers of quality has helped to gain the confidence of the academia. Peers who participated in the assessment visits could experience the rigor of the process and they were the ambassadors to convince their respective institutions.

Contextualising Assessment

During NAAC's early studies it was found that instruments and standards set should not be followed blindly. They may provide an external point of reference for evaluating the quality of the processes of the institution under assessment, but they cannot be interpreted in void. Contextualising, synthesising and sensitising the data to objectives are essential, and for this, peer assessment is inevitable. For example, the student–library book ratio may be very favourable in an institution. The library may have long working hours, open access system and book bank facility. If the team goes by those aspects alone, for library facilities, the institution may come in the top bracket. But a closer scrutiny may reveal that over the years, the institution has accumulated books but the quality of the books, currency, implementation of the book bank facility, support services of the library, linkage with other libraries, and maintenance need a lot of improvement. As one can see, for some of these aspects quantification in terms of ratio is possible and for the others it has to be a qualitative judgment. The peers have to synthesise both qualitative and quantitative inferences to arrive at a holistic value judgment, in the context of the institution. In other words, the peers have an important role in analysing and moderating the credits, synthesising the outcome on individual indicators to arrive at an overall assessment and also in evaluating the contextual framework of the institution. Accepting peer assessment as a vital component, the Frame of Reference for Peer Assessment was developed to focus peer attention on key issues. It is a framework where the peers have to record the justification for taking a certain value judgement on aspects that have a direct bearing on criterion assessment.

Enhancing the Professionalism of Assessment

Having accepted peer assessment as an integral part of its methodology, NAAC brings in consistency among the peers by appropriate safeguards, training strategies and discussions. A notable effort towards this direction is the development of the 'National Cadre of Assessors'.

The assessor's main responsibility is to visit institutions to assess the quality of education offered there. To do this job professionally, experts from different parts of the country are selected through nomination and advertisements and through a rigorous selection process. For the assessors thus selected, NAAC organises a 3-day residential training programme to induct them into the 'National Cadre of Assessors'. This training strategy has given a professional dimension to the National Cadre of Assessors. The trained assessors are not full-time employees of NAAC but join the assessment teams on invitation by NAAC. They would be on the active roll for a period of five years and participate in four to six visits of three to five days each per year, for which there is a nominal honorarium.

At the end of the training programme, the resource team evaluates every participant of the training programme, for the various competencies required of an assessor. In general around 90 per cent of the trained assessors get a "good" to "excellent" rating. Around 5 per cent may have to be dropped due to serious lacunae. Though there may not be a formal intimation to such assessors, they do not get invited for any team visits. The other 5 per cent are the ones who may be strong in some areas and whose weaknesses have to be balanced appropriately by others in the team. When the newly trained assessor is inducted into a team for the first visit, these remarks become the guidelines for the NAAC officers. Further, when an assessor goes on the first visit, it is almost like a mentoring programme. Care is taken to see that the others in the team are well experienced. This makes the first assessment of the new assessor a smooth learning experience. More importantly, it ensures that the consistency in the frame of reference of the team is not affected by inducting new members (although they are already trained for the job).

To assess the effectiveness of the training strategy, after completing two training programmes, NAAC invited an international observer to sit in one of the assessment visits. The feedback was useful in fine-tuning the training strategy. The areas that need to be strengthened were identified. The feedback had substantial influence on the planning of the peer team visit as well as on the training strategy.

Making the Purpose Clear to Stakeholders

Further, it was found that clarity in purpose paid rich dividends. When there were different and at times non-compatible expectations from different interest groups, NAAC made its stand clear. Instead of trying to be defensive, NAAC was explicit in reiterating that its process was by and large designed to serve the prime objectives in the first cycle of assessment and may be expanded to include improvements to serve more beneficiaries during the next cycle. The voluntary nature of the process, the self-improvement purpose of accreditation and the intrinsic benefits were discussed. Institutions understood that there might not be any immediate monetary benefits, with the tacit understanding that the fund-giving agencies may use the assessment outcome for their decision-making. This avoided unrealistic expectations from the assessment outcome.

Activating the Internal Mechanisms

Emphasising the significance of the self-study report as the beginning of quality assessment and insisting on the participatory process also nurtured the feeling of ownership. The internal quality assurance mechanisms of the institutions were encouraged and involved, which also facilitated to a large extent the participation of the members of the institution in the process. In fact during the first three years, NAAC promoted the concept of "Internal Quality Assurance Cell (IQAC)" with guidelines to set up the internal structures to review quality as an ongoing process. The guidelines for IQAC suggested a methodology of self-evaluation similar to the one required for accreditation by NAAC but without the external peer review. Many institutions initiated IQACs, felt confident about the process of self-evaluation and later volunteered for accreditation by NAAC. The real benefits of accreditation have been the impact it has had on establishing/making the internal quality assurance mechanism functional and robust, which strengthened the ownership of QA among the institutions.

Building on Work Already Done

While evolving the norms and indicators, the work already done by UGC, National Institute for Educational Planning and Administration and Association of Indian Universities—the national bodies of Indian higher education—was taken into consideration. By updating and expanding the statistics already evolved by these agencies, NAAC could work on its approach. The pilot studies helped in fine-tuning the crude statistics into 'sensitive indicators'.

Pilot Studies and Field Trials

The assumption that at the initial stage, mistakes are bound to happen and field trials and experimentation may help in eliminating the adverse effects of initial errors was reasonably correct. The first ten institutions were assessed for their functioning in ten parameters and the field experience revealed the overlap in many of those parameters. Clubbing the overlaps, NAAC revised the ten parameters into seven criteria that led to a few unhappy notes. The assessment outcome also underwent changes. The initial grading pattern of letter grades A, B, C, D, and E had to be revised to the grading pattern of A with one star to five stars where the letter A denoted accredited status and the number of stars denoted the level of quality. This was again changed to the current grading pattern on a nine-point scale (C, C+, C++, B, B+, B++, A, A+, A++). These changes have led to a few non-comparable outcomes which could have been avoided with enough pilot studies.

Involving the Early Adopters

Capitalising on the 'early adopters' (members of the institutions that volunteered for assessment and the assessors who joined the assessment visits) was also a great support for the efforts of NAAC. Most of the institutions that volunteered for assessment in the beginning were confident of their potential and were eager to know their strengths and weaknesses through an objective external assessment. Some of them were already employing their own institutional evaluation through internal mechanisms. The broad involvement of early adopters who could share their conviction, positive approach and experience enabled NAAC to ensure widespread support from the others. Those who were involved in the assessment visits became the change agents in their own institutions. The early adopters have also helped in pilot studies and in the collection of data for working out the norms and indicators for assessment. This gave an assurance to the academia about the appropriateness of the process and it enhanced the acceptance of NAAC's efforts.

Building on Experience

In the initial stages, building on the experience of every assessment visit and every experience is vital to avoid the repetition of mistakes. Till a pattern was set for the criteria to be followed for team composition, NAAC was particular about regular staff meetings and briefings by the coordinating officers. Amidst all the work pressures, staff members were very particular in sharing their experiences with colleagues in staff meetings. During those meetings any issue of concern that might arise with reference to a particular assessor or a conflicting situation were made known to the other officers. Though very rare, there have been instances where conscious decisions have been taken not to invite a particular member based on the derogatory role s/he had in the peer assessment. Continuous updating of such feedback about the assessors and dissemination of that information among the staff members who are involved in the team visits is very vital to uphold the credibility of the process.

Responding to Genuine Issues of Concern

Responding positively to the genuine concerns of the academia has been the strength of NAAC. Fine-tuning the instrument and methodology and roping in government support towards accreditation costs were the initiatives taken by NAAC in response to the genuine concerns expressed by the institutions of higher education. In fact when institutions became a little doubtful about the status of NAAC and worried whether NAAC would be acting as an arm of the government to cut government grants, NAAC ensured awareness of the independent status of the council and the ameliorative role NAAC intended to play through its awareness programmes. Today, the institutions are convinced of the facilitating role being played by NAAC.

Evaluating Evaluation

NAAC respected not only the concerns expressed by institutions but also the expectations of institutions. The mid-term review held in June 2000 was a response to analyse the expectations of institutions. After assessing about 125 institutions, NAAC carried out an evaluation of its evaluation procedures. The analysis of the feedback was discussed in a meeting and the outcome was published. The overall analysis indicated that NAAC's procedures are workable but may need fine-tuning in a few aspects. The openness with which NAAC carried out the evaluation instilled confidence among the academia. NAAC's efforts at meta-evaluation are not a one-time affair. After the major event of collecting feedback from the first 100 accredited institutions, it has become a regular feature. Any institution that completes six months after getting accredited is sent a questionnaire from NAAC seeking feedback on the different aspects of NAAC's methodology and asking details about the impact assessment has made on the institution. The feedback is analysed to look for aspects to be fine-tuned. After every assessment visit, feedback is collected from the members of the peer team in a structured format for perfecting the peer team visit. A roundtable for chairs is an annual feature where many issues of evaluating NAAC's process are taken up for threadbare discussions. International observers have sat in the assessment visits and given evaluative reports about NAAC's process.

Keeping Pace with International Trends

Being in the mainstream of international trends also added to the acceptance of NAAC. India did not lag much behind other countries in accepting External Quality Assurance as a means to promote quality. There have been many developmental strategies where India joined the mainstream/ international trend many decades later, but not in adopting the EQA mechanism. In most of the countries, except perhaps for USA, EQA is a concept that evolved very recently and India is already in the mainstream. International linkages established with other countries for sharing of information and experience, teleconferences with international experts, bi-national conferences, joint research and publication programmes, academic exchange programmes, participation in international events and presence of international observers and experts in some of the events of NAAC have enhanced the status of NAAC. Membership in the International Network of Quality Assurance Agencies in Higher Education (INQAAHE) and the organisation of the sixth biennial conference of the INQAAHE network in 2001 at Bangalore have further strengthened NAAC's image. As an active member of the Asia-Pacific Sub-network of INQAAHE, with Prof. A. Gnanam, Chairperson of the Executive Committee of NAAC as the co-chair of the sub-network, NAAC is working towards strengthening regional cooperation in quality assurance.

The Lessons Learnt

The lessons learnt may be summarised as follows:

- Assessment of quality cannot be the answer to all quality-related problems.
- Quality assessment is a complex issue and hence should be used to address issues of high priority.
- Quality assessment to a large extent depends on peer judgment and not just on quantitative indicators.
- For quality assessment, a combination of self-study and peer review offers an appropriate strategy.
- The unit of assessment chosen should be viable, feasible and practical in the national context.
- Assessment outcome can be useful only for institutions that have the desire to improve and are anxious to do so. Hence the internal quality assurance mechanism has to be activated.

- The feeling of ownership of the process has to be developed among institutions.
- Emphasising the significance of the self-study report makes the internal quality assurance mechanisms functional and robust.
- A combination of focused core group workshops and broad national level consultations ensures the appropriateness of the strategy.
- Bringing in people from various backgrounds to discuss quality issues enhances the insights of the group process.
- Experimentation and field trials may help in eliminating the adverse effects of initial errors.
- Transparency in all the efforts enhances the acceptability of the strategy.
- A multi-pronged approach is essential to ensure the support of academia.
- Assessment of quality need not rely heavily on quantitative indicators.
- Peer assessment is vital in contextualising the assessment.
- Clarity in the frame of reference is important to guide peer assessment.
- Guiding peer assessment through pointers of quality and quantitative indicators with caution is rewarding.
- Capitalising on the 'early adopters' is of great help to promote the acceptance of the process.
- The role of the EQA agency in steering the assessment processes has to be finalised at the start. The balance between the co-coordinating functions and steering the assessment processes is an important issue to be finalised before venturing into assessment.
- The reporting of the assessment in line with the prime objectives has to be taken care of.

- Stakeholder decisions play a vital role in promoting assessment.
- The information requirements of stakeholders and their legitimate expectations should be taken note of.
- The strength of peer assessment depends to a very large extent on the professionalism of the experts and an appropriate training strategy has to be evolved to enhance professionalism.
- The objectivity of peer assessment has to be ensured through appropriate safeguards.
- Responding positively to the genuine concerns of the academia strengthens the acceptance of QA.
- Involving the institutions in fine-tuning the instrument and methodology is rewarding.
- Roping in government support towards accreditation enhances the benefits of accreditation.
- The success of the process depends on respecting the expectations of the institutions.
- Being in the mainstream of the international trend enhances the acceptability of the process at the national level.

The experience of NAAC has to be seen in the light of the national context and the objectives for which NAAC has been established. It is obvious that the instruments and methods adopted by one country in assessing the quality of higher education may not be totally applicable to another. Even within a country, one agency may have a different mandate from another because any strategy has to necessarily take cognizance of the contextual conditions. Further, successful strategies for achieving a result may not be intrinsically good but depend on a multiplicity of factors and the task of quality assurance is no exception. The Indian experience has to be seen with this understanding.

Part II
Challenges for the Council

Quality Assurance is an evolving mechanism and new challenges emerge as the system evolves. To develop a suitable model, countries must start the quality assurance initiatives with a reasonably good structure and make improvements based on field experience as they progress. Countries may not benefit if they wait for a perfect system to be evolved by others. However, after starting the quality assurance mechanism, too many changes too soon, in the name of fine-tuning, may send wrong signals about its preparedness to the stakeholders and they would tend to wait until the system stabilizes. The system will also lose its credibility. Hence, clarity about the critical elements as well as the degrees of freedom to make changes is essential. It is in this context that the experiences of other countries are of great value. The Indian system made a good beginning and carried out further fine-tuning as it progressed towards professionalism. This part deals with the five major challenges that are emerging in the Indian context – overcoming post-accreditation complacency, fine-tuning the policy on eliminating the conflict of interest, evolving procedures on substantive changes, enhancing the professionalism in the process and diversifying the protocols to include distance education provisions. It also highlights how the Indian system is getting ready to balance the core methodological elements of quality assurance with the ground reality of the national context without losing its credibility at the global level.

5. Policies on Conflict of Interest and Substantive Changes

Quality Assurance has the danger of becoming subjective and biased if not handled with care. QA agencies should be careful in evolving safeguards and protocols to eliminate biases and to ensure the credibility and integrity of accreditation. One of the safeguards is to eliminate the conflict of interest among everyone involved in the process. Another policy issue that needs to be firmed up is the policy on substantive changes. The peers generally recommend the accreditation status based on certain evidence available at the time of the assessment visit. The accreditation decision taken by the agencies is largely based on the peer team recommendation and it is valid for a specific period. During the validity period, if there are substantial developments in the institution that may affect the status to which it belongs to, what should be the course of action to be taken by the quality assurance agency? These two issues should be addressed carefully as the credibility of assessment depends on them.

The protocols and procedures used for assessment should eliminate the chances of subjectivity and uphold the credibility of the accreditation process. The process draws its strength from the clarity in policies and the built-in checks and balances in the procedures. To be tuned to the developmental needs of the evolving process of accreditation, close attention should be paid to policy development on two areas, namely, eliminating conflict of interest and handling the issue of substantive changes in institutions subsequent to accreditation.

Conflict of Interest

The significance of peer review in quality assessment, is still under debate, but a better alternative has not been found, in any of the quality assurance agencies. The qualifications and talents of the people who constitute the assessment teams are critical to the credibility of the whole process. It is not enough if the institution has confidence in the expertise of the peers; more than anything the institution should be able to trust the peers. It is in this context that the policy on "Conflict of Interest" has to be evolved by the quality assurance agencies.

The Audit Manual of Australian Universities Quality Agency (AUQA) classifies possible conflicts as *personal, professional* or *ideological* (between which there may be some overlap). *Personal* conflicts could include animosity, close friendship or kinship between a peer and the head or other senior official of the institution or if a peer were excessively biased for or against the institution due to some previous event. That is why it is normally preferable to avoid having graduates of the institution on an assessment panel. *Professional* conflicts could occur if a peer had been a failed applicant for a position in the institution, were a current applicant or prospect for a position in the institution, were a senior adviser, examiner or consultant to the institution, or were with an institution that is strongly competing with an institution being assessed. An example of an *ideological* conflict would be a peer's complete lack of sympathy for the style, type or ethos of an institution.

International experience indicates that quality assurance agencies have to work further to eliminate conflict of interest. For example, it is debatable who should take responsibility for identifying and reporting the conflicts during or after the visit – the peer, the chair, the council staff or the institution. Even if one of the above brings it to the notice of the council, issues that need more reflection are: who are to be involved in solving the conflict, what procedure is to be followed, who are to be excluded from the discussions, what part of the discussions is to be confidential, etc.? As of now, in most of the QAAs the assessors and the institutions are entrusted with the responsibility of bringing any information that may appear to be a conflict of interest to the notice of the council before the visit commences.

NAAC has clearly defined what it means by "Conflict of Interest". It primarily deals with having interests or associations that compete with one's official actions or duties in the accreditation process. As in the case of international experience, the conflicts that emerge "during and after" the visit might pose new challenges to NAAC. To avoid any confrontation with uncomfortable situations, in which a real conflict of interest jeopardises the legitimacy of the accreditation process, there is a need to have a comprehensive and explicit policy on any conflict of interest that can possibly surface at pre-, during and post-assessment visit stages. Such a transparent policy framework is essential, not only to help avoid procedural problems, but also to enhance the credibility of the entire process.

In practice, the institution is consulted on the panel of experts who are being considered for constituting the visiting team. If the institution has any justifiable reservation against any member, it may be brought to the notice of NAAC without suggesting any alternative. In fact, the institutions have to sign a 'no conflict of interest statement' which reads as follows:

> *This is to certify that, the peer team members have no involvement with our institution, directly or indirectly through their close relatives, in the past or at present, as either an employee or a member of any official body, or a consultant or even a graduate. Further, none of the members of the proposed team will be appointed at least for a year for any important assignment in the institution.*

Where reservations are justifiable, NAAC constitutes the peer team out of the other members of the panel, removing the individuals in question from the team. Once the choice of the peers is made, NAAC finds out from them whether they have any conflict of interest with the institution to be assessed. Though the peers are experts known for their integrity, to ensure and assure objectivity, they too have to sign a *no conflict of interest statement* which reads as follows:

This is to certify that, I have 'no conflict of interest' with the proposed institution as detailed under:

- I have no involvement with the proposed institution, directly or indirectly through my close relatives, in the past or at present, as either an employee or a member of any official body, or a consultant or even a graduate.
- I do not belong to the same state in which the institution is located.
- I have no affiliation with an institution competing directly with the proposed institution.

Similar procedures are followed by the other QAAs. Although the explicit cases of conflicts are thus eliminated by the QAAs at the pre-visit stage, instances of "apparent conflict of interest" might emerge during the on-site visit. Therefore, a clear comprehensive policy on conflict of interest is of vital importance. It is very important that even the appearance of conflict of interest is avoided to maintain the credibility of accreditation. There are many instances when the conflict of interest is noticed only during the visit or after the visit is over. Here are a few hypothetical cases.

Case 1: One of the members, say, Prof. AX, had served in the high level committee of the region where the institution was located. Since it happened a decade ago and also since it was seen as an honorary academic assignment, the peer did not perceive it as a conflict of interest and did not bring it to the notice of the QAA. During the team discussions, the member often mentioned of that role to emphasise his better understanding of the higher education scenario of the region. This made the other members feel uncomfortable and the Chairperson had to be very tactful in not allowing this to look like a conflict of interest. Especially when the member's evaluation differed greatly from the other members of the team, it made the team discussions unproductive.

Can we say that the member had a conflict of interest? Was he obliged to inform the QAA about his role in the past in the high level committee? Had he informed, what should have been the decision of QAA? Should such experts be excluded from the team or should it be seen as an advantage to know the higher education scenario of the state better? Can we say that all this could have been sorted out if the member had been more diplomatic in asserting his knowledge and understanding about the state? If he had been diplomatic can we say that it had really eliminated the conflict of interest? What should the Chair do in such cases? Report to the QAA? What could be the appropriate role of the council staff in that situation? If that member had not agreed to the evaluation of the others and recorded a dissent, what procedure should be followed? Quoting the "apparent conflict of interest" can the member's dissent be disregarded? Who could decide about the "apparent conflict of interest"? Should the Chair and the QAA go by the majority opinion?

Case 2: During the interaction with the Department of American Studies, the expert Prof. AY found out that the department needed more exposure to current developments and to identify its thrust areas. After listening to some of his suggestions and impressions, the department invited him for a series of lectures. The QA agency's policy insists that experts do not accept any assignment from the institutions visited by them for at least one year. But, accepting a lecture series may not be equated to consultation or an assignment with high remuneration. Prof. AY agreed to give the lecture series.

How should such an invitation be handled? Can the assessor accept that invitation? Should he suggest another colleague who may be equally competent? Should he consult the Chairperson of the peer team on this invitation? What should be the QA agency's stand on this issue? Did a conflict of interest exist? If there are problems in arriving at consensus about the final institutional score, in what way could this invitation be perceived differently and as a source of 'conflict of interest'? Even if such a problem does not arise, would this set an unhealthy precedent for other situations? Should the institution bring such issues to the notice of the QAA? On the site, what should have been the role of the agency staff on this issue? If the issue of invitation comes to the notice of the QA agency through another institution much after the visit, what action should be taken by the agency to inform the concerned institution and the peer?

Case 3: In the initial stages of the agency's development, a well-known educationist, Prof. AZ, had often voiced his opinion that the agency's grading system needed a thorough change. According to him only institutions of international standing should be given the top grading. Further, he was of the opinion that there could be no top category institutions in India. However, as quality assurance gained the acceptance of the academia and more and more institutions were accredited, he ceased to voice his criticism. After two years of his silence, the agency thought that he had been convinced of the assessment process and wanted to use his expertise for the assessment exercise. When the agency invited Prof.

AZ to join an assessment team, he decided to join the team to know more about how the process was implemented and where the agency might be going wrong. The institution did not record any objection since it knew only about the member's reputation as an educationist and did not have a clue about his reservation on the QAA's grading.

The peer team discussions were very uncomfortable for the chairperson of the team. There was a wide gap between the assessment of AZ and the rest of the team. The arguments of AZ were about the conceptual mistake in the grading and not on substantiating his evaluation. The QA agency staff explained that the evaluation framework of the QAA was not international standards. But AZ was not ready to accept the evaluation framework that aimed to classify the national HEIs into a few categories depending on their quality. Since there were no top grade institutions in India, according to his opinion, he wanted to place the institution two levels below where the others had placed the institution. After a lot of discussions which brought out the different (personal) frame of reference AZ had, the group decided to go by their "QAA's frame of reference". AZ recorded his ratings separately and a consensus could not be reached.

Was it ethical on the part of AZ to sign the "No Conflict of Interest" statement and join the team? The members of the assessment team are expected to leave their personal baggage behind and act on behalf of the agency. They are expected to assess the institution with respect to the agency's frame of reference and follow the agency's guidelines. It is commonsense that no system can evolve a mechanism that is 100 per cent acceptable to all. Many a times a huge diverse system like ours goes by collective decision-making and honours the majority opinion. It is with this understanding that many who had difference of opinion at the personal level joined the agency's activities and acted on behalf of the agency. But Prof. AZ decided to go by his personal agenda. While joining the team itself was seen as unethical,

AZ went ahead to complain and criticise the agency's process. Some of his remarks were even against the confidentiality of the evaluation the peer team was supposed to maintain. How should such cases be treated? Will a mere diplomatic approach be enough in such cases? Or should the agency make it clear to the other peers and HEIs that what AZ had done was unethical? If AZ's breach of confidentiality is exposed by the QAA, will it be harmful to the image of the agency? Or will it add to the credibility of the protocols followed by the QAA?

Case 4: Prof. AP was from a premier institution that was yet to undergo assessment. He was sure that his institution deserved a top rating. He thought only institutions close to his own institution deserve the top grade and voiced his opinion during discussions with the council staff. When he joined an on-site visit he was determined to see how close standing that institution was to his own institution. In other words, his institution was his frame of reference. The chairperson of the team had a difficult job balancing AP's fault-finding behaviour. He felt that the team spirit was affected very much by the arguments of AP who always had his own institution as the model to be emulated. Was there a conflict of interest? Should AP be involved in future visits? Can we say that all this could have been sorted out if the member had not been considered at all in view of his assumption about the grading his institution deserves? In addition, if that had been done, would it mean that the agency was biased in choosing members? A whole lot of questions given under case-1 emerge in this case also.

Case 5: Prof. AQ was very concerned about some criticism he came across from a colleague that the agency's grading was liberal towards a particular group of institutions. During the interaction with agency staff, he was also informed that the management of that group of institutions did an internal analysis and submitted only the best of their colleges for the first phase of assessment. However, when he joined the peer team to assess one of those institutions he decided to be very rigorous in his assessment and see for himself whether QAA's assessment was liberal or not.

During the peer team discussions, the other members of the team felt that Prof. AQ was not in tune with the QAA's frame of reference that had been followed so far to other institutions. To cite an example, the institution did not have a formal career guidance cell. But the Dean of Students Welfare was coordinating those services. In similar instances in other institutions, the teams have accepted the effectiveness of the strategy in vogue in the institutions and did not consider it as a weakness. To cite another example, the institution had just activated its alumni association and collected feedback from the alumni on their campus experience. In other instances, the very initiative had been seen as a healthy practice. However, Prof. AQ did not agree with the others. While all these differences in perceptions added up to a greater magnitude, the agency staff also felt that the frame of reference for evaluation was different for Prof. AQ. The team Chair expressed his opinion that the evaluation framework should not be changed mid-way of the review and it was for the QAA to decide on these policy matters. What should be done?

Case 6: Conflict of Interest that is known after the visit. After the assessment visit, the council staff came to know that one of the peers (say Prof. AR) might have used the team visit for a personal benefit. A few weeks after the on-site visit, a close relative of Prof. AR, introduced to the head of the institution during the informal dinner on the first day of the visit, had been appointed in a responsible position in the institution. Another member of the visiting team, seeking guidance whether such instances would be acceptable to the QAA, had brought the information to the notice of the council. The council staff was appreciative of the qualifications of the relative in question. But, the relative's presence with the peer during the on-site visit, although it was during an informal dinner, after he had appeared for an interview for a position at the institution but much before a decision was made about the appointment, seemed to be a conflict of interest. What should the council do? What are the guidelines to be evolved to avoid such instances?

Case 7: Role of the Members of the Council. The international practice varies in the way the agency staff is involved in the process. The Commissioners and Directors lead the teams in some agencies. In Quebec, one of the three Commissioners of CEEC leads teams and writes the reports. Staff members of the agency serve in the teams of QAA, UK. In South Africa, the managers of the audit directorates have the responsibility to write the audit reports. No council staff accompanies the team in the case of the North Central Association for Schools and Colleges of USA. Staff members of the agency join the teams as coordinators in NAAC visits. Members of the Executive Committee of NAAC who are the decision makers on accreditation outcome join the teams as members or lead the teams as Chairs. Though these practices help in maintaining the consistency in the evaluation framework and also provide rich feedback about the process to the decision makers, there are arguments in other agencies about unknown conflict of interest or internal conflict of interest entering into the process. In Australia, Board members do not normally act as auditors to avoid these conflicts. AUQA believes that "*problems could arise for an AUQA Board member who had been a member of an audit panel, if the Board raised serious questions about the performance or result of the audit, or the auditee were to attempt to appeal to the Board against the conclusions of the audit report. Therefore, Board members do not normally act as auditors; if they were so to act, they would be excluded from any subsequent related discussions at Board meetings. Also, any Board member associated with a particular institution or agency is excluded from any discussion of that institution or agency at a Board meeting.*"

Some agencies argue that conflict of interest may arise in the case of council staff even if they serve on teams only as coordinators since the agency and the staff have access to a lot of sensitive and confidential data that might influence the quality assessment and while handling the data conflicts might arise. Therefore, the policy on conflict of interest should spell out what could be the conflicts of interest for the council staff and its decision makers.

If the hypothetical cases discussed above seem to be trivial ones, that assumption needs to be corrected. We do come across instances where peers sign the no conflict of interest statement as a routine and later when the situation arises, do not even recognise the conflict. In one of the regional accrediting agencies of the USA, there was a situation which came to light after the whole visit was over. After the visit when the team members were finalising their travel plan to reach the airport, one of the members revealed that she did not have to worry about it since she was the wife of the President of the institution. The accrediting agency had invited her for the assessment visit based on the one-year old curriculum vitae which was in her maiden name and the council had no idea that she was the wife of the President of the institution to be assessed. The reviewers from UK have a few instances similar to this. In one of the assessment visits, a reviewer expressed his reservations to interact with a particular staff member of the institution and it was then that the Chair came to know that the staff was the ex-wife of the reviewer. Of course, the concerned agencies handled those situations well; nonetheless these are examples to indicate that specific guidelines are necessary to deal with such conflicts.

As the hypothetical cases indicate, to eliminate conflict of interest at the personal and professional levels, before the commencement of the on-site visit, the existing practices of QAAs are satisfactory. But the ideological conflicts and the conflicts that emerge during the visit need more reflection. As NAAC works on fine-tuning its procedures and protocols, this area will be given due attention.

Apart from the conflict of interest, one more area that has to be firmed up is the policy on substantive changes.

When an institution is accredited, the accreditation is based on conditions existing at the time of the assessment. However, after accreditation, the institution may introduce changes and some of them may change the character of the institution significantly. The policies to deal with those changes are very important to institutional accreditation more than any other form of quality assessment like programme assessment, mainly because institutional accreditation covers almost everything done in the name of the institution.

Substantive Changes

The accreditation outcome basically depends on the recommendations of the peer team. It is valid for a specific period. That is the period when an institution may not drastically change its characteristics but make improvements. It might go up or down slightly in the quality continuum that will hopefully be taken care of in the next assessment. In fact, if an institution acts on the assessment report, changes are expected to happen. If the changes enhance the quality of the institution, that may lead to a better grading in the following assessment. An institution that falls into slumber after accreditation may decline in its standards, which will again be noted in the next assessment. But the reality is not as simple as it seems to be.

Subsequent to accreditation, institutions bring in changes. Many changes, such as adding or dropping courses, innovations within existing programmes, recruiting more personnel, etc are not substantive, and therefore may be included within the scope of the institution's accreditation without additional formalities. But there may be changes that significantly alter the operations or status of the institution and they should be taken note of at an appropriate time instead of waiting for the next assessment. But how do we define substantive changes?

In the USA, HEIs have the obligation and responsibility

to keep the accrediting agencies apprised of plans for certain important proposed or actual changes in their operations and status. In the case of the DETC, even a change in marketing approach is considered to be a substantive change, since the marketing strategy has a central role in distance education provisions. The Middle States Association has the following policy: *"Institutions should report changes that*

- significantly alter the mission, goals, or objectives of an institution;
- alter the legal status, form of control, or ownership;
- establish instruction constituting at least 50 per cent of a degree programme in a significantly different format/method of delivery;
- establish instruction at a new degree or credential level;
- replace clock hours with credit hours;
- increase substantially the number of clock or credit hours awarded for successful completion of a programme;
- establish instruction constituting at least 50 per cent of a degree programme at a new geographic location;
- relocate the primary campus or existing branch campus;
- otherwise affect significantly the institution's ability to support and to continue the support of existing and proposed programmes."

The discussion on substantive changes should not be viewed as an effort to inhibit such activities nor to diminish creative approaches to them. While the decision to modify an institution is an institutional prerogative and responsibility, the quality assurance agency is obligated to determine the effect of any substantive change on the quality, integrity, and effectiveness of the total institution.

There are also concerns expressed about cases where adverse actions hidden from the peer teams come to surface after the accreditation result is made public and the judgment about the status of accreditation in such cases may require a drastic change. How to go about in those situations? Let us consider a few hypothetical cases of new facts emerging and major changes in the functioning of the institution.

Case 1: Six months after grading the institution in the top category, a major scandal broke out in the institution in the evaluation of exam papers. Thousands of answer scripts of students were found missing and the institution did not handle the crisis well. A lot of queries came in about the impact this scandal could have on the accreditation status. What should be done?

Case 2: In another institution, soon after accreditation, there was a change in leadership and the new leader initiated many of his pet projects that had only an adverse impact. What should the quality assurance agency do?

Case 3: That the data on faculty and staff welfare were false came to the notice of the peer team chair after the announcement of the accreditation result. There was evidence that academic freedom and faculty development were at stake in the institution and the data presented to the peer team were false. What should be the implications?

Case 4: There were criticisms that one of the institutions raised the fee structure very high and indulged in marketing its high accreditation grade for unaccounted "donations" from parents. The Parent Teacher Association made a representation to the quality assurance agency to advise the management of the institution. Should the quality assurance agency interfere? Should the quality assurance agency insist that it is obligatory on the part of the institutions to inform the agency before raising the fee structure beyond a certain per cent, say 10 per cent?

As a proactive measure, if the agency has to evolve a

strategy to tackle substantive changes, what could it be? Should the agency ask the institutions to give annual reports? If yes, what are the aspects to be highlighted in the report? Will it end up as another annual report on the achievements of the institution or should it highlight the change and progress made by the institution based on the assessment report? How should the report be analysed – in-house or by involving external peers? What would be the guidelines to review the reports? What are the guidelines to take a value judgement on whether there has been a substantive change or not? One should bear in mind that not all changes, positive or adverse, are substantive. How do we define them?

This is only a beginning. In spite of the mechanisms to report and review substantive changes, if there are issues that are not brought to the notice of the agency by the institution, what should be the consequences to the institutions? If someone else, a third party, may be a stakeholder, brings an adverse development in the institution to the notice of the agency, how will that be dealt with? When other stakeholders bring adverse developments to the agency's notice, what are the issues that could be considered as genuine for which the agency's intervention in the accredited status would be necessary?

In the case of affiliated and autonomous colleges in the Indian context, should a part of the monitoring activities of post-accreditation substantive changes be entrusted to the parent university? Can the parent university be requested to monitor and report to the quality assurance agency when the developments cause some concern? In fact this raises a very important issue that has a bearing on defining the affiliating functions in the post-accreditation period. The parent universities and NAAC should work in partnership to monitor substantive changes. If not done consultatively, it may lead to the criticism on overload of assessment. Instead of promoting academic autonomy, it might lead to more controls. A similar situation exists in other countries also.

It is difficult to proceed with imaginary doubts and hypothetical cases. At the same time it is important to reflect on those situations and evolve broad safeguards proactively. In any mechanism, there are advantages as well as disadvantages; what is needed is clarity on policies. When the policies are made transparent and clear, the procedures can be simplified to the extent possible, avoiding overlaps and overloads.

Based on the experience of the QAAs of different countries, even an emerging QAA can quickly firm up and formally record the core policies on conflict of interest and substantive changes. The core policies should include the essential criteria to be taken care of, action to be taken on matters of concern and the responsibility of the parties involved in the process. As the QAA gains field experience, based on the contextual requirements, it may fine-tune the policies and make them public documents for all stakeholders to refer to.

6. Enhancing Professionalism in Assessment

The quality assurance agencies the world over are undergoing changes. After initiating a mechanism, if there are too many changes too soon, the system will lose its credibility. At the same time not responding to the changes in the national and international context of quality assurance would make the system irrelevant. Hence, the clarity on the critical elements to be followed as well as the degrees of freedom for change that the quality assurance mechanism can enjoy is essential. While the experience of other QAAs would indicate the critical elements to be adhered to, the field experience contributes to building on degrees of freedom. This paper deals with NAAC's efforts to enhance the professionalism of assessment by constantly fine-tuning its safeguards, without losing sight of the critical elements.

Quality Assurance is an evolving mechanism. There are no set priorities and standards to follow. Every system has to evolve its own model taking into consideration both national and international developments. To initiate a suitable model, countries may not benefit if they wait for a perfect system to evolve. Waiting for a perfect model might make the QAA a non-starter. What is best is to start with a reasonably good structure, and make improvements based on field experience. It is easier said than done. Once a strategy is implemented, if the field experience calls for changes, how far can changes be effected? True that further fine-tuning is necessary since the whole process is still an evolving one; but the consistency in the focus and frame of reference of the strategy should be maintained. These two aspects—Making a Good Beginning and Fine-tuning—are the factors that depict the larger picture of a QAA.

Making a Good Beginning: Adhering to Critical Elements

Two major aspects, the national context and the objectives for which the mechanism is to be set up, dictate a good beginning. These two aspects provide the basis for the quality assurance mechanism of a particular system. As discussed in the earlier chapters, while it is essential to evolve the methodology to suit the national context, it is equally essential to ensure that it is in line with international trends. For any strategy to be successful it is necessary to identify the "if and only if" conditions and the degrees of freedom the system can afford—aspects where deviation must be avoided and areas where changes can be introduced towards improvement. The "if and only if" conditions may be termed as critical elements. Despite differences in national contexts, the critical elements of quality assessment are bound to be the same. A slight oversight of critical elements will put the QA system in a situation where drastic changes may be necessary soon after initiating the QA mechanism and it will be a threat to the credibility of the mechanism. The core elements have to be broadly adhered to, to conform to the international norms and NAAC is well in line.

Incorporating the critical elements in its methodology, NAAC applied multi-pronged strategies at various levels – awareness programmes to familiarise the academia and educational administrators with the concept of assessment, debate on critical issues, workshops on development and research, training the experts for assessment, discussions with administrators to mop in government support and the like and made a good beginning. There are also areas where the agencies enjoy more freedom and most of these aspects are taken care of while fine-tuning.

Fine-Tuning: Building on Field Experience

Of all the efforts made by NAAC, the one that had the most significant impact in stabilising its process is the fine-tuning of the instrument and methodology, taking field experience as the key. Although NAAC's process had been evolved taking cognisance of the international experience and the Indian context, at the practical level, many new issues came up during field experience and they formed the basis for further fine-tuning the manuals, guidelines and the methodological elements. Some of those initiatives deserve a mention here. Guiding peer assessment through Benchmarks, Pointers of Quality and Frame of Reference, clear role description of peers, firming up the reporting strategy and appropriate training strategy for peers are the noteworthy initiatives that significantly enhanced the objectivity of peer assessment.

Benchmarks

NAAC followed Best Practices Benchmarking. Establishing benchmarks through processes and practices is not a new concept in higher education. The Association of Commonwealth Universities (ACU) has already tried it. In 1996, Commonwealth Higher Education Management Service (CHEMS), a subsystem of ACU launched an international "University Management Benchmarking Club" for universities from the Commonwealth. This Club focuses on the effectiveness of university-wide processes and not narrow departmental functions. The CHEMS approach to benchmarking goes beyond the comparison of data-based scores and conventional performance indicators and looks at the processes that achieve results. By using a consistent approach and identifying processes that are generic and relevant, irrespective of the organisation and how it is structured, it becomes possible to benchmark across sector boundaries (location, size, mono or multi faculty, etc.)

In CHEMS methodology, the first stage of the benchmarking process is the identification of aspects and processes to be addressed. Members of the benchmarking club are then required to supply a written submission, backed up, if necessary, by supporting material from the university's existing documentation, highlighting anything perceived to be a strength or weakness on their part. As regards the assessment process, the assessors award scores in respect of the strength of responses. The reports detailing acknowledged strengths and areas for improvement are provided to each member, together with a composite model of good practice. These are then discussed to arrive at some consensus as to what might be regarded as best practice. It is this process that the club believes encapsulates true benchmarking, *i.e.* in the absence of predetermined benchmarks, the aim is to establish benchmarks through the process.

NAAC has attempted a similar methodology. In its assessment of quality of education, NAAC's methodology looks into how the various policies and processes of the institution are geared to facilitate the educational provisions and the resultant quality in its offerings. The focus is functioning of the institution as well as the outcome. To facilitate the process mapping, in the initial stages, NAAC adopted ten parameters that encompass every aspect of functioning of the institutions of higher education. They are: Goals and objectives, Curriculum design and review, Teaching-learning and evaluation, Research and publications, Consultancy and extension activities, Organisation and management, Infrastructure facilities, Support services,

Student feedback and counselling and Generation and management of financial resources.

For each parameter, best practices that contribute to the efficient and effective functioning of the institution towards quality offerings were identified and defined and they were called as criterion statements. Instead of identifying the practices of the 'best-in-class' institutions, the experts who worked on the criterion statements focused on a typical institution. Under desirable conditions, the best practices we can expect in a typical institution were identified as criterion statements. These criterion statements served as best practices benchmarks. The criterion statements/benchmarks thus evolved were modified latter to suit the revised seven criteria. Further, each criterion has been spelt out into key aspects. The key aspects and the criterion statements are given in the appendix. Once the key aspects were identified, the need to agree on the levels of quality and the indicators emerged and that resulted in the efforts to identify pointers of quality.

Pointers of Quality

The development of the pointers of quality has already been explained in Chapter 4. The pointers of quality for two key aspects – programme options and feedback mechanism – of Criterion-I of an affiliated college is given below:

What is the range of programme options available to the students for awards such as degrees, certificates/ diploma?

For every 3 programmes – 1 point
(Not exceeding 5 points)

Is there any mechanism to obtain feedback from academic peers and employers on the teaching programmes and how is the feedback used in the initiation, review and redesigning of teaching programmes?

Peer assessment	
Good	– 2 points
Satisfactory	– 1 point

After a thorough discussion with a group of experts, the Pointers of Quality were piloted on a few institutions. It became clear that for initial focus on aspects of importance, the credits were useful as the referral point.

Frame of Reference for Peer Assessment

Field experience strengthened our initial assumption that the credits could not be added-up to arrive at the credit score. In the light of the standing of the institution with respect to these pointers, the peers had to give an overall 'criterion score' and as such they were not meant to be converted into criterion-wise scores. Hence a format was evolved to synthesise peer assessment. The Frame of Reference for Peer Assessment for criterion I is given at next page.

The review conducted by NAAC revealed that the use of this format has greatly improved the objectivity of peer assessment. Benchmarks, pointers and frame of reference help in focusing peer team assessment and in giving a quantitative dimension to it. Once the quantification is made as objective as possible, expression of peer assessment in the assessment report, which is qualitative in nature, becomes the next challenge. NAAC has succeeded in this stupendous task also by its appropriate reporting strategy.

The Reporting Strategy

In NAAC's methodology, sharing the report with the head of the institution has a very significant role that has influenced the whole methodology in many ways. Towards the end of the on-site visit, the draft report is given to the head of the institution for checking factual accuracy as well

The frame of reference	*Evaluation (score in per cent) Upper limit exclusive*									*Justi-fication*
	55-60	60-65	65-70	70-75	75-80	80-85	85-90	90-95	95-100	
Criterion I: Curricular Aspects This aspect requires value judgement on the practices of the institution in initiating and redesigning courses that are relevant to the regional and national needs. It also focuses on how the curriculum design of the institution offers diversity and flexibility to learners. This can be best done by judging where the institution stands with reference to the following aspects: • Compatibility of programmes with goals and objectives • Initiation, review and redesign of programmes • Feedback on programmes and interaction with academic peers and employers • Programme options • The system which enables the above										

as for feedback on the evaluation of the peer team. This gives an opportunity for the head to differ from the opinion of the peer team and present the point of view of the institution. Sharing the draft report makes the job of the peer team very challenging. "Looking for evidence" is always kept in focus from the start of the assessment exercise. Nonetheless, there are still issues of concern.

There is no second opinion that the report should be commensurate with the grade awarded. However, there are criticisms that the report does not seem to be discriminating between institutions of different rating and whether an institution is given a top rating or a lower rating, the content and vocabulary of the reports seldom vary substantially. In the words of one of our reviewers, "assessment runs the risk of settling into stereotyping". To avoid these pitfalls, the peer team takes adequate care to collate the data that forms the basis for the evaluative remarks especially the "hard remarks" which are likely to be objected to by the head. Interestingly, what NAAC sees as its major strength is viewed with the following doubts: What if the burden of sharing the report with the institution affects the truthfulness of the evaluation itself? Will the major task of the team be that of completing the on-site visit without any confrontation with the institution, rather than presenting a truthful evaluation?

It is true that the peer team expresses hard remarks in a positive tone. It avoids high-sounding words and a magisterial and condescending tone. For example, the team may not say, "The functioning of the departments X and Y is poor" but would say that those departments need to be strengthened or might say that those departments cause some concern. This tendency to be gentle has led to the criticism that there is "ambiguity in the evaluative language". The critics say that the softening of the remarks might not present the true evaluation. Very often with the good intention of not hurting the weak departments, the team might become so soft in its remarks that the outcome could be misleading. In NAAC's experience, there have been rare instances where the institution agreed with the report and later complained that the grade awarded did not match the report. Out of around 500 assessment exercises done so far, not even 5 per cent have complained on this issue. In fact, balancing the evaluative language and ensuring the correlation between the institutional score and the report is a challenging responsibility of the peer team.

NAAC insists that there must be clear, uncontentious, sound evidence for every evaluative statement made. As the members collect evidence during the on-site visit, they spend time individually as well as collectively on reflection and team discussion. During team discussions on drafting the report the team keeps the following questions in mind:

- Is the report evaluative?
- Is the message clear?
- Are the judgements supported by evidence?
- Does the writing match the institutional score?

Focusing the attention of the peers on the key aspects of assessment through structured formats and pointers and the emphasis given at every stage for collecting evidence and recording the justifications for inferences drawn have greatly facilitated the quality of the report. The editing done by a language expert who is also well experienced in the assessment visits as a reviewer further ensures that the report becomes a 'NAAC Document' before it is included in the NAAC website. Statements based on mere impressions, commendations that may violate existing governmental or institutional norms and remarks that are not in line with NAAC's stand are eliminated at this stage.

Role Description of Peers

Even the most highly qualified team can be thwarted in its work if the accreditation agency is not clear in its expectations of the team. Having accepted peer assessment as a critical component of accreditation, NAAC has evolved clear role descriptions of peers to uphold the professionalism of accreditation. The peers are expected to "evaluate the institution being assessed" with utmost objectivity according to the philosophy of NAAC. They have the following three responsibilities:

- *Before the visit,* every member of the team analyses the self-study report and makes a tentative evaluation. NAAC sends the self-study report to the peer team members well in advance. The peers go through the self-study report thoroughly and based on the analysis of the data, arrive at a tentative evaluation of the performance of the institution.
- *During the visit,* the team looks for evidence to validate the self-study report and collects additional inputs to assess the standing of the institution. The visit varies from 3 to 5 days depending on the size and complexity of the unit to be assessed. As the team collects evidence, the *tentative individual scores* are revised and fine-tuned to *provisional team scores* in percentage.
- *At the end of the visit,* the team makes a collective assessment about the strengths and weaknesses of the institution, records the justifications for the inferences drawn, agrees on the criterion scores and finalises the highlights of the assessment report. The team discusses the "issues of concern" with the head of the institution, for observation and reaction. Through this interaction, any discrepancies and gaps in information are eliminated. After a discussion among the team members on the feedback, the modified/corrected report is given to the head of the institution. At this stage, the head may go through the report and bring to the notice of the peer team any factual errors. If the institution agrees upon the evaluative remarks of the team, the peer team as well as the head of the institution signs the report. In the Exit

meeting that follows, the chairperson of the team shares the highlights of the assessment, (not the scores which are confidential till they are processed and approved by the Executive Committee of NAAC) and hands over the draft report officially to the head of the institution. This 'draft report' is only for internal use by the institution till it is finalised as a NAAC document. The report is passed on to NAAC to be placed before the Executive Committee (EC) of NAAC, along with the confidential recommendations of the team. The decision of the EC is final.

In brief, the roles and responsibilities of the peers are clearly spelt out as follows:

Before the Visit (As individuals)

- Understand NAAC's Process
- Analyse the Self-Study Report
- Identify the Strengths and Weaknesses
- Arrive at Criterion-wise Tentative Scores with Justification

During the Visit (As members of the team)

- Share the analysis of the report with the Team Members
- Agree on Issues that Need Further Probing
- Accept Responsibilities to Collect Evidences
- Interact with the Management, Head, Teachers, Staff and Students
- Check Documentary Evidence
- Cross Check Non-documentary Evidence
- Validate the Self-Study Report
- Agree on the Provisional Criterion-Wise Scores

At the End of the Visit (As a team)

— Write a Clear Report
— Share the Draft Report with the Head of the Institution
— Arrive at the Final Scores
— Share the Highlights of the Draft Report in the Exit Meeting
— Hand-over a signed copy of the Draft Report to the Head of the Institution
— Hand-over the Draft Report and the Confidential Score Sheet to NAAC

One can see from the above expectations that "assessing quality" is a rigorous task. It requires the ability to hold face-to-face interactions effectively, maintain interpersonal relationships and be objective and open-minded in taking decisions. Sometimes the peer may have to lead a sub-group, or may have to work independently and assist the chairperson of the team. This can be done in a professional manner only if the peers have the ability to work in as well as lead a small team. This also calls for the ability to work to tight time schedules and strict deadlines, ability to write clearly and effectively and record evidence systematically. NAAC identifies people who have these abilities to be included in its pool or database of experts and trains them appropriately.

The Training Strategy

Over the years NAAC has relied heavily on nominations, database of other national bodies and informal ways of identifying the peers. Five years ago there was an effort to advertise in newspapers and experts were selected after a thorough scrutiny. We should remember that experts might not like to apply even if they agree on the importance of the assignment. However, the nominations have worked very well. The Vice-chancellors of universities and the state representatives have nominated the right kind of people. Proven peers have suggested names and during the assessment visits the council staff members identify potential assessors.

Since NAAC focuses on the institution as a whole, it looks for peers who understand and appreciate the institutional context. The database of experts has a large number of experts who, although accomplished in a special field or discipline, can serve as "generalists". Care is taken to select only those experts who are known for their integrity. NAAC brings in consistency and objectivity among the peers thus selected by appropriate safeguards, training strategies and discussions. A notable effort towards this direction is the development of the 'National Cadre of Assessors' through the national training strategy, already discussed in Chapter 4.

For instance, an expert in Indian Languages who is well recognised for his contributions as well as analytical skills may not be good in report writing in English. He might be a good input to the team for assessing an institution strong in the "Indian Languages". However, the team composition should be balanced with others who will have good report writing skills to support the Chair. Such evaluation about the assessors is recorded in a structured format and made available to the NAAC officers. If one goes through the feedback given by the resource team of the training programmes, one can see comments like "Good for the Hindi speaking belt", "Can lead a team to college after one or two visits", "May not be acceptable to assess universities", "Domineering. Should be balanced with a strong and diplomatic Chair", "Will be an excellent team leader", "Does not respect time management", etc. When the newly trained assessor is inducted into a team for the first visit, these remarks become the guidelines for the NAAC officers.

The Chair and the co-ordinating NAAC officer record the feedback about the performance of the assessor at the end of the team visit, if it happens to be different from that of the resource team or something more than that.

To assess the effectiveness of the training strategy, after

completing two training programmes, NAAC invited an international observer to sit in one of the assessment visits. The feedback was useful in fine-tuning the training strategy. The areas that need to be strengthened in the visit and therefore to be taken care of during the training strategy were identified as follows:

- Adherence to the timetable for the visit
- Balancing the intensity of the visit programme
- Provision for more reflection and writing time for the team members
- Using the evaluation framework and the key aspects to provide an agenda for meetings and interactions
- Increasing the number of parallel visits
- Increasing the opportunities for the sharing of experience among the peers
- Management of meetings, the skills of asking questions, report writing and forming judgements
- The relationship of the final criterion scores to the number and seriousness of the issues noted in the report

The feedback had substantial influence on the planning of the peer team visit as well as on the training strategy. Today, NAAC has reached a stage where the other EQA systems are appreciative of the professionalism with which NAAC carries out its accreditation process. The enhanced professionalism of NAAC's procedures has been well accepted. In fact, it reflects in the collaborative arrangements NAAC has established with the Distance Education Council and the National Council on Teacher Education to assess the distance education and teacher education units of the country.

7. Quality Assurance of Distance Education

Distance Education with a long history of serving isolated and remote learners, is now emerging as part of mainstream education. With the amazing developments of technology and its integration into education, it is becoming possible to provide learning opportunities that are flexibly responsive to learners' needs. With the potential of distance education becoming recognised well, the quality related issues – differentiating the good from the substandard—have come to the forefront. The concern for quality in distance education and the need for external quality assurance have brought NAAC and the Distance Education Council of India together to develop the broad methodology for assessment and accreditation of distance education units. There is considerable dialogue about the methodology to be followed for assuring quality of the distance education provisions and how far the methodology should be different or similar to that applied for formal educational system.

Trends in Distance Education

Technology has been integrated into almost all forms of education making the distinctions between various forms of education less clear. With online delivery systems and approaches being employed for both distant and on-campus students, distance education and on-campus instruction are converging. Today, on-campus students can take a part of the programme or courses through "online" or "e-learning" routes in the campus or away from the campus. This combination has narrowed down the gap between the on- and off-campus students and has resulted in the use of the more broad-based term "distributed learning".

Very soon the term "distributed learning" may replace "distance education" because distance is too restrictive a concept. Distributed learning can occur either on- or off-campus, providing students with greater flexibility and eliminating time as a barrier to learning. Regardless of whether students are on- or off-campus, by integration of technology into education, learning becomes distributed. In fact, the "anytime, anyplace" nature of distributed learning has its greatest impact on campus instruction in countries where online courses are in vogue. Some universities advertise that their online courses cost less and encourage the campus students to earn part of their credits through online courses. Consequently, distance learning needs to be redefined. It may be seen as a subset of distributed learning, focusing on students who may be separated in time and space from their peers and the instructor. It is a system and a process that connects learners with distributed learning resources. It takes a wide variety of forms and use of electronic media is not necessarily required. However, it is the technological development in electronic communication that has enabled distance education to emerge as part of mainstream education globally. Due to the developments in the world-wide-web (www), the reach of distance learning is not confined to the country of origin anymore.

Growth in Distance Education

In US, large public universities such as University of Maryland University College (UMUC) are especially active in distance learning, providing distance learning opportunities on a global scale through online courses. The percentage of US universities with distance education courses has grown from 34 per cent in 1997-98 to about 50 per cent in 1999-2000 with significant activity in online courses. Thirty-three states in the US have a statewide virtual university and 85 per cent of the community colleges are expected to offer distance education courses by 2002. The International Data Corporation (IDC) released a report in January 1999 titled *Online Distance Learning in Higher Education, 1998-2000*. The report estimates that 2.2 million college students will be enrolled in online courses in US institutions by 2002.

In Australia, nearly 14 per cent of university students study at a distance. The Australian Government has planned to spend more than $100 million over the next five years on a programme aimed at bringing education and skills training to developing countries via the internet. This programme will link up with an $800 million World Bank plan to use the internet to help developing countries avoid becoming victims of the "digital divide" as the developed world goes online.

A $3.3 billion "e-Learning Action Plan" has been adopted in March 2001 by the European Commission (the Executive Body of the European Union) to promote the development of online education by European Universities. The German government has initiated a joint programme between the Federal Ministry of Education and Research (BMBF) and the Deutscher Akademischer Austauschdienst (DAAD) to support the export of German universities' study programmes. In Canada, 57 per cent of Canadian Universities were offering online courses – with 3,000 courses offered in all, in 2001.

In UK, the Open University (OU) undertakes activities worldwide which include setting up partnership arrangements with overseas academic institutions, selling copies of the best-selling Good Study Guides and other Open University course material and licensing Open University TV programme to broadcasters all over the world. Courses are available throughout Europe and, by means of partnership agreements with other institutions, in many other parts of the world. Over 25,000 learners are studying OU courses outside the UK. United Kingdom Telecommunications Academy (UKTA) and the National Training Organisation for the UK Telecommunications Industry are the other initiatives that provide global access to the combined training capabilities of the leading communications companies and selected universities in the United Kingdom.

In Japan, 34 per cent of 4-year institutions use the internet for online learning and 23 per cent more plan to, and 123 institutions have installed a communications satellite system for organising lectures, seminars and academic meetings. The Mexican Virtual University of Monterrey uses teleconferencing and the internet to reach 50,000 students spread allover Latin America. In Thailand and Turkey, the national open universities enroll respectively 41 and 38 per cent of the total student population in the home country.

In India, the Madurai Kamaraj University has been using the All India Radio to reach thousands of its distance education students since the 1960s. The Indira Gandhi National Open University (IGNOU) reaches its students through radio and TV programmes along with the traditional mode of study guides. The videoconferencing experiments of IGNOU, the Virtual University launched by the Birla Institute of Technology and Science (BITS) and the Tamil University are notable developments in the use of multimedia-based technology in recent years. The open universities like IGNOU, Maharashtra State Open University and Bhoj University, along with a large number of distance education units of traditional universities including Madurai Kamaraj University, Annamalai University, Madras University and Pondicherry University have gone global with overseas study centers in other countries. Here too convergence of traditional and distance education programmes is taking place. In the Pondicherry University, students have the option to accrue credits through courses by the Indira Gandhi National Open University as well as the Community College and the Directorate of Distance Education (DDE) of the Pondicherry University. In other words, a regular campus student of the Pondicherry University can accrue a part of the credits, studying at a distance in IGNOU or DDE. This is an example of distributed learning.

The growth of distance learning poses several challenges too, and soon India has to tackle such problems. Whether offered by the conventional universities or by other providers, distance education introduces new conditions and structures to the higher education environment. The faculty role is different, the course management becomes different and the library and learning resources may require more electronic access. Coursework can now provide material in highly interactive audio, video, and textual formats at a pace set by the student. These attributes are very exciting, but drastically different from the traditional classroom-based education. How good are these learning environments? How differently do we have to examine these processes that deviate so markedly from what has been practiced for hundreds of years? Who will assure the quality of these education providers? In brief, there is considerable dialogue throughout academia about what constitutes quality in distance education.

Challenges

It is worth noting the survey conducted by the Distance Education and Training Council (DETC) in 1998. DETC based at Washington DC is a National Accreditation Agency but has global membership and undertakes accreditation of distance education institutions world over. The survey by

DETC revealed that the following are widely held beliefs within the DETC membership:

- Higher education will be turning to distance education as a "mainstream delivery medium"
- Regulatory interests will increase, as hundreds of new "providers" create more activity and "problems" for quality assessors.

With regard to the first belief, although one may argue that it might not happen in the near future, the broader concept of "distributed learning" is gaining momentum. The increase in the number of online courses and student enrolment for e-learning indicate that distributed learning is emerging as mainstream education. In the case of the second belief, emergence of the new providers and the various forms of delivery through new forms has caused serious concern to governments all over the world. It has caused concern about the safety of the national systems, legitimacy of the new providers, protecting the public from fake providers and the quality of the offerings. These initiatives affect India, as it is a huge market for these global operations.

Quality Concern

There was a time when "courses at a distance education" were considered substandard on the counts of poor quality, not being on par with the regular courses, lower standards of students who enroll, and being detrimental to the planning of higher education in the country. The supporters of distance education used to argue about improving access, the wide choice of learning opportunities, the possibility of competitive pricing, the advantages of not leaving home to take courses and the healthy competition that could be promoted to offer quality courses. With technological developments and adequate awareness about ensuring quality, the questions are of a different order now. For example, the adequacy of student support services and the missing element of interaction with teachers, researchers and other students continue to be issues of concern. Of course, supporters of distance education brush away these reservations by reminding others of the situations in the traditional classrooms where hundreds of students move between large lecture halls of unintellectual atmosphere without any interaction with teachers. They contend that distance education is just like any other form of traditional education; it can be done well or badly. Proponents argue that many research studies have proved conclusively that distance education is "as good as" traditional education if conducted properly.

With technological developments and adequate awareness about ensuring quality there is a growing consensus that distance education can be made very effective. But it is easier said than done. Exploiting the potential of the distance education mode to offer a quality programme is a complex issue in itself—much more than merely installing gadgets to arrive at simple and straightforward solutions. If that is so, how to assess how good it is, against what standards?

Several different organisations have developed principles, guidelines, or benchmarks to ensure quality of distance education. The Institute for Higher Education Policy of USA has come out with 24 benchmarks considered essential to ensuring excellence in internet-based distance learning—Institutional Support, Course Development, Teaching/Learning, Course Structure, Student Support, Faculty Support and Evaluation and Assessment. With the increasing interest of the federal and state governments to ensure the quality of the distance education modes, the regional accreditation agencies in dialogue with the Council of Higher Education Accreditation (CHEA) are revising their standards to include the distance education and electronic course offerings into their assessment procedures. The regional accreditation commissions have agreed on certain standards that cover the areas that include Evaluation and

Assessment, Curriculum and Instruction, Library and Learning Resources, Student Services, Facilities and Finances, against which the evaluation of electronically offered programmes will be done.

In UK, the Quality Assurance Agency (QAA) has published new guidelines for distance learning in higher education. The guidelines start from the principle that the quality of distance learning needs to be assured in the same way as any other form of higher education. The guidelines are arranged under six headings: 1) System design, 2) Programme design, approval and review, 3) The management of programme delivery, 4) Student development and support, 5) Student communication and representation, 6) Student assessment. Each one deals with an aspect where quality assurance is likely to require attention in a particular way when study is by distance learning.

In India, the Distance Education Council has evolved various guidelines to promote quality in distance education offered by the Indian HEIs. But efforts towards its external quality assurance have just begun.

Indian Scenario of Quality Assurance in Distance Education

In recent years, distance education in India, long regarded to be a 'poor cousin' of the conventional form of education, has gained acceptance and has emerged as a possible alternative to the formal variety. Being flexible, distance education has been projected as an answer to the problems of access and equity (Powar, 2001). There are two types of institutions that offer distance education programmes—the correspondence course institutes (CCIs) attached to the conventional universities, and the open universities (OUs). The first were promoted largely to meet the rapidly increased demand for higher education in the years immediately following independence; the second to provide a flexible and open form of education. The distance education programmes were launched in the form of correspondence courses, way back in the year 1962. During the last four decades, there has been considerable expansion and diversification of distance education. It has been estimated that at least one-fifth of the total student enrollment in higher education is through distance education. As the demand for distance education programmes is rising, an increasingly large number of institutions is getting involved with distance education. Of the 298 university level institutions, 64 have established their distance education units. (In the Indian context, open universities are understood as synonyms for distance education. Open learning is essentially without any restriction of age or entry qualification for pursuing higher education leading to a degree or other awards. It deviates from the traditional distance education in providing open access. Further, flexibility in terms of age and entry qualification can be integrated in formal education as well. Nonetheless, as the open universities and distance education institutions operate in the distance mode, they are discussed together.) At present, there are ten open universities – IGNOU (1985) as the National Open University and nine State Open Universities (SOUs). Today, both forms of distance education are firmly established.

At the turn of the millennium there were 600,000 students in the 64 CCIs. The total cumulative enrolment in the ten open universities was over 1,700,000 with the registered strength being 618,000. Thus about 16.5 per cent of registered students in Indian higher education belong to the distance education stream (Powar, 2001). The number can increase greatly through proper promotion. The programmes offered through the distance stream are no longer confined to the arts, social science and commerce streams. Advances in communication technology has now made it possible to offer management, science, engineering, agriculture and even medical programmes through the distance mode. It is significant that formal institutions (*e.g.* the Birla Institute of Technology and Science, Pilani) have already entered the 'virtual class' mode. It is expected that by the end of the first decade of the new century, virtual classes will be common.

As discussed in chapter 2, the Distance Education Council (DEC), established in 1985 by an Act of IGNOU, has the mandate for promotion and maintenance of standards in distance education. NAAC-DEC deliberations have resulted in the agreement that the following seven criteria will serve as the basis of the assessment procedures:

- Curricular Aspects
- Teaching-learning and Evaluation
- Research, Consultancy and Extension
- Infrastructure and Learning Resources
- Student Support Services
- Organisation and Management
- Healthy Practices

The criteria are the same as the ones used for traditional institutions but the unique characteristics of distance education are taken care of in the details. With due consideration to the distinctive aspects at the subcritical levels of distance education, the same three-stage process followed for the traditional institutions for assessment and accreditation is to be followed:

- Preparation of the Self-study Report by the institution, to be submitted to NAAC
- Validation of the Self-study Report by the peers by visiting the institution, and
- The final decision of NAAC based on the Self-study Report and the recommendations of the team of peers.

Final outcome

On studying the institution under the seven criteria the peer team will do the marking for each criterion depending upon what the institution has achieved and/or is doing. The weightage for each criterion is given below with respect to Open Universities (OU) and Distance Education Institutes (DEI) separately, as most of the open universities in the country are standalone institutions, while DEIs are not.

Criteria	*Weightages (%)*	
	OUs	*DEIs*
Curricular Aspects	10	10
Teaching-learning and Evaluation	30	35
Research, Consultancy and Extension	10	05
Infrastructure and Learning Resources	10	10
Student Support Services	20	25
Organisation and Management	10	05
Healthy Practices	10	10
Total	100	100

The assessors will give the raw score for each of the seven criteria and the weighted score will be arrived at in accordance with the weightages stated above and the Total Weighted Score for the institution will be arrived at.

There is considerable dialogue about the implementation of this methodology and many issues to be discussed further have emerged. An attempt is made in the following section to explore some of those aspects where distance education is different from the traditional setting.

Tensions that may arise

The purpose of this section is to explore a few issues on quality assurance of distance education so that the distance education community will continue to reflect on them. The focus is not to discuss the problems of quality assurance in general. For example, quantification of quality is a bone of contention everywhere and the debate will continue in the context of distance education also. This section does not touch upon those issues. Only the aspects that are distinctly related to distance education and the very basics that are yet to be clarified in the context of distance education are discussed here.

a) Is it as simple as it appears?

Although there is a growing consensus towards the point of view that the basic methodology of quality assurance would be the same for both traditional and distance education, there is disagreement on the extent of modifications needed. Distance education tests conventional assumptions, raising fresh questions as to the essential nature and content of an educational experience and the resources required. For example, the requirement of one of the professional councils in India on student-staff ratio and a few other aspects for distance education programmes was a burning issue two years back. The distance education units that used to admit thousands of students with various arrangements with local institutions could not comply with those requirements and many of them discontinued their programmes in those areas of studies.

The example of what is happening in US is contrary to the Indian experience. In March 1999, the North Central Association of Colleges and Schools (NCACS) accredited Jones International University, the first institution to be accredited by a regional accrediting body that offers its courses and services on a global scale entirely over the internet. The Distance Education and Training Council (DETC) that has a well structured policy and practice for distance education accreditation has also accredited the Jones International University along with the US Open University and the Western Governors University (WGU). In the case of the Jones International University, accredited by both NCACS and DETC, of the 56 faculty members employed by the university, two are full-time, and the other part-time members generally hold academic posts at other universities. Content experts help develop the subject matter and structure for the courses, and teaching faculty execute the courses from locations around the world. Accreditation of Jones was criticised too. The American Association of University Professors (AAUP) sent a letter describing its concerns about the accreditation of Jones to the executive director of NCACS. The protest was based upon what AAUP saw as a lack of quality particularly given the high number of adjuncts the university is using. In addition, AAUP cited the short duration of the university's courses, the lack of learning resources – such as libraries and research laboratories – and the small proportion of students who seek degrees from the institution. But accreditors have stated that Jones met the requirements in other ways.

The implication is that distance education may present extraordinary and distinct challenges to the traditional methods of quality assurance in some aspects. The big question for implementation is "Do we need a drastically different approach?"

b) Criteria and Focus

Any assessment and subsequent accreditation should be made with reference to a set of criteria. Even if we agree that the criteria to assess the quality of educational offerings are basically the same for both traditional and distance education offerings, the subtle difference in the context needs to be spelt out. A few additional aspects may have to be included or deleted to suit the context of distance education. In distance learning, learners take increased responsibility for control and direction of the learning process. If we look at the international developments, there is growing consensus that existing standards and criteria that often focus on learning input fail to acknowledge the many forms that effective learning can take and therefore, the focus needs to be on learning outcomes.

CHEA and Commonwealth Higher Education Management Service (CHEMS) have designed and tested an alternative approach based on competencies that places significant emphasis on student outcomes and delivery via distance education. The competency standards are organised in three main areas of institutional performance: Student outcomes and attainment; Responsiveness to students and Organisational alignment and support. The focus is to see how the institution's graduates meet clear standards of achievement demonstrable through explicit assessments of performance and how the institution facilitates effective student outcome. In a similar development, the Guiding Principles for Distance Learning in a Learning Society suggests the following major dimensions that focus more on learning support and outcome: Learning Design, Learner Support, Organisational Commitment, Learning Outcomes and Technology.

NAAC-DEC deliberations have resulted in the agreement that the same seven criteria used for traditional institutions will serve as the basis of the assessment procedures for distance education. It has also been agreed upon that although the criteria are the same, the unique characteristics of open and distance education will be taken care of. However, it is the actual implementation of the process that would reveal more fine-tuning to be done. For example, aspects like the "adequacy of infrastructure", "quality of learning resources" and "effective management of support services" would acquire new meanings depending on the context of the institution. The challenging task is evolving clear guidelines on these aspects to be used by those who would be involved in the assessment process.

Another issue may relate to some of the basic terms like 'good educational experience', which depends on the definition of the target group. Distance education requires motivated and self-disciplined students. Providing good educational experience to such a target group depends on optimum utilisation of available technologies and techniques and their judicious combination to effect maximum learning. It cannot be justifiably done through study material alone. Thus the definition of good educational experience should respect these two factors – differences in the characteristics of the target learners and the potential of technologies and techniques. These issues lead to the question of what the frame of reference should be.

c) Frame of reference

There is a point of view that distance education can be as good or as bad as traditional programmes. In India, the stigma attached to distance education, as second-grade cannot be denied. Will quality assessment undo this stigma and identify the quality institutions that can provide distance education programmes of comparable quality? While assessing quality, is it expected that the distance education programme will be assessed with the same rigor that has been applied for traditional institutions? In the UK, the USA and Australia this has been well established. The certificates given by the George Washington University and many other universities in the USA do not differentiate between the on-campus and off-campus students. Australian Universities of repute have been awarding indistinguishable degrees to on-campus and off-campus students for decades. In the UK, Open University degrees are recognised as representing rigorous, thorough British education.

Since the responsibility to provide evidence for quality assessment rests with the distance education institutions, it is essential that the stand of the council is made clear to the distance education community. While insisting on quality and its assessment in a way as rigorous as the traditional setting, the distinctive features of distance education cannot be overlooked. Distance education should make a respectable place for itself. The question is on 'recognising the unique features of distance education' without compromising the rigor of the process. This makes the need for benchmarking crucial.

d) Benchmarks and Indicators

The crux of the problem related to quality assurance of distance education lies in identifying suitable benchmarks which will make the assessment clear to both the quality assurance agency and the distance education institutions. For assessing traditional institutions, NAAC has evolved suitable benchmarks and similar efforts are needed with reference to the seven criteria for distance education.

Further, to use the benchmarks to make value judgements, indicators become necessary. For example, without specific indicators, the benchmark statement "Instructional materials are reviewed periodically to ensure they meet programme standards" does not tell us whether a particular level of functioning is best or just adequate. To take another example, student support system is mentioned in one of the criteria listed above. The corresponding benchmark statement may state as follows: "The institution has well-run student support services." This benchmark statement does not spell out clearly what characterises effective student support and what indicates different levels of effectiveness. Either quantitatively or qualitatively, for each aspect of assessment, it is essential to spell out what characterises the different levels of performance. Otherwise, the differences between 'we also do it' and 'we do it well' may become ambiguous and affect the objectivity of assessment.

Here again what NAAC had done for the traditional institutions to develop 'pointers of quality', already discussed in Chapter 6, is worth mentioning. As an example, one of the pointers thus developed under the criterion 'Curricular Aspects' is as follows:

Percentage of total budget allocated to academic programmes other than salary component:

>3% would get credit points	2
1% to 3% would get credit point	1

These pointers were used only as guides and as such they were not converted into criterion-wise scores. Experience has shown that the pointers have been useful to focus the attention of the peers on key issues that have a direct bearing on quality. A similar effort may be needed for distance education.

This is a challenging task due to the ambiguity surrounding what are best practices in distance education. The best practices and, consequently, indicators of quality for traditional institutions are well understood and accepted. For example, computer facility with easy access to even non-computer science students is a mark of quality learning resources in a traditional institution. The open access system in the library with online library facilities is a good practice under the management of learning resources. A traditional quality institution is expected to have a functioning counselling center and a placement office. Student seminars and projects are aspects to be encouraged under avenues of learning. When it comes to distance education, the picture is not as clear. This is an area where we need to take stock of what is possible under best conditions, what is happening in most of the distance education units right now and what could be the benchmarked performance for different levels of judgement.

e) Re-defining the site-visit

With due consideration to the distinctive aspects of distance education, the same three-stage process – self study, peer review and final decision by the council—followed for traditional institutions for assessment and accreditation is to be followed by NAAC for distance education also.

In this three-stage process, the "site visit" is the one that is likely to undergo a lot of changes. The basic question for the site visit raised by June Lester in 1991 still holds good – "How do you translate a process that was designed to evaluate a bricks and mortar environment into one that works for distributed sites that include one person's living room and another's kitchen?" June Lester identified five basic purposes of the site visit – to evaluate the institution or programme in the context of the learning environment, to conduct the interviews, to evaluate physical resources, to observe instructional delivery and to examine records. Some of these purposes could be achieved with simple adaptations. The quality of the instructional materials can be assessed independently by subject experts without a site visit and their evaluation may be provided to the assessment team. Examination of records and documents could be achieved centrally at the administration site for most of the data. However, the other purposes need to be translated carefully.

In the traditional setting, the site visit enables the peers to get a feel of the institutional ambience. What is the concept of institution for distance education? We tend to think of the institution as composed of a complex of physical buildings, faculty, staff and students. This definition of the institution obviously doesn't work for distance education where the learning environment becomes physically distributed. The key elements of the new environment are the supportive and responsive intellectual access to the counsellors and information resources. Peers have to cope with this "distributed site".

Another reason for the site visit is that it is the efficient way to interact with a cross-section of the constituents of the institution – management, faculty, students, alumni, and parents that constitute a major means of data gathering by the peers. How can this be achieved in distance learning? One of the obvious answers could be through electronic mail, computer conferencing, two-way video and audio, and the telephone. Although all these modes could be used for traditional institutions also if one would like to avoid site-visit, in assessing distance education these modes have a significant place. A member of the assessment team can watch an e-mail conferencing going on without the need to move from his/her office or home and make an assessment about the effectiveness of the interaction. Is it sufficient? Is it viable? How well co-ordinated the distance education providers are to face the assessment this way? How well trained are the peers to assess the institutions in this "new way"? It is worth noting the methods adopted by the NCACS and the DETC. To assess the Jones International University, the NCACS team went into the virtual mode. DETC still conducts a wide-ranging survey through contacting hundreds of agencies, along with online interactions. In addition, the commission surveys students whose names are randomly selected by mail to get their opinions as well.

The third activity of the site visit is observation of the quality, availability and utility of resources. Evaluation of facilities like library could be easily checked but access to resources in different sites and the responsibility of the provider are issues to be debated. To what extent can the institution be held responsible for the necessary access to resources? How do we deal with the criticism that the distance education providers have become parasites of some of the local campuses for computer and lab facilities for their students? How do we define the adequacy of resources?

f) Defining the Boundary

As the providers of distance education integrate more and more online courses, the need for a physical site is decreasing. The borderless and boundaryless distributed learning has already become a reality. However, most of the Indian institutions that offer distance education still rely on physical sites. They operate through study centers/sites/campuses spread over different geographical locations including overseas arrangements. Assuring the effective functioning of the overseas offerings needs careful reflection on the policy as well as the methodology. With many distance education providers of India having study centers abroad, the policy on those centers should be made clear. The Directorate of

Distance Education of the Pondicherry University has launched its programmes in the United Arab Emirates, Qatar and Kuwait. The Indira Gandhi National Open University (IGNOU) offers its programmes in Kuwait, Dubai, Abu Dhabi, Sharjah, Al Ain, Doha, and Muscat for a total of 325 students. Arrangements with Seychelles and Maldives are being finalised. Negotiations are underway for launching IGNOU programmes in Nepal, Mauritius, Saudi Arabia and African countries. A few more distance education units have joined this group.

When NAAC accredits a traditional university that has a distance education unit offering hundreds of programmes through various overseas study centers, the distance education unit is assessed as one of the many departments of the university. The peers do not go to any of the sites other than the main campus. In most cases the main campus might have only the administrative office. NAAC also makes it clear that the outcome of such an assessment is for the whole institution and the distance education unit cannot claim that as its specific evaluation. However, some of the distance education units throw the cloak of accreditation around to advertise their courses.

The question is: Should NAAC adopt the policy of assessing all activities conducted in the name of the institution in India as well as abroad under its sponsorship or should it be restricted to the offerings in India? This issue is discussed in detail in the later chapters on quality assurance of transnational education.

g) Final Outcome

The final outcome is another aspect that needs further reflection. The NAAC-DEC deliberations have resulted in a clear model of assessment up to the calculation of the institutional score. But what should be done after that stage needs a critical thinking. Should the outcome be an overall institutional grade similar to the current nine-point scale that is followed for traditional institutions? If yes, with only ten could be different, will the difference send conflicting signals about non-comparable assessment outcomes? Or should it be a two-point scale – accredited/not accredited? Since all the Open Universities have been established and supported by governments that ensure the minimum threshold level of quality of the universities, is it likely that all Open Universities will be accredited? If yes, does the two-point scale have any meaning? If it is expected that there may be Open Universities that may not be accredited, what could be the implication of non-accredited status? Can the final outcome be in terms of only institutional score? Are the instruments and methodology of NAAC-DEC fine-tuned enough to make a public disclosure of the institutional scores?

The primary focus of NAAC-DEC assessment and the direct beneficiary also needs to be well articulated for the benefit of the distance education providers and accordingly the reporting strategy has to be fine-tuned. If distance education units are the prime beneficiaries, the reporting elements may focus more on quality enhancement strategies to build on strengths and overcome weaknesses. If the distance education learner is also in the target group, according to the differential nature of the distance education learners, useful elements have to be incorporated into the report. If there would be government sanctions, since DEC is involved, the implications need to be discussed with the distance education institutions. Striking the right balance is not an easy task. What part of the report is for public, what is for follow-up, what part is for the institutions to act upon, etc., need to be deliberated.

h) Who will assess?

The next major problem is going to be the "pool of experts" that would assist NAAC and DEC in assessing open and distance education. There are many members in the higher education community who still look at distance education not as desirable mainstream education but as a problem to be solved. It will be a tremendous task to remove such traditional thinking from their minds. The concept that 'distance education should closely resemble conventional on-campus education, and is deficient in so far as it is dissimilar to the conventional' has to be removed from the minds of everyone associated with the task. At the same time it should not lead to dilution of standards. This calls for a well-informed group of experts, comfortable with the functioning of distance education in the country and abroad to be involved in the assessment process.

However, there are adequate number of academia already associated with the huge distant education units of the country – 10 open universities and 64 or so distance education institutes. Many of them are well experienced as distance education in India is not of recent origin. They can be suitably trained as peers and involved in quality assuring distance education provisions.

Successful distance education initiatives have proved how quality can be sustained in the distance education mode. Dissemination of this information to those who would be involved in the assessment is important because many experts in higher education may not be familiar with what could be achieved in successful distance education initiatives. While most of the assessment team membership will be from the distance education background, there would also be those with a different background. Once the pool of experts is identified, a dissemination strategy should be attempted to bring all of them to the same comfort level they may have with traditional higher education. Not all experts can be trained or invited for an orientation programme. This needs a multi-pronged approach, especially for those who are too senior to fit into a training programme or too busy to attend an orientation or a round-table discussion.

i) Minimum Vs Healthy Practice

In the case of accreditation of traditional institutions in India, time and again we have been saying that accreditation is different from the existing regulations, inspections, affiliating functions, etc. The institutions know that it is the excellence that is assessed and not the minimal threshold level. What is the stand for distance education? Since the distance education units have been established either by legislature or under the university acts, it is reasonable to expect that the minimum requirement will have been taken care of by other existing mechanisms and the NAAC-DEC initiative is meant for assessing excellence.

This will clarify what could be considered as the healthy practices that need to be commended which is very important for the assessment teams. For example, in all the government colleges of Tamil Nadu, there is a requirement that the colleges maintain files on individual students, each faculty member is allotted a group of students under the tutor-ward scheme, etc. That system may be documented on paper because the colleges have to comply with it. However, if it is done well in spite of the workload and other pressing demands for faculty time, that would certainly qualify to be a healthy practice. It would set a good model for the other institutions to emulate but not if it is only on paper.

Translating this experience to distance education requires more careful reflection. It implies that one needs to have a clear idea about the minimum requirements to be ensured by other regulatory mechanisms, the various good practices of different distance education providers, good initiatives possible under favourable conditions in India and the ones that stand out. Now that our institutions are becoming global with overseas study centers, we should also have a clear picture of what is offered by the other countries and where our institutions stand on those issues in terms of healthy practices. DEC has evolved certain guidelines for offering quality programmes. After extensive dialogue with AICTE and NCTE, it has already entered into MoUs. These initiatives may form the basis for further discussion on what the minimum expectation is and what is to be commended.

j) Know Thyself

What are the commonly voiced ailments of distance education and how do we collectively overcome them through quality enhancement strategies? The distance education in India suffers from all kinds of problems, from staffing to sustainability, not leaving any aspect untouched. Although the distance education community might brush aside this observation as a sweeping statement and generalisation, one would agree that there is truth in some of the issues related to quality. While IGNOU has a research group to analyse the quality of its programmes through various methods, in most of the other units they are of recent origin mainly promoted through the incentives of DEC. Instead of just running in the race and getting locked up in the routine, our distance education institutions should take time to take stock of the situation. It may do good to reflect on them collectively also with other interested parties who will bring in new perspectives into the quality assurance initiatives of distance education.

How do established distance learning institutions ensure quality? How do the quality assurance agencies view the distinction between traditional programmes and the distance education programmes? Are we interested in quality assurance in terms of minimal standards or in terms of quality enhancement? These are the questions that need the reflection of all parties interested in higher education.

A beginning has already been made to address the general scenario. The NAAC-DEC seminar held in June 2001 was a right step where the national consultative committee was formed. It has to be continued with the specifics in focus, once the national consultative committee firms up its recommendations. It should be borne in mind that, as developments elsewhere indicate, the emergence of the different dimensions of distance education is likely to change the nature of quality assessment mechanisms. It is doubtful that the philosophy, principles and standards routinely applied to evaluate or accredit traditional units can be used without significant adjustments to assess the quality and effectiveness of distance education. The tasks that are ahead of NAAC-DEC are substantial and challenging. The National Consultative Committee on Distance Education is working on these details. With the experience of having assessed around 500 traditional institutions and the academic guidance of the consultative committee, NAAC and DEC are well positioned to carry out this substantial and challenging task.

8. Challenging the Post-accreditation Complacency

One of the purposes of accreditation as an external quality assurance mechanism is to promote conscious efforts among the higher education institutions (HEI) to enhance the quality of their provisions. But in reality post-accreditation complacency is seen among some institutions and the issue of "complacency versus continuous improvement" is emerging as a new challenge. Reasons for this inaction, on the part of the institutions, are many such as pre-occupation with routine work, crisis management, relatively long intervals between successive assessments, short tenure of the institutional leadership, etc. Despite these factors, to make the optimum use of accreditation, HEIs should think of moving to a higher level of quality enhancement taking the assessment report as a starting point. This chapter is an expression of concern about the post-accreditation complacency and suggests ways to overcome it.

As external quality assurance gains acceptance as an integral part of the education system, new challenges emerge for the quality assurance agencies and the system develops choices. In India, the choice is not between success and failure in solving the problems of survival. Presumably NAAC will be in place for the long foreseeable future. Rather, the choice is about balancing competing priorities to expand horizontally as well as to develop the processes more meaningfully. There is an increasing need to include more number of institutions, to serve more stakeholders, to explore unchartered areas like distance and open learning provisions, to assess the transnational provisions, to keep pace with the international forums and, above all, to make the process more meaningful to institutions. One of the priorities for NAAC towards making accreditation more meaningful is to promote strategies that would lead to "continuous quality enhancement". But in reality post-accreditation complacency has already set in among some institutions and the issue of "complacency versus continuous improvement" is emerging as a new challenge, the focus of this chapter.

Quality Assurance versus Quality Enhancement

The hundred and odd quality assurance agencies that are members of the International Network of Quality Assurance Agencies in Higher Education (INQAAHE) follow different strategies for quality assurance and quality enhancement for various purposes. But they all can be seen as different combinations of two variables – quality assurance (summative) and quality enhancement (formative). The emphasis on either one of the two varies between different countries, depending on the degree of accountability required by the various authorities. The inherent tension created by accreditation's dual purposes of quality assurance and quality enhancement (judging versus helping) is well recognised the world over.

In the case of NAAC's process, it should be understood that accreditation does not provide a continuous supervision or review. It is, rather, an assessment of an institution at a given time, resulting in a grade and a report about the quality of education offered in that institution at that time and its potential of maintaining that quality. Due to this characteristic, NAAC's process at present is particularly well suited to serve 'assessment of quality' and 'quality enhancement' is not addressed directly. This is not a situation unique to NAAC; this has been the international experience in the developmental process of many other quality assurance systems as well.

However, as has been the international experience, quality enhancement has been a by-product of the assessment process itself. The participation of the faculty members, administrative staff, students, parents and alumni has led to new initiatives. The preparation of the self-study report has served as a catalyst for institutional self-improvement. Interaction with the peers has provided a means for the wider dissemination of information about educational development. Further, the impact analysis conducted on the accredited institutions reveals that NAAC's process has made a significant change in the pedagogical, managerial, administrative and related aspects of functioning of most of the accredited colleges. Institutions took up initiatives beyond the mandatory minimal requirement of the affiliating system. Management was often able to bring in major changes on the grounds that it would demonstrate a commitment to quality. Introduction of need-based programmes and curricular reforms were observed. Student support services and learning resources were greatly improved. Initiatives that require confidence, self-reliance, team spirit and potential bloomed. There was a change in the perception of the management on issues of faculty workload, supporting the research culture and encouraging faculty development. The interpersonal relations between the management and the faculty improved. All these changes had a direct bearing on improving the quality of education and they had been achieved as a byproduct of the accreditation exercise. As assessment and accreditation activities continue, and as the validation period of many of the institutions are coming to an end, a new set of questions emerges. Should quality enhancement still be left to be a byproduct? Has accreditation ensured that institutions investigate "educational quality and institutional improvement" as an integral part of their functioning?

Value Addition versus Complacency

Ideally, the self-study process should add value to the robust functioning of the institution. The self-evaluation of the institution should never end and it should be an ongoing process. Here comes the problem, especially in the case of highly rated institutions. When an institution gets a high rating, everybody celebrates the great achievement. The Vice-chancellor tells the Steering Committee Coordinator what a great job s/he did and promptly reassigns her/him to whatever position that was previously held. The administrative officials feel relieved and return to their daily routine. In brief, all those who might have been deeply involved in the self-study process and have the potential to be 'change agents' get locked into the routine. There are institutions that got into this slumber a few years back and wake up now to get ready for the next assessment visit.

NAAC's accreditation is valid for a period up to five years. The greatest mistake an institution can make is to wait till the end of the validity of the accreditation status to think about the next assessment. Although the institution might have been highly commended by the assessment team, there might be numerous things noted in the report for further development of the institution. The best time to begin to address these concerns is soon after the assessment visit. Unfortunately, the high rating generally leads to an equally high level of complacency. If this period of complacency goes untreated, it can lead to consequences that would affect the grading during the next assessment visit. The response of the institutions towards the assessment report in the case of some institutions needs a mention here.

Response to the assessment report

First, the impact of accreditation has been very significant on marginal institutions just above or just below the mid-level grading. With such institutions, the influence has often been great. On institutions that are well above the mid-level, its impact though found to be good in the beginning, loses its momentum, and complacency is evident as the initial impact wears off.

Second, on interacting with faculty from institutions that have undergone the process of accreditation, one would realise that the recommendations of the accreditation process, in general, have not received their adequate attention. Given the immense amount of thought, effort, and commitment that has gone into the process, the fact can only be regarded as stunning. Although it might sound like an exaggeration, it amounts to the inference that the accreditation report is forgotten by the faculty. HEIs should remind themselves that quality enhancement cannot be achieved as an administrative process. As in the case of the self-study, acting on the assessment report should continue to be a participative endeavour involving all the units of the institution, especially the faculty.

Third, even the institutions rated very high because of their overall performance have within them pockets of poor performers. At times, the pockets are not small. These quality problems are not sufficient enough to raise questions about the grading the institution deserves, but nevertheless, for the potential for improvement they have, these problems are significant. Do the highly rated institutions take the remarks of the assessment team about these pockets of poor quality seriously? In many cases, these institutions have not paid any extra attention to these pockets of poor quality. In fact, there are criticisms that the reports of the highly rated institutions paint a rosy picture and present the pitfalls in such sugar-coated words that the momentum to initiate quality enhancement is lost. However rosy the picture is, it is reasonable to expect that the discriminating heads can see through the report as to what their weaknesses are and how serious they are.

Fourth, it is worth noting that the institutions do take seriously their areas of strength but recommendations of the assessment report do not seem to be treated with the same seriousness. For example, there are institutions that are well known for their research outcomes. It is a fact that research performance is sharply subjected to external review and evaluation – often in a rather harsh way. As a result, research activity in these institutions is highly energised and much more adaptive than is the activity involving teaching and learning. Similarly, there are institutions that are well known for their athletic activity. They are highly charged and active in maintaining their strength in those areas. It is a fact that athletic activity is also subjected to frequent public review and evaluation. But one could not say for sure that the same seriousness is attached to the assessment report relating to teaching. In general, despite the fact that institutions are keen on getting accredited by NAAC, the assessment reports are seen as documents that endorse their achievement rather than as documents to be acted upon.

There are institutions that do act on the report very sincerely but not adequately. Institutions may assign the task of addressing the issues to a few members of the faculty and staff without adequate support. For example in a university with six hundred faculty members and two hundred administrative and support staff, ten or twenty may be involved in the process while the other seven hundred and eighty begin to head towards complacency.

Fifth, some of these institutions have not realised the potential of the assessment report to move towards focussed institutional improvement. HEIs should realise that accreditation and the report should challenge them to go beyond adequacy towards excellence in all their endeavours. Every institution should be energised by the assessment report to compete against its own past performance and maximise its potential. What does accreditation have to offer that is unique and valuable to the accredited institutions, especially the highly rated institutions that already have a fair understanding of their quality? There is indeed something: the external evaluation and judgment. As an institution evolves and develops its healthy traditions, it also inherits some bad elements that would not welcome any move to change the existing practices. The resistance from such elements would make the institution stagnate in the long run. External evaluation can be a much-needed agent of change to tackle the resistance from these elements.

Finally, some of the reputed institutions have treated the assessment report with defensiveness. In general the assessment reports recognise and respect the capability of the institutions to contextualise and manage their affairs well and do not make prescriptive suggestions about what is to be done to address the problem areas. It does not mean that they have nothing to improve.

An analysis of the assessment reports of highly rated institutions indicates that the reports have recorded a lot of initiatives for further quality enhancement. True that some of them have been acted upon by some. One of the recommendations noted in most of the reports is on strengthening the internal quality assurance mechanisms. Except for the traditional planning and development sections or their equivalents, which are predominantly administrative in nature, how many institutions have made a move to initiate or strengthen an internal quality assurance mechanism?

In sum, although institutional accreditation by its very nature provides an excellent vehicle for stimulating change directed to the improvement of quality in higher education, there are institutions that have largely thrown away this opportunity and allowed post-accreditation complacency to set in. Nearly four years have passed since the first list of accredited institutions was announced. During the coming year, the institutions should see how the remaining opportunity could be maximised. Three strategies that would help to overcome the post-accreditation complacency are outlined for possible adoption. They are: 1. Institutional research to improve institutional effectiveness. 2. The re-accreditation process with elements to assess the progress made on the recommendations of the earlier report. 3. The pro-active role of NAAC. Each strategy needs an in-depth analysis; but this chapter makes an attempt to very briefly point out what could be done under these three strategies.

Institutional Research

An institution that is ready to commit itself towards continued improvement will find it useful to take 'institutional effectiveness' as its focus for research. Traditionally our institutions have been concentrating on subject-oriented areas of research and not on institutional effectiveness related research. There are exceptions like the University of Hyderabad, the University of Roorkee and the Birla Institute of Technology and Science that have carried out research on different dimensions of their effectiveness. But they are rare examples to be proud of.

True that the Planning and Development section collects a lot of reports and data from different units of the institution. The data and reports are mainly used to project or justify the budget and manage the routine administrative functions. But are the inputs used for institutional research on institutional effectiveness? Of course, the most usual reaction to proposals about such initiatives is to say that they sound fine in theory but are infeasible in practice. A warning response may be in order: it is a mistake to look for significant results from timid strategies and miniscule efforts. It requires a lot of commitment. The highly rated institutions have the potential to make the commitment and initiate significant moves to develop this area of research and set a model for the others to follow.

To begin with, institutional research might focus on how the assessment report could be used to make essential improvements and to plan for the future. For all accredited institutions, self-study had been a period of intensive examination conducted internally and subsequently reviewed by external peers. That should encourage institutional self-examination to become a continuous process rather than a periodic event. The concept of Internal Quality Assurance Cell (IQAC) promoted by NAAC had this task in focus and more than 44 institutions of higher education have established IQACs in their campuses. NAAC has evolved detailed guidelines to facilitate the functioning of IQAC. As an outcome of accreditation, a few more colleges have taken this step and IQAC provides a good forum to take up the institutional research responsibilities.

At present, in most of the institutions that formally initiated an IQAC, it functions only when the institution begins the self-study process and lacks trained personnel who understand how to maximise the value of IQAC for institutional improvement purposes. If implemented well, there are ways in which IQAC can avoid post-accreditation inactivity and support further accreditation processes. Giving a leading role to IQAC in facilitating every unit to work towards demonstrating improved performance is one of those strategies. That would avoid the complacency that is likely to set in during the post-accreditation period. IQAC can also play a critical role in keeping the institution tuned to the next assessment visit and contribute to the self-study process. If the right person is given the responsibility to lead IQAC, it would facilitate in organising the evidence and supporting documents for the accreditation activities. For example, an IQAC coordinator has to be familiar with conducting surveys and special institutional studies. S/he should be able to guide the other units on appropriate documentation and analysis of data to demonstrate their improvements. S/he has to be well versed in analysing data from national databases to provide comparative data and information; ensuring data used in the self-study and the institutional decision-making are reliable, consistent and accurate. This would reduce the anxiety and confusion that often accompanies accreditation activities.

Further, if the above-mentioned efforts are extended to analyse the effectiveness of institutional functioning with respect to different dimensions, the outcome would result in institutional research on institutional effectiveness. This is an area that has the greatest potential to promote continuous quality enhancement but is yet to be explored by the IQACs.

Institutional research for continuous quality enhancement

Institutional research essentially involves a systematic comparison of different dimensions of institutional performance to institutional goals. Any short fall in achieving the goals may be due to various reasons and one of the purposes of institutional research is to identify the root cause and to evolve suitable corrective action. The effectiveness of an institution may be conditioned by a number of factors, but a weakness in one area may offset all other efforts. Hence, identifying the limiting factor becomes crucial for institutional improvement and it may require detailed analysis of all the available data. Once the limiting factor is identified, the remedial measures may not be difficult to find. In some cases, the reason for ineffectiveness may be obvious and the remedy may not be simple. Institutional studies might be able to evolve alternate strategies that would work equally well.

To do this, the assessment report that is based on the objective and systematic analysis of institutional data over a period of at least three years is a good starting point. The recommendations given in the assessment report, in essence bring to the attention of the institution "the limiting factors" in institutional improvement. It is not sufficient that the assessment report is just circulated to members of the institution. IQAC should use the assessment report to discover what should be done in the near future. An internal discussion and analysis of the report would indicate what works and what does not work towards quality education in the institution. That should trigger a continuous formative evaluation of the institutional functioning.

For example, we may consider student learning. Semesterisation has greatly improved continuous evaluation of students, provided it is implemented well. The pass percentage of students and the number of first class or distinctions have been used for demonstrating curricular effectiveness and for improving teaching-learning. But are they used to analyse further the areas that need more attention? Do institutions have a well-conceived plan to assess the following?

— student evaluations of course and instructional quality
— measures of student satisfaction with the quality of the curriculum
— measures of students' personal and affective development
— measures of student retention, and students' interest in their educational programme
— measures of student involvement in academic and co-curricular activities
— faculty peer evaluations
— measures of alumni achievements
— evaluations of alumni work performance
— evaluations of student support services

The above-mentioned areas are vital to quality enhancement and institutional research should focus on these issues. This could be achieved well only if the head of the institution provides the active leadership necessary to ensure that every unit of the institution is clear about what its goals are and works towards improving its performance in achieving the set goal. A major institutional commitment is required to initiate and maintain this comprehensive effort. In part, the commitment involves providing the personnel, time, and financial resources necessary to support the process. Even more significant, however, is the commitment to use assessment results in making improvements in areas that are ineffective. It may be in changing programmes or optimal use of limited resources. Unless the outcome of the institutional research is taken seriously in decision-making, the other units will down play and ignore them. There also may be active opposition from departments that are not in a very favourable position in the assessment and institutional research, though the likelihood may be reduced through constructive uses of institutional research to guide efforts for institutional improvement.

In countries like the UK and the USA, similar efforts have been found to be very successful. In the UK, the Teaching Learning Enhancement Unit takes care of teaching–learning related research and supports the various assessment activities. In the USA, the Institutional Research Office manages these functions. Even in South Africa where the Higher Education Quality Committee (HEQC) has been established just two years ago and where the new method of accreditation is yet to take off, HEQC has been successful in strengthening the role of Quality Managers in the institutions of higher education. The members of the ASEAN University Network (17 universities from the ASEAN countries) have appointed Quality Officers with adequate support in its member institutions. Indian institutions of higher education are already in the mainstream through the IQAC. What is needed now is to develop feasible plans for IQAC to work towards continuous institutional improvement. The apparent challenges and requisite commitment will be made worthwhile by the benefits that would accrue to institutions.

While these are the steps to be taken by the institution to facilitate its smooth transition into the next assessment visit, there is an area where both NAAC and the HEIs should work together and that concerns the framework for the re-accreditation process.

Framework for Re-Accreditation

It is proper and educationally sound to expect that the re-accreditation process will bring to light how institutions have progressed over the period of five years with accredited status. For any institution that comes again for re-accreditation, it would be reasonable to expect that it would demonstrate how well it has used the earlier assessment outcome and how well it is engaged in an ongoing quest for quality. In the first phase of assessment, many institutions reported that they did not have certain formal mechanisms and that they were being achieved informally anyway. For example, student feedback, career counselling, skill development of students, etc. were areas where one could find four major lacunae: 1) Many institutions did not have formal mechanisms in place. 2) Those who claimed to have formal mechanisms had initiated them very recently. 3) Documentation and support structure for those mechanisms were not adequate. 4) Even in cases where such mechanisms existed, efforts and evidence towards demonstrating the effectiveness of such mechanisms were absent.

There was yet another phenomenon that was observed in some institutions in the first phase of assessment – the copycat syndrome. In spite of explaining that institutional uniqueness will be taken care of, institutions had started copying the top bracket institutions. The manuals developed by NAAC to facilitate the preparation of self-study report had also contributed to this. The manuals give a generic format for data collection, which may contain a few questions that may not be relevant to a particular institution. Forgetting the generic nature of the format, for any aspect questioned in the manual the institutions hurriedly initiated those mechanisms. Further, not all questions have value addition; some are only for data collection. Yet institutions hurried to put all mechanisms in place and tried to project themselves as tailor-made to the manual.

NAAC could understand that, at times, those who met the peers had been carefully coached. In some institutions, the interactions with a representative group of students or staff turned out to be sessions of eulogising the management or the head of the institution. Experts had been consulted on preparing documents. Some had spent much time preparing documents and plans, which they thought would impress the peer team. In other words, some institutions created the semblance of quality rather than effecting quality assurance by trying to please the assessment team. However, the peer team always had a balanced composition of academia that could appreciate the new initiatives of the institutions and at the same time differentiate gloss from reality.

However, in an effort to contextualise assessment and promote healthy practices, the assessment teams had not taken a penalising stand on those issues. The very existence of such mechanisms – formally or informally – was taken as a healthy practice. At the same time, it is reasonable to expect that during re-accreditation, the institution would be able to demonstrate that these drawbacks had been set right. For all those hurriedly initiated mechanisms, the institutions have to demonstrate how effectively they are being sustained.

What has been discussed above is only an example. An analysis of the assessment reports would indicate a lot more areas where institutions have been expected to act at the earliest. Since the issues are contextual and differ from institution to institution, this chapter does not attempt to discuss all of them. But the message is that when institutions get ready for re-accreditation these issues need to be approached carefully and differently. Unlike the first accreditation where the existence of certain mechanisms itself was considered to be a healthy practice, during re-accreditation the institutions will have to provide evidence to demonstrate the effectiveness of those mechanisms. The implication is that institutions will have to work hard to improve their effectiveness in these areas and a superficial attempt may not fetch them credit. Both NAAC and HEIs will have to work jointly to spell out the expectations of this dimension.

Role of NAAC in the Post-accreditation Period

It should be noted that the institutions have no obligation to act on the recommendations of the accreditation report of NAAC. In the case of the Professional Bodies that do licensing and programme approval in their areas of specialisation, the reports have a different status. If the institutions are given recommendations, they are expected to report back on the action taken. With varying period of validity, the institutions are also expected to send reports to the concerned bodies. This ensures that the recommendations of the agency/body to ensure the satisfactory functioning of the institutions and the norms laid down by them are taken seriously and ensure the threshold level of quality they have set forth.

The recent UGC Committee on NAAC's Policy and Procedures approved in March 2002 has recommended as follows: "*The efforts and money expended on the assessment exercise will be worthwhile only if the post-assessment activity is attended to seriously. Institutions should be encouraged to work on the recommendations of the peer teams and the healthy practices suggested during the visit. Institutions should be motivated to develop new approaches to deal with changes and simultaneously equip themselves on a continuing basis. NAAC should develop a formal mechanism to get annual feedback from accredited institutions and help them to develop internal monitoring mechanisms*". However, as of now, the follow-up is left to the institutions themselves with the understanding that the self-study process would assist every institution to develop plans for continuing improvement that can be incorporated into ongoing planning and development efforts. To make this assumption a reality, NAAC has taken steps to play a supportive and facilitative role.

One group of academia shares the view that any assessment and accreditation is essentially for the use of its stakeholders, namely, government, funding agencies, students, employers and the society at large. Institutions that undergo assessment may benefit by the outcome of the assessment and the report, if they are serious about enhancing the quality of their provisions. However, it may be of no use, if the major providers are not interested in using the outcome for enhancing the quality. They argue that NAAC has given the stakeholders the indications about the strength and weakness of the institutions and the others – the regulatory bodies, advisory bodies, fund providers, etc. should act on it. NAAC can't simultaneously be the owner of the system trying to directly promote quality enhancement and also be an impartial assessor for assuring quality. In their point of view, the major responsibility in overcoming the post-accreditation complacency lies with the other stakeholders. However, the fact that NAAC has an important facilitative role to promote the stakeholder usage of assessment outcome cannot be denied. It is with this spirit that efforts have been taken to strengthen the benefits of accreditation to institutions that would be catalytic in nature to overcome post-accreditation complacency.

Ensuring that the governments take the assessment outcome seriously for their decisions is one such strategic role. NAAC has succeeded in roping in the support of the important bodies at the center as well as the states. UGC's decision to link the development grant with accreditation status is evidence to this fact. The enthusiasm of some of the state governments discussed in Chapter 3 needs a mention. These initiatives have made institutions realise the trend that more and more stakeholder decisions will be based on assessment outcome in future. However, a more organised relationship between accreditation, policy decisions of the governments and the decisions of the other funding agencies, mainly for quality enhancement schemes is yet to emerge.

The three aspects discussed above have the potential to greatly reduce the post-accreditation complacency. However, the impact will be significant enough to arrest post-accreditation complacency only when the triad – NAAC, institutions of higher education and governments – sustain their efforts and work in partnership. Much depends on the initiatives of the institutions themselves.

In sum, it is time that the accredited HEIs realise the potential of accreditation as a change-agent and take the assessment report as a starting point to overcome post-accreditation complacency. NAAC also has a facilitative role in this and the international experience indicates that these concerns are part of the developmental stage of any quality assurance mechanism. The way NAAC and the HEIs would proceed further is bound to enrich the international development of quality assurance.

Part III
The International Dimension

Globalisation of economies, initiatives to promote education as a tradeable service through GATS protocols, and advent of new forms of education that transcend national boundaries have brought higher education to the center-stage. Rapid expansion of higher education, undertaken in many third world countries, emergence of transnational providers to play a significant role in this expansion as a supplement to the fund-starved national efforts and the like have brought the concern of quality of education to the forefront. Although nations are busy in preparing a national regulatory framework, the quality assurance agencies will have a significant role in self-regulation of both national and transnational education. Transnational education is a two-way process and is inclusive of both export and import of higher educational offerings for many countries including India. This brings new challenges to the quality assurance agencies that are oriented to the national context and they are discussed in this section.

9. Developments in Transnational Education

Borderless distributed learning has already become a reality. With more and more transnational providers that offer borderless education being born every day, assuring quality of education in those provisions has become an issue of concern. What is the role of national quality assurance agencies in assuring quality in transnational education (TNE) provisions? With the current discussions on GATS, what will be the role of national quality assurance agencies in the larger perspective of assuring the quality of higher education to include foreign providers and foreign students? This chapter is an attempt to initiate a discussion on these issues that need serious consideration.

The environment in which higher education institutions and quality assurance agencies operate is changing rapidly. There are six features that characterise the new environment. Firstly, all over the world, more and more private initiatives in higher education are coming up. Secondly, there are private initiatives that go beyond national borders to offer transnational educational provisions and different countries deal with transnational education differently. Thirdly, transnational education takes a variety of new forms and some of the developments are massive. Fourth, the new forms of transnational education are beyond the existing traditional regulatory framework of the national governments, creating new interdependencies between the existing national regulatory framework of nations and the emerging quality assurance systems at the international level. Fifth, the dependence of nations on national QAAs is being accelerated by the growing demand to ensure quality and mobility of students at the international level. Sixth, the vigorous lobbying of WTO towards progressive liberalisation of trade in education is adding a commercial flavour to educational service and the perception of education as a public good is changing. These features generate a number of crucial challenges to governments, QAAs and the providers of educational services and they are briefly discussed in the following pages.

1. Increase in Private Initiatives

As each country begins to realise that more of its population educated at higher levels is essential for national development, expansion of the higher education system gains priority. However, educational analysts strongly believe that the expansion of higher education will not be matched by a proportional rise in public expenditure. This is due to budget limitations, the changing role of government, and increased emphasis on market economy and privatisation. Regardless of the extent of a country's wealth, no country can sustain expanding its state funded higher education system, especially those that are tuition-free. The implication is that this would lead to an increase in private provision.

India is a typical example of how private initiatives came to be encouraged in developing countries. When the country became independent from the British rule in 1947, there was a dearth of educated and skilled work force to undertake the massive nation-building activities. Therefore, it became essential and urgent to generate adequate human resources for the diverse sectors. As most of the population could not afford higher education, the government decided that providing education at all levels would be a national responsibility. Accordingly, the then national government virtually "nationalised" all the universities and colleges – both private and public—and commenced funding them directly. The government approved for state support to all educational institutions including those institutions that were originally established and maintained by private philanthropies. These institutions have come to be known as grant-in-aid institutions as against government colleges and public universities. By the late 1980s the number of colleges increased from 500 to about 5,000. By then, the resources of the government reached the limit and most of the state governments were forced to stop establishing or funding new colleges. In the same period, the preferences of students also shifted from academic disciplines to professional programmes of studies, particularly areas related to engineering, medicine, management and computer science. The combined effect of these two factors has resulted in the emergence of a new category of private institutions which are run with student fees, without financial support from the government. The government encourages the establishment of these private institutions and regulates them under the academic regulations of the universities in the area. This new crop of private initiatives locally called 'self-financing' institutions now outnumber the public ones in most of the states, more so in the southern states of India.

This seems to be the trend in many other countries, particularly in the Asia-Pacific region, where privatisation is seen as a means to increase access to higher education. China has nearly doubled its higher education institutions since 1999 and there are already more than 1000 *min ban* (people-run) institutions in China. In Japan private higher education accounts for 77 per cent of the higher education in the country. In Philippines, among the total of 1,353 HEIs, 1,189 are private institutions, which educate 70 per cent of the students in higher education (Kim, 2002).

2. Transnational Providers

As the national private initiatives establish their roots in the country, avenues are also opening for second country providers to offer higher education services. They are categorised as transnational educational services. Transnational education is a term that is being used to describe real or virtual movement of students, teachers, knowledge and academic programmes from one country to another (Knight, 2002).

China, which educates but 3-4 percent of its 1.2 billion people, has in recent years approved a large number of linkages with its state universities and in recent months has recognised certain state universities to provide online education with the assistance of second country providers. Malaysia in the 1980s recognised that it would be unable to educate more than 6 per cent of its population through its own institutions and began partnering with international institutions to supplement its system of higher education. In recent years, this has led to the authorisation of foreign universities on Malaysian soil. Japan's education ministry has decided to allow universities to grant credit for online courses. The education ministry of Japan is also setting specific rules for online courses. The revamped standards will allow Japanese students abroad to take course credits, and they will also allow students in Japan to earn credit for some courses taken online from foreign universities (Lenn, 2002).

There are also countries not favourable to second country providers. The government of Greece has passed a change to its constitution that no longer recognises universities and education providers in its country which are not Greek. The Greek government allows these colleges to function and classifies them as "laboratories of free studies" and regulates them under the Ministry of Commerce instead of the education ministry.

In India, there have been strong criticisms that the foreign providers establish collaborative arrangements with mostly substandard institutions. The government has not given recognition to the awards of such linkages. Efforts to regulate this situation through appropriate quality assurance measures are in the initial stages.

3. New Forms of Transnational Education

Today, with developments in science and technology, especially with the internet, we see transnational education taking new forms. While there may be some conceptual differences between transnational education and borderless education, they are often used interchangeably. The 'business of borderless education' comprises various forms and developments, among which also combinations are possible, such as the following:

- Distance education programmes that are delivered through satellites, computers, correspondence or other technological means across national boundaries
- Twinning arrangements – in which a degree is gained through study in more than one country as a result of agreements between institutions in different countries to offer joint programmes
- Study abroad semester or credit earning arrangements similar to the twinning programmes
- Branch or satellite campuses set up by an institution in another country to provide its educational programmes to foreign students
- Sale of proprietary materials such as books, courseware or testing, together with associated services
- Franchised operations – using a third party to give degrees – for example a computer company delivering a university computer science degree

- Partnerships for overseas offerings where institution A in one country enters into a collaborative arrangement with an institution B in another country to provide one or more of its programmes to students in B's country
- Free-standing programmes operating outside the country of the provider with or without a combination of the above mentioned arrangements
- Virtual Universities

These developments shape an environment in which new providers can successfully expand the supply of educational services. Universities from North America, Europe and Australia take initiatives to reach out their educational provision to this international higher education market, by active recruitment of international, fee-paying students to the home institution, by establishing branch campuses or franchising and twinning agreements with local institutions, or via distance education and e-learning and other transnational activities. As a result, an exciting but rather complex, picture of higher education provision is emerging. Many of these new providers extensively use the internet as a delivery channel; in some cases they develop into real 'cyber-universities' with a very limited physical presence. The best universities of any country can reach out across borders using the internet or satellite communication links, effectively competing with any national university in its own territory. India, South Africa, China, Malaysia and Hong Kong are seen as big markets for these new provisions.

4. Beyond the Traditional National Regulations

The educational provisions and developments mentioned above differ markedly from conventional education. In most countries, the traditional viewpoint still is that higher education is a public responsibility, that institutions have to be publicly recognised and financed, and that it is the nation-state that gives formal public validity to their degrees. The transnational educational delivery arrangements do not fall in line with this viewpoint.

Further, most of the national context and consequently the mechanisms and schemes have been put in place to regulate and control the domestic providers and not the transnational activities. Increasingly, the national governments feel that they no longer can control the transnational providers adequately with the existing mechanisms, resulting in tension in the national regulatory framework of the countries.

In countries where the national QAAs are functioning or emerging, this tension is coupled with the expectation that what escapes the regulatory governmental framework should be covered by QAAs. In other words, it creates new interdependencies between the national regulatory frameworks and the QAAs and the national QAAs are expected to cover the transnational activities of the national providers as well as second country providers. It results in a set of new conditions under which the QAAs and the transnational providers have to function, which causes concerns among the second country providers.

5. Need for Quality and Mobility at the International Level

Academic mobility for students, scholars, teachers and knowledge workers has been an integral aspect of higher education for centuries. But the picture is changing now. In the globalised scenario, not only more people but also academic programmes and providers are moving across borders. This results in an increasing demand for international transferability and recognition of qualifications. In the simplest form, transnational education through collaborative arrangements between two countries implies the need for recognition of quality and of qualifications in both the countries. Quality becomes central to the issue of recognition. The increasing number of joint awards, which are given by institutions in different countries, has given rise to similar needs for mutual recognition of the qualifications between countries and therefore the need for mutual recognition among the quality assurance systems in different countries. This requires an appropriate and reliable mechanism to reassure the public that the courses, programmes and degrees offered by the transnational arrangements meet acceptable academic and professional standards and that they will be of value in other countries also.

6. Implications of GATS

The General Agreement on Trade in Services (GATS) is the first ever set of multilateral, legally enforceable rules governing international trade in services. It came into effect in 1995 and is being negotiated under the auspices of the World Trade Organisation (WTO). GATS considers education as one of the 12 tradable services. The decision-making body of WTO, called ministerial, in its meeting held at Doha in November 2001, has resolved as follows: "The negotiations on trade in services will be conducted with a view to promoting the economic growth of all trading partners and the development of developing and least-developing countries. ... Participants shall submit initial requests for specific commitments by 30 June 2002 and initial offers by 31 March 2003" (WTO, 2001). It has also resolved to focus on increasing the participation of developing countries in trade and the members entering into successive rounds of negotiations towards progressive liberalisation.

GATS has two broad categories of rules. The first category lists general rules which apply, for the most part, to trade in all services. The second category lists rules applicable to national commitments in specific service sectors. The most significant general rule is about 'Most Favoured Nation Treatment' (MFN). MFN means that countries must give equal and consistent treatment to all foreign trading partners. WTO describes this as 'favour one, favour all'.

Under the other category of rules where the countries can list limitations, the rule on National Treatment is important. National Treatment means equal treatment for foreign and domestic services or service suppliers.

Under the provisions of GATS every country is expected to list its commitments with respect to different sectors and sub-sectors, and also the activities therein. They can also list out limitations on market access and national treatment. The guidelines for negotiations also specify that due respect will be given to the national policy objectives, the level and development and size of the economy of the individual member country and the needs of the small and medium sized service suppliers, particularly those of the developing countries.

Those who consider that education is not a tradable commodity, and that higher education should remain a public good and a public responsibility, perceive GATS as a threat to national sovereignty and culture and as a serious attack on the core values of the university and the quality of teaching. Altbach (2001) argues that the overriding goal of WTO and GATS is to guarantee market access to educational products and institutions of all kinds and that the negative impact of WTO control will be greatest on the developing countries. One of the initiatives by non-government organisations supporting this view is the Joint Declaration on Higher Education and the General Agreement on Trade in Services developed and signed by four organisations: Association of Universities and Colleges in Canada (AUCC), American Council on Education (ACE), European University Association (EUA) and the Council for Higher Education Accreditation (CHEA). The declaration encourages countries not to make commitments in Higher Education Services or in the related categories of Adult Education and Other Education Services in the GATS. Instead it supports the notion of reducing obstacles to international; trade in higher education using conventions and agreements outside of the trade policy regime (Knight, 2002). Trade promoters, on the other hand, try to point to its benefits – competition, motivation for traditional institutions to innovate, establishment of professional networks, providing enhanced opportunities for access to higher education, etc.

With these developments, preserving the safety of the national systems, ensuring the quality of higher education, promoting access to quality education and protecting/ empowering the learner become key issues in response to these phenomena. As a result, there are many challenges to face by all parties involved—the national regulatory systems, QAAs, the transnational providers and the consumers.

The Tensions and the Challenges

Problems of the providers

Looking from the point of view of transnational providers, governments are not supportive and governmental regulations are based on mistrust. Customs regulations limit the movement of education and training materials across borders. In some cases, telecommunication laws inhibit the flow of educational context. For example, Mexico has telecom laws that restrict the use of national satellites and receiving dishes. Visa procedures for students and faculty may become difficult. Foreign currency controls limit the investment by the foreign provider.

Knight (2002) lists the following as barriers faced by transnational providers when they engage in educational delivery through branch or satellite campus, franchise and twinning arrangements:

- Inability to obtain national licenses to grant a qualification
- Limit on direct investment by education providers (equity ceilings)
- Nationality requirements
- Restrictions on recruitment of foreign teachers
- Government monopolies

- High subsidisation of local institutions
- Difficulty in obtaining authorisation to establish facilities
- Economic needs test on suppliers of these services
- Prohibition of higher education, adult education and training services offered by foreign entities
- Measures requiring the use of a local partner
- Difficulty to gain permission to enter into and exit from joint ventures with local or non-local partners on voluntary basis
- Tax treatment that discriminates against foreign suppliers
- Less favourable treatment to foreign partners than other organisations
- Excessive fees/taxes imposed on licensing or royalty payments
- Rules for twinning arrangements
- Lack of transparency in government policy such as the following:
  — domestic laws and regulations are administered in an unfair manner
  — subsidies are not made known in a clear and transparent manner
  — when government approval is required, long delays are encountered
  — when approval is denied, no reasons are given for the denial

TNE providers argue that in the global market, the consumers have the right to quality education and they should be empowered to make their choices. They point out how even the most competent provisions welcomed by consumers suffer bottlenecks at the governmental level due to general mistrust.

Concerns of the Students and the Public

Students who join these transnational provisions generally do not qualify for government benefits. Students face difficulties in translating degrees obtained from transnational providers into national equivalents in many countries. There are transnational providers who aggressively market their courses by assuring equal treatment and recognition of their awards in the provider country. But the student experience indicates that the awards do not give them any competitive edge or benefit in further studies or employment as of now. More cases of questionable providers who collect the fees but are unreachable when the student finds out he or she has been deceived are being reported. Thus the issues of consumer protection are real and the governments have a genuine concern to protect the public.

Government's concerns

The safety of the national values and the in creasing amount of student fee that goes into internet courses offered by foreign providers that are below minimum standards is emerging as an issue of concern to the governments. For example, Hong Kong spends one billion Hong Kong dollars each year on offshore courses. The governments are concerned about the exploitation of the public and the safety of the national systems. The WTO's efforts to progressively liberalise trade in higher education has made the national governments give priority to these concerns and look more closely at the role of the government in the following:

- Licensing and regulation procedures for foreign providers
- Quality assurance and accreditation for imported and exported education services
- Funding protocols including subsidies and scholarships
- Qualification recognition and credit transfer systems

(Nigavekar, 2002)

For many of these issues, "quality" becomes the central point. There have been instances where the quality of some of the transnational providers, even in cases of having physical campuses or with collaborative arrangements, has been questionable and this has made the governments more rigid in their policies and practices on transnational education. In Greece and Israel there is an almost total refusal to include non-national providers in the national higher education system or to recognise their diplomas and degrees.

While realising the need to regulate transnational provisions, governments also feel that their capacity to monitor these developments is inadequate. Even in the US, which has a century-old history of accreditation, regulators struggle to crack down on fake transnational providers. Louisiana now requires that any higher education providers should have a physical presence in the form of offices and personnel. About 50 diploma mills that claimed Wyoming as their home and advertised themselves as American HEIs to attract both American and transnational clientele, were forced to move away after the state passed a law that required institutions to have a physical presence in the state.

When one state tightens the screws, they often simply change mailing addresses. Since the providers of transnational education integrate more and more online courses, the need for a physical site is decreasing and the governments' regulation on physical campus is easily bypassed. As the situation becomes unwieldy, and too difficult to be corrected by national regulations, the governments start depending on the QAAs. More state legislatures in the US are approving bills that allow only accredited universities to establish bases in the state. It is important that the QAAs take note of these interdependencies and take steps to maximise the benefits and minimise the threats to a robust and quality higher education system.

QAAs' Concerns

Obviously QAAs are concerned about providing reliable assurance to stakeholders about the quality of TNE. QA may be easier when programmes are offered at a site in a country rather than solely on the internet. The web presence, which the fake HEIs rely on both for advertising and in some cases for offering courses, poses a problem even to well established QAAs. Many of the web-oriented institutions have the ".edu" websites trying to project an educational image. They have a long list of programmes. Some mention about the accrediting bodies that have been created by the fake HEIs themselves. The problem is serious with the diploma mill distance-education institutions that use the internet to prey on foreign students.

In the US, there are reports that unaccredited institutions that target students from the US and the other countries have established dozens of accrediting bodies that are not recognised by the US Department of Education. These new accrediting bodies themselves lack the infrastructure and standards that they would need for official recognition from the Department of Education. But they are started by the unaccredited institutions with the hope that that would help them gain legitimacy. American Council of Private Colleges and Universities, Association for Online Academic Excellence, World Association of Universities and Colleges are a few to mention. When these institutions expand their scope, often students from countries where accreditation is not a familiar concept become victims. Even for the enlightened public, the way accreditation works in the USA and in other provider countries may not be very clear and the fake transnational providers thrive on these loopholes.

The experience of the UK also reveals that quality assurance of transnationals is a challenging task even if they have a physical site or arrangements with partners in other countries known as overseas educational provisions. The Higher Education Quality Council commenced a series of audits of transnational provision, *i.e.*, of programmes validated or run by British institutions of higher education at locations outside the United Kingdom. In 1996, a pilot series of overseas audits considered a sample of such activities in particular countries, including Hong Kong, Singapore, Malaysia, Greece, and Spain. In 2001, QAA had to make a special enquiry about the collaborative arrangement of one of the UK institutions of higher education with an institution at Israel based on the complaints it received. One may wonder how many cases of deviating from the 'code of practice' get noticed anyway. The redeeming feature is the importance given to such quality audits. The developments with regard to quality assuring transnational education are discussed in detail in the following chapter.

10. Quality Assuring Transnational Education

There have been various efforts by different agencies to develop methodologies, principles or codes of practice to address the quality dimensions of transnational education. The common feature in the various efforts is that management aspects and quality of learning resources are given more importance. As the quantum of transnational education and the issues related to its delivery increase, the assurance by QAAs on these aspects and the cooperation between QAAs in providing reliable assurance are emerging as an imperative. This chapter discusses those developments.

The visibility of Trans National Education (TNE) is increasing now in all countries and new issues of concern are emerging. Basically they can be classified under two categories – TNE operations of domestic institutions exporting education services to other countries (export of education) and TNE that is imported into the country from other countries (import of education). For instance, the various twinning arrangements of American institutions with Indian HEIs to offer awards of American institutions come under import into India. The twinning arrangement of the Christ College, Bangalore with the Western Michigan University, Illinois is an example of import into India. The campuses abroad of the Manipal Academy of Higher Education (MAHE) come under export of Indian HEI. MAHE, one of the oldest self-financing colleges established in 1950s, has grown to 8 colleges and three campuses within the country (at Satna, Pune and Surat) and many others abroad. Campuses abroad are located in Malaysia, Dubai and Nepal and additional ones are being established in Sri Lanka, Uganda and Mauritius. Each mode of TNE has its own implications depending on the clientele and the perspective of the country. What we have discussed in the earlier chapter, to a large extent, reflects the concerns of the nation from the point of view of the education services that are imported into the country and hence the issues of protecting the national system, safeguarding the public and students, etc. It is also necessary to think in terms of the quality of export from the country. Consequently, the confidence the country can place on the quality of both export and import of education and the role of QAA in supporting that value judgement needs a discussion.

Quality Assuring the Export of Education

In 1995 the world market for higher education was estimated to be US$ 27 billion and was expected to touch the figures of US$ 50 billion within a decade. The principal exporter of education services is the US; other major exporters are France, the UK, Australia and Canada (OECD, 2001). In the USA, the education sector ranked fifth in terms of services export revenue, accounting for 4 per cent of total services revenue in 1999 and over US$ 14 billion of export receipts in 2000.

While the QAAs of the USA, Australia and the UK are particular about the quality of export from their countries, most of the other countries are concerned about protecting themselves from questionable imports. Since the number of exporters and importers is lopsided, with only a few in the club of exporters and the rest of the world at the receiving end, work done on quality assuring TNE is also skewed towards imports. There are intergovernmental and international initiatives that are free from country perspectives and assess the quality of educational service from a neutral stand like IIQ, GATE, ISQ and ISO (which are discussed in the later part of this chapter); but such successful initiatives are sporadic.

In the United Kingdom, external scrutiny of the institutional quality assurance arrangements for transnational programmes, have been considered either as part of "standard" institutional audits, or, when the scale of activity is substantial, as separate additional audits. The British practice of quality audit of transnational activities has been guided by the Code of Practice for Overseas Collaborative Provision in Higher Education (HEQC, 1996). This document deals with the code of practices under some twenty headings, indicating the purposes of collaborative links and the allocation of responsibilities for quality assurance. Many items focus upon more detailed facets such as quality control, advertising materials, the duration of studies, and the conducting of student assessments. Under the management aspects of TNE, QAA focuses on the following: Conformity to Local and UK Law; Partner Selection Procedures; Development and Execution of an Audible, renewable Formal Agreement which includes Provision for Termination and the Use of Agents; Host Country Recognition of Awards; Policy for Differing Titles of Awards and Recording Location of Study on Certificates; Sending institutions Control of Publicity and Information; Financial Arrangements. The QAA expects that all higher education institutions will be able to show that they are adhering to the principles of the 'code of practice' to ensure the quality of overseas offerings. Failure to demonstrate that best practice is being followed will be highlighted in the institutional reports published by the QAA. This initiative is designed to help provide enhanced confidence in the work of British universities and colleges operating outside the UK.

In the US too, the regional accrediting agencies require institutions to submit their off-campus initiatives for assessment. The prevalent mode of cross-border educational arrangements are of two types; one in which the students of the American institution would spend a semester or so in an institution in another country commonly known as study abroad semester and accrue credits. The other arrangement is the educational delivery of the American institutions in non-US locations through various arrangements. Both these initiatives are covered by the regional accrediting bodies. For example, where study abroad programmes are included in an institution's offerings, the Middle States Association (MSA) has the practice to conduct on-site evaluations. Since 1981, hundreds of visits have been made to programmes sponsored by member institutions to review whether academic credit earned through study abroad are comparable to that earned on-campus. Travel programmes *per se* or commercially sponsored study travel or independent foreign study programmes which are not related to the curricula of specific colleges and universities in the United States are not evaluated by MSA. The on-site evaluation is not an accreditation visit but a review of an overseas offering reflecting the quality of education offered by the sponsoring institution. The MSA will evaluate all study abroad programmes, regardless of size or location, on a schedule roughly approximating the decennial evaluation cycle, unless problems are identified which require more frequent review. Newly initiated study abroad programmes are evaluated within three years of their establishment and then on a 10-year cycle, always assuming that no special problems are discovered.

"Characteristics of Excellence: Standards for Accreditation" of the Middle States Association of the Commission on Higher Education describes institutional responsibility for off-campus offerings as follows: "Ultimately, the integrity and credibility of an institution's educational programme rests directly on its acceptance of responsibility for all activities conducted in its name or under its sponsorship. (p.17)" The Commission takes seriously its charge to insure the quality of off-campus programmes at its members' off-site locations. In order to do so in an informed and systematic way, the Commission asks every member college and university with off-campus offerings to prepare a report on these offerings as a regular part of the self-study process for the ten-year evaluation team visit. This report serves as the basis for peer assessment by evaluators who are assigned to serve on evaluation teams after being trained especially in the assessment of off-campus programmes.

In Australia, the Australian Vice-Chancellors' Committee (AVCC) has evolved a Code of Ethical Practice in the provision of Offshore Education and Education Services. The code includes the following aspects of management of TNE: Notification of Australian Diplomatic Missions; Accuracy of Promotional Materials; Competence of Agents or Partners; Compliance to Local Laws; Explicitness of Fees and Refunds, Student Support Services, and Staff Support. The Australian Universities Quality Agency (AUQA) established in 2001 is conducting the first cycle of audits. However, its policy is clear that it would include the auditing of overseas offerings of the Australian Universities.

Although the major exporters have good QA mechanisms in place, their impact on TNE arrangements is not very clear. For instance, in India in 2000, out of the 144 newspaper advertisements about TNE services that appeared over a period of 8 months, as many as 31 per cent of the foreign providers are not recognised/accredited in their own countries. As many as 89 per cent of their Indian partners are not affiliated to any Indian recognised university or other institutions, suggesting that they have entered into collaboration with doubtful partners (Powar, 2001).

The benchmarks followed by the QAAs of the exporting countries in reviewing the export of their HEIs also raises questions. Do they assess whether the educational service provided in the importing country through TNE operations is comparable to the service provided to the campus students in the provider country? Can they assure to the clientele that the awards given to students of the host country through such TNE operations are comparable to the awards of the first country students? Do they have the provider country standards as the benchmark? Or is the national standard of the host country the point of reference for review and if that is the case is it made clear to the students of the host country? Or does the QAA follow a different set of compromised benchmarks for the TNE operations of their HEIs?

Quality Assuring the Import of Education

The international scenario indicates that a wide range of methods are employed to quality assure TNE imports including: comparison of programmes offered abroad with equivalent programmes offered in the home country, comparison of provider with host country standards, comparison with their own published standards and mutual recognition. In some countries programmes have to be approved before they are initiated. Some countries allow providers to set quality standards without review. A few exclude all foreign courses from approval.

Third Party Assurance

While the efforts of national QAAs – either from the point of view of export or of import—have the mandated and regulatory approach, there are various guidelines and codes of practice evolved by international and inter governmental interest groups. There are also institutions and programmes that seek certification at the international level – external to both the provider country as well as the importing country—for various reasons. Presently, international bodies like the International Institute for Quality (IIQ), Global Alliance for Transnational Education (GATE), and International Association of Continuing Education and Training (IACET), are taking the initiative. IIQ and GATE are emerging as multinational external agencies for the purpose of assuring the quality of education offered in any country through a certification process quite similar to those of the national EQA agencies, but with international standards.

The International Institute for Quality (IIQ) is the initiative taken by two international academic bodies – Quality Assurance International and CINDA – which are, in turn, dedicated to quality related issues. The IIQ manual indicates that "The International Institute for Quality is devoted to the assurance and improvement of quality in higher education through reviewing and accrediting institutions in relation to widely accepted international standards. The core services offered by the organisation are commissioned consultancies and independent institutional reviews against specified international standards." In these procedures, there are some modifications both in the criteria used and in the composition of the peer team that visits the institution to validate the claims. But a cursory survey of their processes would indicate that there is not much difference between their evaluation process and those of other national EQA agencies. In fact when they undertake the certification process of an international education programme that are designed for overseas clients, they involve the members of the other national accrediting agencies or their expert nominees who have wide experience in the accreditation process.

The GATE Certification Manual notes that, "GATE's primary purpose is to address the assurance and improvement of the quality of education that crosses national borders" (GATE, 1999). Now GATE has moved away from mainstream to assess only electronic learning. GATE principles look into the following aspects of TNE management: Conformity to Laws and Approvals of the Host Country; Disclosure of Pertinent Information to Learner; Adequacy and Sustainability of Resources, Learner Support Services, and Facilities; Roles, Expectations and Obligations Covering Agreements with Third Party Agents; Professional and Employment Recognition and Restriction of Awards; Record keeping.

IACET guidelines for managing TNE include the following: Defined Unit or Group for Administering Activities, Courses or Programmes; Responsibility and Control; Award System; Maintenance and Availability of Records; Learning Environment and Support Systems; Demonstrated Financial and Administrative Commitment; Staff Training and Development; Record keeping; Intellectual Property.

Another development is the application of the ISO family of standards. An elaborate process for ISO 9002 implementation in educational institutions has been evolved and the outcome is expected to assure a certain level of quality. A few educational institutions in India have already got the ISO certification through the national bodies that have the ISO membership, with a hope that their education would have worldwide recognition. The ISO 9000 series emphasises the following: Procedures for Contract Review and Modification; Defined Relationship with Funding Bodies, Awarding Bodies, and Franchisees; Internal and External Document Control; Assessment of Sub-Contractors; Procedures for Identifying Non-Conforming Product and Corrective Action; Materials Handling; Training and Staff Development.

Among intergovernmental initiatives, the UNESCO's code of practice deserve a mention. UNESCO and the intergovernmental Council of Europe formed a working group on transnational education and the group has evolved some principles of good practice to be followed by transnational providers. According to those principles, institutions that plan to export educational services, whether physically or virtually, should ask themselves the following few basic questions (Lenn, 2002).

Mission: Does the programme or degree reinforce the college's mission? Who at the providing institution knows that the programme is being exported? Who else needs to know?

Control: Are the academic programme, staff, and other key operations within reasonable control of the institution?

Academic programme and teaching staff: Are the instructors qualified to teach the curriculum? Do they have equivalent qualifications to those working at the home institution? If tutors are used, are they well trained? In what language will the instructors teach the curriculum?

Learning resources: Do the library, laboratory, and instructional materials and equipment adequately support the curriculum?

Students: Can they complete the programme? What is the language requirement for students? If it differs from the home institution's requirements, can that be justified?

Student services: To support the academic programme, does the institution provide such services as advising, hostels, and other support networks?

Physical resources: Unless it is an online programme, is the physical infrastructure for the educational entity adequate and well maintained?

Financial resources: Is the home institution in control of those resources? Are appropriate fees, including tuition, being asked for services rendered? Are revenues invested in maintaining a good programme as well as providing a financial return to the home institution?

Although significant developments have taken place, the question of effective implementation of quality assurance of TNE using these guidelines still remains.

Ground Realities

The problem is not just how to assess the quality of learning in transnational provisions, but how to define the area of operation, how to redefine the concepts of QA that have the root on the traditional education and how to coordinate assessment exercises by various national quality assurance agencies across national borders. The major questions facing the emerging QAAs are: Should the QAA adopt the policy of assessing all activities conducted in the name of the institution in the home country as well as abroad under its sponsorship or should it be restricted to the offerings in the home country? Should the QAA take a via media giving importance to domestic offerings and ensure a remote control for international activities? Depending on the stand taken by the national QAAs, the HEIs would also take a stand regarding their responsibilities in 'crossing the borders'. If the overseas offerings are to be given a prominent place in the assessment protocols, it would further influence the issues on criteria, frame of reference, benchmarks and indicators, site-visit, etc. since the stakeholders of the outcome of assessment become the international audience. For example, will the peers visit the overseas sites? Will they visit all the sites or only a few? What would be the implications for the resource requirement for such a visit? Will the criteria and benchmarks be raised to the international standards? Will the benchmarks be set to the level of the host country? The answers to most of these questions depend on the approach the QAAs would like to take.

At this juncture, there are two questions that have to be answered. One is whether TNE should be within the national QAA's area of operation. The other is whether the national QAA will have a substantial role to play at all in the issues of TNE.

Area of Operation

We need to look at two arguments with respect to whether NQAAs should worry about TNE at all. One argument is that NQAAs need not worry about TNE since the volume of TNE in any country is very low. The other argument is that whether significant or not, any regulation or quality assurance of TNE should have a significant place for an NQAA and therefore an NQAA should reflect on its role. If quality of provisions and protecting the country from substandard providers and exploitative agents is the cause of concern, a national quality assurance agency should have a due role in the discussions on TNE right from the beginning. In fact the NQAA has to be the resource base for such discussions and hence the need to worry about the issues related to TNE.

Let us take the first argument. As of today, if one has to go by the figures on the volume of activity, it is true that TNE is not a substantial activity in most of the countries, compared to the size and spending of the national system of higher education. Among the various modes of transnational education, the contribution of the mode that moves educational delivery across the national boundaries is a minor one compared to the movement of international students to study at foreign universities. The bulk of students who opt for an award from other countries travel to the provider countries and join the formal national educational systems there. For instance, in 1998, the US was host country to 32 per cent of foreign students in OECD countries, followed by the UK, Germany and France. Such provisions where students cross borders are already covered by the national QAAs of the providing countries. Take the case of India for example. From the data pertaining to the number of persons who have been issued students visa in India for the years 1988 and 1999, it is estimated that about 24,000 students migrate each year to pursue their higher studies in foreign universities. This is not a significant number as compared to more than 8 million students enrolled in the country. The number of students enrolled in the collaborative provisions is not available and it may not be much. Therefore, it can be concluded that the quality assurance of the national stream of education, with or without the overtone of internationalisation is adequate to serve the majority of stakeholders across the national boundary as well.

Those who argue in favour of serious attention to TNE cite the developments in GATS. In their opinion, in view of the developments in GATS and the lobbying of WTO, TNE operations are already on the increase and the role of QAA in quality assuring those provisions will become important. The implication is that although the volume of TNE may be low as of now, it is likely to increase due to the developments in GATS and NQAAs should take note of the quality related issues of TNE.

Transnational education is an under-researched and often misunderstood area about which no systematic information can really be found. The activities developed in different multilateral frameworks and by professional organisations are overshadowed by the WTO and the GATS promoting trade in educational services (Stamenka, 2002). Irrespective of the GATS related developments, NQAAs have to take a stand on the international activities of the HEIs of their countries and especially of the HEIs that are covered by the quality assurance activity of NQAAs. If NQAAs intend to cover all activities of the institutions, it should pay attention to TNE as well. And, it should be in line with the international trend. The international trend is to have a strong component of quality assurance mechanism. Therefore, as a policy NQAAs may have to take a stand about TNE and the international trend would pressurise NQAAs to take TNE seriously. This answers the first question.

The second question is whether the NQAA will have a significant role at all in TNE. In most of the countries, efforts are underway to evolve a set of basic codes and criteria for the imports, especially the operation of foreign education institutions. Discussions are also going on about promoting the export of education services by domestic institutions. Quality is central to the promotion of export and import of education. To attract foreign students to local campuses as well as to export education, HEIs need a certification about their quality. Obviously, the national quality assurance agency should have a significant role in these developments. The NQAA should provide reliable assurance to the foreign markets about the quality of the educational services exported from the country. This answers the second question and the NQAA will have a substantial role in the quality assurance of TNE.

But one cannot be certain that the current approaches to QA as practiced can stretch adequately to regulate these new international endeavours. The issues to be addressed in this regard are discussed in the following pages.

Co-operation Among QAAs

International developments indicate that nations have realised that national regulatory frameworks may not be adequate to oversee education provisions that cross national borders. Similarly, QAAs also have realised that the traditional QA framework is not adequate to quality assure transnational provisions and they cannot make any progress if QAAs operate in isolation. The problem is not just how to regulate and quality assure TNE, but how to coordinate the regulatory and quality assurance exercises by various agencies across national borders. Mutual cooperation among the various national QAAs is seen as a possible solution. For example, the Audit Manual of the Australian Universities Quality Agency (AUQA) notes as follows: "AUQA will also establish links with foreign quality agencies to obtain their assistance in relation to Australian operations overseas". (www.auqa.edu.au/qualityaudit/auditmanual/chapter02/index.shtml) It may seem to be a simple statement but it is loaded with a lot of implications. Reflection on what the NQAA would do in such circumstances is necessary.

How will the NQAA go about in the following six situations is worth analysing:

— Domestic HEIs with TNE operations
— Cooperation the NQAA would expect from QAAs of receiving countries in the above
— Cooperation the NQAA would extend to QAAs of receiving countries in their QA efforts of import into their countries
— TNE offered in the country by foreign providers
— Cooperation the NQAA would expect from QAAs of the provider countries in quality assuring the import into the country
— Cooperation the NQAA would extend to QAAs of provider countries in their QA efforts of export by their HEIs

The above-mentioned issues can be clubbed under two major categories – quality assurance of TNE imported to the country and quality assurance of TNE exported by domestic HEIs. Having agreed that TNE operations of HEIs should be given a due place in the NQAA's QA procedures, the extent of significance to be attached to the various components of the procedure need attention.

Generally, in the case of domestic operations, the NQAA's policy evolves over a period of time. For instance, in NAAC's procedures, the place to be given to the constituent colleges, the distance education units, the teacher education units, the individual departments and the satellite campus in institutional accreditation was not very clear in the beginning. Today, it is made clear to the HEIs that the grade of the university does not include the quality of the constituent colleges and that managing the constituent and affiliated colleges through the affiliating functions is seen as a part of the organisation and management function of the university. Although the distance education units may have substantial activities, it is taken as one of the many departments of the university and for the assessment of distance education *per se* there is a separate mechanism in collaboration with DEC. The same is true for the teacher education colleges and departments. The institutional grade is not the average of departmental grades and for departmental accreditation there is a separate mechanism. These delineations did not emerge overnight but with field experience of eight years during 1994-2002. It is still an evolving process. A similar delineation is necessary for the TNE operations, though we may not wait that long.

The specification of the approach to be followed and the cooperation needed from other parties raise a series of questions. Should the NQAA decide that since TNE operations differ markedly from national provisions, they should be assessed separately? If yes, will it be similar to the QA procedure for national provisions? If an integrated approach is preferred, will TNE operations of domestic HEIs be treated similar to departmental initiatives? If no, will it be treated as another form of campus expansion? Can we assume that if an institution has long experience in effectively administering satellite campuses, there may not be too many new issues in the commencement of overseas operations? Along with the integrated approach, should the NQAA get ready for a separate mechanism as in the case of departmental accreditation or programme accreditation or institutional accreditation? Will the NQAA choose the approach depending on the level of TNE operations of the HEI? Will it be a case-by-case approach? What will be the criteria to decide about the approach and how will that be made known to TNE providers? What kind of cooperation and collaboration should the NQAA look for with other parties in the country? What will be the role of professional bodies, if the TNE operation is in a professional area of study?

What will be the outcome of the NQAA's approach to TNE operations? Will it be in terms of whether the offerings are good or substandard? Will it indicate whether the TNE operations are accredited or not? Will it pass a judgement whether institutional accreditation can include or exclude the TNE operations? Can it say that the TNE operations should cease to be offered? Will the outcome be directly linked to approval or denial of permission to offer TNE service? In systems where accreditation is voluntary and in systems where accreditation has so far not served the function of approval or recognition, is it in a position to serve that function for the endeavours of TNE operations?

The stand on the outcome has implications for the guidelines to be given to the HEIs. At what point should the NQAA state that the institution's operations are substandard? When can it say that the institution's operations are not accredited? When can it say that the institution's overseas operations must be excluded from accreditation? At point can it declare that the institution's overseas operations should cease to be offered? What are the guidelines and code of practice the NQAA would give to domestic HEIs that engage in TNE operations? For example, there are institutions that have arrangements with host institutions abroad to guarantee acceptance of their credits and this kind of articulation arrangement alone makes the institution a viable TNE provider. These arrangements cannot ensure mobility or recognition beyond the two partners and the quality of student support services may be at stake in some of these arrangements. How should the NQAA look at these articulations?

Many nations lack a clear approval process by which the legitimacy of the collaborating partner can be recognised. In many nations the laws about higher education are those which establish and regulate the state-controlled system of higher education. In fact, in some nations no legal concept of private higher education exists. Is it acceptable that the domestic institutions contract with establishments that are not recognised in the host nation as educational entities?

The discussion reveals that new dimensions are to be added to quality assure TNE. Evaluation of e-learning provisions, quality of the learning materials, qualification of the authors of e-material, formal training in e-education, etc., are many new dimensions. It may involve new ways of doing things also. The most important new dimension is doing it collaboratively within the country as well as with the counterparts abroad. Evolving a code of practice becomes essential at this juncture.

Code of Practice

The code of practice suggested by UNESCO and the ones that are being practised by other agencies have been given in the earlier chapter. The framework for assessment itself has to build on that code of practice. Obviously the framework of assessment has to be made known to the TNE providers.

From the point of view of the NQAA, in the transnational setting quality assurance of education is perhaps best reduced to the ability to ask the right questions about the transnational arrangement. Tom Clawson lists a set of questions under four categories with reference to transnational professional ventures and some of them are worth a mention in the context of general TNE arrangements:

- What are the current social, political, economic, and cultural issues facing the country involved in the partnership?
- What is the history of the particular offering in the partner country?
- What is the make up of its clientele?
- How do the clientele get their educational experience?
- By what process do the clientele gain the awards?
- What are the requirements and/or conventions of certification?
- What are the most important qualities in the identification and selection of a partner?
- What are the motivating factors for each partner in the establishment of a transnational joint venture?

- What is the day-to-day management and overall governance structure under which they operate?
- What legal requirements need to be followed?

Apart from providing the code of practice for HEIs there is a need to agree on the code of practice of the quality assurance of the NQAA itself with respect to the cooperation it expects from other QAAs and the support it would be willing to extend to other QAAs. Council for Higher Education Accreditation of the USA has developed four principles for United States Accreditors who undertake reviews of institutions and programmes operating outside the US. They are intended to strengthen the working relationship among the US accreditors and international quality assurance agencies and encourage and enhance ongoing cooperation and communication. The first two principles relate to accreditation of non-US institutions and programmes and the next two are about the US exports. The principles 3 and 4 that relate to the accreditation of the US exports is given below:

Principle 3: Accreditor Expectations of Providers of the US online and Web-based Instruction and Programmes Exporting to Another Country.

US accreditors will:

- Work closely with the US institutional and programmatic exporters of online and Web-based education to assure quality, as offerings are made available in a variety of countries, especially when Web-based and online offerings involve instructional strategies that are unfamiliar to the host country;
- Work with the US exporters to inform potential students of the language expectations and requirements associated with online and Web-based courses, programmes and degrees;

- Work with the US exporters to review language, literacy and study skill levels of the target audience for online and Web-based offerings, preparing separate or supplemental material to meet special needs if appropriate.

Principle 4: Responsibilities of the US Accreditors Working with Non-US Institutions and Programmes to Students and Colleagues in Another Country.

US accreditors will:

- Work with other countries to provide the most comprehensive and accurate information available about the US exports to avoid "accreditation mills" and "diploma mills";
- Develop, working with international colleagues, an information protocol that can be used to assist countries in reviewing imports from the US.

Source: www.chea.org

While working in collaboration with the agencies within the country itself is yet to materialise in many areas, leading to territorial claims, collaboration at the international level that will have major implications needs more reflection. As of now the NQAA of a country assures prospective students that an institution is providing quality educational programmes and that it will continue to do an acceptable job in the future. As it reviews the new trends in TNE, the NQAA should consider whether it can provide with confidence this assurance to foreign students. In this context, this paper highlights some—certainly not all—of the significant challenges the NQAA may have to confront. They are challenges to the accrediting community world over. Most defy a quick solution or an easy answer. Because the national QAAs will have to respond soon, there is some urgency in these discussions.

11. Indian Scenario of Quality Assurance in TNE

In India, NAAC, being the national external quality assurance agency, may have to extend its concerns to include transnational provisions. Although the volume of transnational education in India is still very low, if NAAC has to contribute to the quality assurance issues of those provisions, how big is that responsibility? Although most of the TNE offerings fall under just one or two areas of studies – especially under computer science and management, as a part of institutional activities they may have to be given a due place in the overall institutional accreditation. This chapter does not propose a particular set of policies to be adopted by NAAC but it outlines the developments in TNE in India and the challenges of quality assuring those provisions – whether offered by Indian HEIs or by foreign providers.

Increasing TNE presence

As of now, there is no foreign university or their campuses in the country. However, the presence of TNE providers from abroad is very much in evidence through their active campaigns, either to enroll students for studies in their home institutions or to the new provisions they offer in collaboration with local institutions through twinning or franchise arrangements. There has been a spurt in the activities of foreign educational institutions since the 1990s and their promotional drive is focussed mainly on attracting students for studies in their home campuses. Powar (2001) carried out a detailed analysis of the TNE presence in the country. More than 80 per cent of the newspaper advertisements published by the TNE providers scanned over a period of 8 months in 2000 relate to attracting students to enroll in their home institutions and only less than 20 per cent devote to their provisions offered with local partners. A cursory analysis of these advertisements brings out some disturbing trends. In the 144 ads (appearing between 1st July and 31st December 2000) analysed, as many as 31 per cent of the foreign providers are not recognised/ accredited in their own countries, the highest number coming from the USA. As many as 89 per cent of their Indian partners are not affiliated to any Indian recognised university or other institutions suggesting that they have entered into collaboration with doubtful partners whose motive could only be commercial gain. The countries that are active in attracting Indian students are the UK, the USA, Australia, Canada, New Zealand, Bulgaria, Cyprus, Hong Kong, France, Ireland, Mauritius, Nepal, Romania, Russia and Switzerland.

In 2000, TNE providers, chiefly from five countries, offered programmes mainly at the master's level, mostly in the areas of engineering and management through franchise or some such arrangements with many Indian institutions. Typical examples of institutions in such collaborative arrangements are the Christ College of Bangalore, SNDT University of Mumbai and Guru Nanak Dev University of Amritsar. More than one hundred collaborative twinning arrangements are currently active offering a number of academic programmes in the universities and colleges throughout the country. In recent times, a large number of private institutions like Sri. Ramachandra Medical University, Vellore Institute of Technology, Manipal Academy of Higher

Education have also established such links with Australia, the United States of America, the United Kingdom and France and offer programmes jointly leading to degrees of either of the co-operating universities.

In August, 2002, based on the information collected from advertisements and articles in newspapers, USEFI made an attempt to identify the offshore activities by American institutions in India. According to that data, in the year 2002 there were 26 American institutions that had offshore activities in collaboration with Indian institutions. Two of them were not listed in the Directory of Accredited Institutions of Post Secondary Education published by American Council on Education (ACE). Most of the collaborations were in information technology and management-related programmes, with the exception of two – one in Journalism and the other in Art in Design.

Existing Regulations

As of now there is no ban or regulatory control on transnational providers offering their programmes in collaboration with local partners or through virtual modes. They can extend their services in all the modes of supply under the WTO formulation except for establishing the universities and colleges in the country. There is no bar in the movement of persons and materials for educational services. Even the foreign exchange regulations and repatriation of funds from India are liberalised in line with the policy evolved for other economic activities. There are also no cultural and linguistic barriers as the country is well exposed to other cultures and the medium of instruction has been English at the higher education level for more than a century. Besides, India is a signatory to the WTO convention and is therefore obligated to liberalise further any existing barrier. India has also submitted proposals to WTO seeking easier market access for professionals in several sectors, including health, information technology, accountancy, education and communication as part of its drive for liberalisation of trade in services. This proposal comes under 'Movement of Natural Persons', one of the four modes of trade in services identified by the GATS document By sending this proposal, .India has made an initial commitment to the principle of trade in educational services.

Regarding the export of education, there are some procedural obligations on the part of the Indian partners in establishing links with their international counterparts. The Government of India regulates their participation in collaborative agreements through the External Affairs and Education Ministries. By and large the government is supportive of such international co-operation, whether twinning arrangements or franchise deals.

Although both the Government of India and its agencies like UGC, AICTE, etc. recognise foreign degrees studied abroad, they do not, as yet, recognise the identical programmes if studied in India by whatever means as transnational programmes. For example, a student who obtains a degree from University X of the UK has the qualification formally recognised whilst the same degree is not recognised if obtained by studying in India through the distance mode. Even if University X and the UK government maintain that both programmes are identical, they do not enjoy the same status in India. This appears to be a major hurdle for transnational providers in expanding their operations. In any event, overseas institutions have no regulations to abide by, either prior to establishing their ventures or thereafter. Thus, transnational provisions remain unregulated and unrecognised but grow in popularity and acceptance. The Confederation of Indian Industries (CII), for instance, works in partnership with the University of Warwick and Indian Institute of Management, Bangalore does so with Lancaster University in offering degrees in management studies in spite of the fact that the degrees offered by the UK Universities in these transnational provisions are not formally recognised. In other words, there is no formal regulatory framework and at the same time there is no legal hurdle for the cross-country providers in entering the education market. The issue of non-recognition of the qualification does not seem to bother the students who are confident of the value of such degrees in the vast job market, both in India and abroad. The non-recognition of the qualifications by government agencies will affect only the prospects of students in getting government jobs, which are in any way not much in comparison with the size of the global job market.

GATS and its Implications

Like other countries, India has also made initial commitments by 31st March, 2003. Without compromising the national policy on education, the country has identified the areas where we have a competitive edge and further discussions are going to negotiate on our strengths. The discussions so far held at policy level indicate that it should be possible to make commitments in higher education with appropriate built-in restrictions that could be sub-sector specific, nation specific and even specific to areas/regions of India.

There have been nation-wide discussions involving the Ministry of Education, Association of the Indian Universities (AIU), Associations of Colleges and at other governmental and non-governmental forums like National Institute of Educational Planning and Administration (NIEPA) and Confederation of Indian Industries (CII) on the implications of bringing higher education as a tradable service as proposed by WTO in GATS. There have also been discussions at the inter-ministerial level involving the ministries of Education, Commerce, Trade and Industry and Finance and the inter-institutional level in this regard. The outcomes of such deliberations are generally positive towards liberalising trade in educational and other services.

Although India is yet to make a firm commitment for the entire education sector including higher education, except the latest proposal for the movement of natural persons, there is a growing awareness about the inevitability of committing to progressive liberalisation. As far as education is concerned, though the government has been a major service provider for years, private initiatives have come to play a larger role in the last couple of decades and they have grown substantially. Therefore, India, as a member of WTO cannot possibly take recourse to Article 13 of GATS that allows exemption to services provided by the government without a commercial purpose and without any competition from private service providers.

However, keeping the national context in view, the general consensus is to liberalise the trade in higher education to begin with, as it is not advisable as of now to make any commitments in the other four sub-sectors viz., Primary, Secondary, Adult and Continuing education and other education. A pragmatic approach is emerging in favour of making commitments in one of the sub-sectors of higher education with suitable saving clauses. The implication is that although the volume of TNE may be low in India as of now, it is likely to increase due to the developments in GATS and the national regulatory framework should take note of these issues of TNE.

National Regulatory Framework

Efforts are underway to evolve a set of basic codes and criteria for the operation of foreign education institutions in the country. In a draft Policy paper prepared by the Ministry of Human Resources Development for regulating the operation of Foreign Educational Institutions in the country and promoting Foreign Direct Investment (FDI) in the Education Sector, the committee constituted for the purpose has outlined the salient features of this policy framework. They are:

- Operations of the foreign educational institutions should not have deleterious effect on Indian culture and ethos and shall be open for practitioners of all religion.

- There shall be mandatory registration of foreign education service providers with a Registering Authority such terms and conditions and following such procedures as may be provided.
- Institutions and programmes offered should be accredited in own countries and awards recognised as equivalent to awards given for their on-campus programmes.
- They shall adhere to a code of practice relating to publicity to facilitate informed decision making by students and their parents.
- They shall avoid gross commercialisation consistent with the principle of no-profit, no-loss for education services laid down by the Supreme Court of India.
- They shall maintain minimum standards as laid down by the concerned agency and *will be subject to external quality review by a designated agency.*
- They shall furnish all information about operations in the country in the interest of transparency.

While the above-mentioned developments mark the beginning of the regulatory approach to TNE, the quality assurance efforts are yet to take any definite pattern in India and without quality assurance stipulations the system to monitor TNE would be incomplete. NAAC has a pivotal role in the stipulation on the "external quality review" highlighted above. The discussions on the role of external quality review are in progress and the policy issues discussed during a seminar at NIEPA in 2000 include 1. Need for a national level mechanism to ensure quality and standards of any education exported or imported and the relevance of registering the foreign providers, 2. Evolving clear guidelines and laws about visa permits for students, migration, work permit, etc., and devolving the powers to deal with these issues to the universities and institutions concerned within the broad framework of national policy, 3. Making NAAC accreditation mandatory for institutions interested in both exporting or importing education and restricting the export option to highly rated accredited institutions in the country, 4. Encouraging universities to offer programmes on the internet and in virtual mode and improving the requisite infrastructure such as internet connectivity for the purpose.

While evolving the national regulatory framework, there are larger issues to be resolved through policy decisions, for instance, who will control higher education in the long run—the nation or international tribunals like WTO? Before making concrete regulatory protocols or reviewing TNE, other generic issues to be addressed are: 1. What will happen to traditional academic values nurtured all these years? 2. How would nations or individual universities maintain their academic freedom in the new competitive environment? 3.Will national universities become part of the international jurisdiction? These are not concerns peculiar to India alone but are common to all the developing countries.

It may take some time at the policy level discussions to define the role of NAAC in the quality assurance of import of education into India. But there is an urgent need to define the role of NAAC in the export of education by Indian HEIs as more and more of them are engaged in overseas educational activities. As a consequence of the initial commitment made by India under GATS, the government will encourage institutions to establish overseas ventures. MHRD has identified the Committee for Promotion of Indian Education Abroad (CoPIE) as the nodal agency to lay down specific guidelines for registration of foreign education service providers consideration in favour of this policy that India with its huge higher education system with many institutions of international standing can benefit both economically and politically by exporting education especially to the third world countries and to those that have a substantial Indian population. Consequently, universities are now permitted to open institutions and campuses abroad significant number of universities are offering academic programmes already in many of the third world countries.

A typical example of an Indian transnational provider is the Manipal Academy of Higher Education. Pune University, Delhi University, Jawaharlal Nehru University and Roorkee University are known for attracting foreign students to their campuses for a number of years now. They have developed the adequate infrastructure, organisational back up and administrative support to handle foreign students. These examples are indicative of the national trend in becoming both the provider and a recipient of transnational education and this trend has a great deal of bearing on the policy and the formulations of regulatory clauses in dealing with international providers

GATS or not, NAAC has to take a stand on the international activities of HEIs that get accreditation. If institutional accreditation intends to cover all activities of an institution run under its name, NAAC should pay attention to TNE and it should be in line with the international trend. The international developments indicate that national quality assurance mechanisms have a significant role in TNE operations. Therefore, as a policy NAAC may have to take a stand about TNE.

What if NAAC does not deem it fit to do so? Probably other mechanisms will emerge to take care of quality assuring TNE. It is not possible to do too many things with a single mechanism and delineating the area of operation is also good for upholding the credibility of the process. For example, course equivalence is not done by NAAC and there are other mechanisms to take care of it. There are many regulatory functions like the affiliating functions that NAAC does not pay direct attention to but only evaluates whether those functions are carried out in a qualitative way. In a similar way, delineating what NAAC intends to do may be necessary. But as of now, NAAC is the national QAA that is positioned well to take care of quality assurance of TNE and hence any move in TNE that is linked to quality is within the scope of NAAC. This new dimension is not free from challenges.

Implications for NAAC

It should be noted that these operations require strong collaboration within the country among the various quality interest groups. Take for example, the type of programmes that are imported to India. Most of them are in the areas of engineering, information technology and management. Where domestic offerings in those areas are concerned, AICTE and NBA have a significant role. Therefore, quality assuring TNE in those areas will warrant a healthy collaboration with those agencies.

Further, as of now, international recognition of qualifications or awards depend on the quality assurance arrangements at the programme level, although discussions are going on to extend mutual recognition to the institutional level and towards mutual recognition of QAAs themselves. Especially in the case of TNE operations in professional courses, to facilitate international acceptance of the joint awards and degrees which result from TNE operations, NAAC may have to firm up its collaboration with professional councils.

While these developments add new dimensions to quality assurance and require NAAC to plan new ways of doing it, simultaneously international developments are exerting pressure on NAAC to fine-tune its methodology to maintain its place as one of the leading QAAs in the Asia-Pacific. For instance, based on the information provided about NAAC's methodology, INQAAHE and IAUP have already accepted NAAC as one of the selected QAAs as candidates for establishing the Trustworthiness. To progress from the candidacy status to the next stage, when the modalities are firmed up, NAAC has to build on its strengths further. It has to meet the standards expected of a Trustworthy Quality Assurance Agency as prescribed by the code of practice evolved by these bodies. Some of the international developments in quality assurance, to which any QAA has to be tuned to, are discussed in the next chapter.

12. International Approach to Quality Assurance

There is an urgent need for national QAAs to work together in areas of common interest and concern and it requires a basis of trust in the quality of QAAs themselves. As a result, there are discussions going on about establishing mechanisms to assure the reliability of quality assurance agencies. Any quality assurance agency that has achieved a reasonable level of success and acceptance among the academia within the country, should explore how to become an international player. It has to stabilise and consolidate its strengths to find a place among the internationally credible quality assurance agencies. Many initiatives are going on to promote this trend, including the formation of the Global Forum, proposal for the World Quality Register (WQR) and the discussion on the International Quality Confederation. This chapter discusses those developments and related issues.

The capacity of any country to protect its citizens from all kinds of imported programmes of poor quality is becoming questionable. This calls for better mechanisms to share information about accredited institutions in each country, questionable providers, standards for review of quality in different countries, and good practices. To put a check on the unhealthy developments in transnational education, an international and sustainable policy framework is needed for dealing with transnational providers that will also protect the interests of national governments, the traditional public higher education sector, for-profit providers, the students and the general public. It calls for developing an international approach to quality assurance and accreditation.

International approach to quality assurance

There is a growing agreement that a transnational approach to quality assurance and accreditation is needed, but there are huge differences of opinion on how to achieve this and which steps have to be taken. Van Dimme Kirk (Kirk, 2002) lists four strategies to choose from. A minimal strategy is to improve communication and exchange among quality assurance agencies of various nations. A second strategy is to develop a soft validation and approval procedure for existing quality assurance systems. A third strategy could be the accreditation of accrediting agencies on an international scale. A fourth strategy is the development of a real international accreditation agency or an international regulatory framework.

The need for strengthening the first strategy – information exchange – has been felt strongly by the agencies that have international activities and many agencies and networks are active in facilitating this development. It is reasonable to expect that this will, in the long run, lead to international benchmarking of quality, standards and methodologies and pave way to the gradual mutual recognition of agencies and their assessment outcomes.

The second strategy will result in more reliable and concrete outcomes. International associations, agencies and networks such as IAUP, UNESCO and INQAAHE are collectively working on establishing a clearinghouse of trustworthy quality assurance and accreditation systems, based on mutually accepted standards and criteria. This is discussed in detail in the later part of this chapter. This strategy seems to be very promising and workable.

The third strategy seems to be unrealistic for the moment since the governments and the quality assurance agencies may not be willing to be subjected to an assessment by a super power and will view any international structure that would coordinate the "accreditation of accrediting agencies" as another power center. There may also be fears that this will lead to a very bureaucratic, costly apparatus beyond the control of all the national governments, quality assurance agencies and the higher education institutions. The countries that are in the initial stages of establishing their quality assurance agencies and the nations that are still building the higher education system will not be comfortable with the concept of "accreditation of the quality assurance agency framework". The fourth strategy – international accreditation agency or the regulatory framework – will also experience resistance due to the reasons listed for the third strategy.

If the emphasis is on cooperation instead of regulation and if the framework is only an "international framework" with a facilitating function, the acceptability will improve.

Regulation Vs Cooperation

The International Regulatory Framework (IRF) for quality assurance has certain inherent limitations. The main constraint would be the imbalance seen in the total number of providers and receivers of transnational education and consequently the regulation that needs to be employed at the provider's end will have very limited scope. For example, only Australia, New Zealand and Japan in the Asia-Pacific region and a few well known Anglophonic countries like the USA, the UK, and Canada from the rest of the world are the main providers to the entire world. It is so because of the increasing recognition of English as lingua franca for all transactions the world over. The major importers of education in the Asia-Pacific region are Japan, India, Indonesia, Malaysia, Taiwan, Korea and China. The major exporters to this region are the USA, France, Germany, England, Australia and Canada, with the USA leading as a major provider. Nearly 58 per cent of the US trade in education is with these Asia-Pacific countries. A common international regulatory agency cannot have much to do except to carry out the watchdog function over some of the unscrupulous institutions from the providing countries that try to sell sub-standard education to others.

Low volume transnational activity in most of the receiving countries will be another problem that will deter any substantial role to IRF in regulating the provisions. If one looks at the annual Global Public Expenditure on Higher Education which is more than 1,000 billion US$ along with the private supplement of at least 600 billion US$, the current level of transnational education as trade at about 40 billion US$, is not very insignificant indeed. In fact even in this 40 billion US$, trade, around 70 per cent is accounted for by the presence of overseas students studying in the developed countries. The mobility of students for studies abroad is an age-old phenomenon. If one makes a correction for this and computes only the amount involved in the international trade through the other modes, it will not be more than 10 billion US$ which is not substantial, as compared to more than 1,600 billions spent annually, to warrant any serious attention.

More than anything else, the International Regulatory Framework should not create any tension between the emerging National Quality Assurance Systems in the region. China for example has a dramatically growing private sector with more than 500 private post secondary institutions, most of which are neither accredited nor formally approved by the government. There are also around 1,000 *min ban* (people run) private institutions that offer vocational education and do not award bachelor's degrees and only around 100 of them have been accredited by the government. A new law regulating this sector will soon be implemented. However, it is evident that a new regulatory national framework is still evolving. It is true in Vietnam, Cambodia and other central Asian nations that were formerly part of the Soviet Union. However, the redeeming development is the effort to establish national quality assurance bodies in all these countries, though the process is not yet complete. Among the major importers of the Asia-Pacific region, Japan, India, Indonesia, Malaysia, Philippines and Hong Kong have well developed national quality assurance mechanisms. In Korea, quality assurance of education is ensured by the Korean Council of Universities, while in China, it is ensured by existing governmental regulatory bodies. The national QA mechanisms in countries like Cambodia, Vietnam and Sri Lanka are at various stages of development and are yet to be operationalised. These bodies have to be firmed up first in their structure and operation so as to be comparable with those of other countries.

The magnitude of cost and effort needed to sustain such a global regulatory mechanism will be another factor that would go against its formation. The viable option is co-operation among NQAAs with a collective strategy based on trustworthiness of the NQAAs and a well-formulated code of good practices. Although establishing a single international accreditation agency or an international regulatory framework faces resistance, there are already multiple QAAs that act internationally and some of them have been noted in one of the earlier chapters.

There are also accrediting agencies that primarily focus on national HEIs with an interest in extending their operations internationally. For such QAAs that extend their operations beyond their national borders, cooperation and collaboration with interested parties in the second country is a major challenge. The Council on Higher Education Accreditation (CHEA) has developed a code of practice to facilitate this cooperation. CHEA is a private US organisation of degree granting colleges and universities and accrediting organisations that coordinates accreditation activity. It has developed two principles for the accreditors of USA who undertake accreditation of non-US institutions and programmes at an international level. They are as follows:

Principle 1: Considerations and Actions for US Accreditors when determining to Undertake Accreditation of Non-US Institutions and Programmes in Another Country.

US accreditors will:

- Assure that they have the organisational capacity to undertake an international review (*e.g.*, language, trained staff and evaluators, budget, experience, basic information about the country);
- Promulgate a clear statement of the scope of the accreditation and the use of US accredited status by an institution or programme in another country, especially with regard to transfer of credit and degree and qualifications equivalency;
- Assure clear understanding of the relationship of the US review to any international agreements that address accreditation and quality assurance;
- Clarify the relationship of international review activity to the priorities of the accrediting organisation;
- Communicate with other US accreditors about international review activity.

Principle 2: Expectations for Conduct of US Accreditation Reviews of Non-US Institutions and Programmes in Another Country.

US accreditors will:

- Inform, consult and cooperate with national quality assurance agencies in countries where reviews are undertaken and seek information and guidance from these agencies;

- Communicate with chancellors, presidents and rectors and other college and university officials at institutions where reviews are undertaken;
- Assure that US staff and evaluators are adequately informed about higher education and quality assurance in the countries in which they are conducting reviews to preclude the appearance of cultural insensitivity;
- Communicate fully and clearly about costs and currencies associated with a review.

Source: www.chea.org

While the strategies with the international dimension mentioned-above and the international regulatory approaches under category three and four mentioned earlier have limited application value in the contemporary context, their value may increase in the years to come. It is also evident that the first two strategies that are based on cooperation among QAAs enjoy more acceptance among QAAs in general. However, the success of the first two strategies lies in the mutual trust that could be promoted among quality assurance agencies in handling issues of transnational provisions. The need to promote trust among QAAs has prompted several different organisations to hold discussions on the international dimension of quality issues of which the initiatives by UNESCO, IAUP, INQAAHE and CHEA have resulted in tangible outcomes.

UNESCO and the Global Forum

UNESCO has always been proactive in such international discussions. An Expert Meeting on the Impact of Globalisation on Quality Assurance, Accreditation and the Recognition of Qualifications in Higher Education was convened by UNESCO in September 2001 to explore the international dimensions of quality assurance and examine the feasibility of establishing an international forum for dialogue among the different stakeholders. The participants of the meeting reached a consensus that a Global Forum should be established under the auspices of UNESCO to bring together different networks dealing with international aspects of quality assurance.

The mission of the Global Forum on International Quality Assurance, Accreditation and the Recognition of Qualifications, established under the auspices of UNESCO in 2002, is to link existing frameworks dealing with international issues of Quality Assurance, Accreditation and the Recognition of Qualifications and provide a platform for dialogue between them. The Global Forum is working collectively to evolve a code as a truly international policy framework for dealing with private and transnational providers, reconciling the interests of national governments, the traditional public higher education sector, for-profit providers and the needs of students and the general public interest. The code may be adopted through an International Accord. The audience targeted by the Global Forum are the different stakeholders of higher education: governments, higher education institutions, students and their families, teachers, business and industry, the public and private sectors of the economy, parliaments, the media, the community, professional associations.

IAUP and the Worldwide Quality Register

In 1999, the International Association of University Presidents (IAUP) initiated discussions on "Internationalisation and Quality Assurance: Towards World-wide Accreditation?" which dealt *inter alia* with international developments in quality assurance in higher education and worldwide accreditation for international higher education. To carry forward the discussions, it established the Commission on Global Accreditation in 2001which in turn convened a working group. The working group consisting of members of IAUP, INQAAHE, UNESCO and experts in international quality assurance from various other organisations has recommended the establishment of a Worldwide Quality Register (WQR), to identify reputable quality assurance agencies (QAAs) around the world. There have been parallel developments in INQAAHE also.

INQAAHE and the Quality Mark

At the 6th INQAAHE conference in Chile, the concept of a quality label for EQA agencies was raised. It was opined that EQA agencies have generally not felt the necessity to assess their own functioning, principally because so many of them are mandated by a government. Nonetheless, it is the responsibility of all agencies to ask themselves the question: *How good are we at the job we are supposed to be doing?* Consequent to this discussion, INQAAHE set up a working group to evolve a set of Principles of Good Practice for EQA agencies. The focus of the code of practice would be to assist member (and other) agencies to answer the question 'how good are we?' and to give them guidance on how to proceed in order to improve. The working group has developed a discussion paper with the aim of establishing the Principles of Good Practice at the Dublin-conference in April 2003. The principles would recognise that different EQAs have different purposes, which include (but are not restricted to) accreditation, assessment and audit. The principles would not lead to the dominance of one specific view or approach, but promote good practices, while preventing bad quality. The draft principles of good practice are as below.

Principles of Good Practice

1. *The Mission statement*: The EQA agency has an explicit mission statement or set of objectives. The statement makes clear that EQA is a major activity of the agency, and that there exists a systematic approach to achieving the mission

or objectives. There is evidence that the mission statement is translated into a clear policy and management plan.

2. *Decision-making*: The EQA agency carries out its assessments in relation both to the institution's own self-analysis and to external references. It respects institutional integrity and autonomy, while being supportive of the institution. The agency demonstrates independent, impartial, rigorous, thorough, fair and consistent decision-making. There is evidence that no party has untoward influence on the outcomes of the decisions. Independence of the evaluators is guaranteed.

The agency makes consistent decisions, even if the judgements are formed by different groups, panels, teams or committees. If the external evaluation leads to an accreditation, the accreditation framework and standards are public and the criteria for accreditation clearly formulated. The rules leading to an accreditation decision are transparent, public and guarantee an equal treatment. If relevant, the agency distinguishes between accreditation (threshold) and extension (improvement).

3. *Resources*: The EQA agency has adequate and credible resources, both human and financial, to be able to organise and run the process of external evaluation, with appropriate provision for development. The agency is economical and efficient.

4. *Documentation*: The EQA agency has public guidelines for self-evaluation and external evaluation, and public manuals explaining its criteria and decision-making processes.

The guidelines for self-evaluation indicate to the institutions of HE what is expected of the self-evaluation, distinguishing clearly between recommendations and requirements.

The guidelines for external evaluation set out the matters covered in these principles, such as decision criteria and methods, reporting format, etc.

The manual for EQA assures clearly that each institution or part of it (*e.g.* subject area) will be evaluated in an equivalent way, even if the external review panels are different.

5. *The external committee*: Where the EQA agency uses external panels, teams or committees, the system clearly ensures that:

- The composition of the committee is adequate
- There are no conflicts of interest
- The committee is instructed clearly about the task
- The committee acts independently.

6. *The Public Face*: In its work, the EQA agency includes, informs and responds to the public. This includes making public and explicit its policies, procedures and criteria.

The agency also demonstrates public accountability by reporting openly on its institutional review decisions, making the outcomes of the evaluation public in an appropriate way. The content of the public report may differ depending on the cultural context and will also depend on the requirements set for accountability.

7. *System of Appeal*: The EQA agency provides a method for appeals against its decisions.

8. *Quality Assurance of the EQA-agency*: The EQA agency has a system for quality assurance of its own activities, emphasising flexibility (in response to the changing nature of higher education) and quality improvements. The agency carries out self-review, based on data collection and analysis, including consideration of its own effects and value.

9. *Collaboration with other agencies*: As far as possible, the EQA agency collaborates with other EQAs.

10. The relation between the EQA agency and the higher education Institutions

The EQA agency

- recognises that quality and quality assurance are primarily the responsibility of the higher education institutions themselves
- respects autonomy of the institutions
- is checking the standards (not prescribing)
- aims to contribute to both quality improvement and accountability

The EQA agency expects the institutions to

- plan with respect to their mission
- have indicators relating to the plans
- assess standards
- provide public information
- carry out self-review and quality improvement

INQAAHE's Position on IAUP's Proposal

In a move to work collaboratively, the Board of INQAAHE met with representatives of the IAUP in May 2002. The representatives of IAUP presented a proposal entitled "Towards a World-wide Quality Register for Quality Assurance and Accreditation Agencies". The document proposed that IAUP, INQAAHE and UNESCO would form a consortium under whose authority a World Quality Register would be established. The document gave the rationale for the Register, and proposed a structure and processes. It also set out an application review and decision-making procedures and suggested external uses of the World Quality Register. It also outlined administrative and financial aspects.

INQAAHE has welcomed the proposal for the establishment of a World Quality Register. It recognises the support and voluntary co-operation of the agencies, the governments, UNESCO and the working sub-networks and regional networks in the development of this proposal.

INQAAHE has also suggested that the WQR may be built on a structure of mutual recognition of quality agencies on a regional basis. INQAAHE will establish essential and elective criteria for a quality assurance agency in higher education. The essential criteria will represent the minimum standards and procedures required for the recognition of judgements of the agency by other quality assurance agencies and by stakeholders generally. The elective criteria will represent additional standards and procedures which are regarded as good practice by the international quality assurance agencies in the higher education community.

The position paper of INQAAHE suggests that a Quality Mark could be introduced to indicate that the agency has reached minimum standards and also indicate which elective standards have been reached. To establish these criteria, it is proposed that a committee consisting of the President, Secretary, one other representative of the INQAAHE Board, and one representative from each of the IAUP and EURASHE, would be established. A similar group could carry out the on-going verification process that would be necessary once such a system were in place.

It is proposed that funding would be sought from UNESCO for the development of this project. In developing this project, INQAAHE will take into account existing projects, such as mutual recognition projects in MERCOSUR and the Nordic countries. Further consultation on this took place among the member agencies of INQAAHE with the intention of putting a proposal to the General Assembly of INQAAHE for adoption at its meeting in April 2003. It is expected that the project will be completed before the INQAAHE General Assembly of 2005 and also before the triennial meeting of IAUP in 2005.

Worldwide Quality Register

The inclusion of an agency in the WQR guarantees that this agency meets agreed standards for trustworthy quality assurance, such as a clear commitment to develop academic quality in the institutions and programmes evaluated by it, fair and appropriate quality assessment procedures, well developed and publicly available protocols, etc. Students, faculty, programmes, institutions and the general public can therefore have reasonable confidence in the academic quality of institutions and programmes positively reviewed or accredited by registered QAAs.

The WQR addresses quality assurance and accreditation agencies that primarily deal with the teaching and learning activities and functions of higher education programmes and institutions. However, contemporary quality education at post-secondary level is closely linked to scientific research. Especially at the postgraduate level, high quality teaching and learning build on state-of-the-art knowledge and recent progress in scientific research. The WQR supports a vision of higher education in which teaching and learning on the one hand and scientific research on the other are clearly linked.

The WQR is conceived not as a discriminatory mechanism, but as an inclusive and developmental framework. The agencies whose application is not reviewed positively at first instance because they do not yet fully comply with the required criteria, will be given a candidacy status. In this status these agencies will receive adequate support and assistance in developing their quality assurance capacities in order to re-apply after a given timeframe. Furthermore, the WQR will support the development of sound quality assurance in higher education worldwide, with special attention to the needs of those countries and higher education systems that have not yet fully developed quality assurance or accreditation arrangements.

WQR Framework

The range of institutions evaluated or accredited by the agency can be both public and private, national and transnational, confined to one discipline or covering many disciplines. The agency must have a minimum of 2 years' experience in the field of external quality assurance or accreditation in order to be in the WQR. A newer agency may be accepted into candidacy status if it meets the other criteria. The following standards are intended to be applied in their entirety in the spirit of their intent and goals; compliance with each individual standard is not required.

- The agency functions autonomously from the institutions or programmes that it reviews.
- The agency addresses primarily the educational function of HE institutions.
- The primary activities of the agency can be defined as quality evaluation, review, audit, assessment or accreditation.
- Those activities are executed on a regular basis and in a systematic way.
- There is evidence of reliance on the agency by the academic community (including students), by employers, by government, or by others.

Agencies must demonstrate their commitment to advancing academic quality in the institutions evaluated or accredited. Fostering high academic quality should be clearly included in the institutional mission of the agency. The quality assurance and accreditation activities of the agency can include the functions of improvement and/or accountability. With respect to the improvement function, the agency should stimulate, encourage or provoke purposeful change towards improvement of programmes and their outcomes. The quality assurance or accreditation activities should also foster and evaluate internal quality assurance, as well as the culture of assessment within the institutions or programmes. With respect to the accountability function, the agency must demonstrate that it is responsible to the public, for example by publishing the final judgment that resulted from its evaluation or accreditation.

The agency that reviews the institutions or programmes must provide reliable information about academic quality to students, stakeholders, the public authorities and the general public. Agencies should require that each institution or programme that they review fulfils its own mission and that its educational quality meets external community expectations for higher education within the relevant field. This may be demonstrated by reference to external benchmarks, by the judgment of visiting peers, or otherwise.

Implications to QAAs

WQR expects that the external assessment by the QAA should be based on a combination of self-evaluation and peer review. The protocol of the agency should provide for autonomy of all processes and committees, even if the agency itself is linked to the institutional higher education sector, the professions, the state, or other stakeholders. The quality assessment processes and decisions must be appropriate, fair, and consistent. The agency must have publicly available protocols or manuals that describe in a transparent way the procedures and standards used in quality assessment processes. Most of the QAAs are well in line with these expectations.

The WQR also expects that the protocols or manuals of the QAA should describe the minimum standards used in its quality assessment process, and the way in which these standards comply with external points of reference. It should also describe how its standards respect each institution's mission. It also requires that the nature of the final judgment and more specifically, the meaning of statements such as 'insufficient', 'sufficient' and 'good' must be clarified. In these areas, the procedures of most of the QAAs may need more fine-tuning in terms of firming up the benchmarks and descriptors of quality to gain international acceptability.

The expectation that the agency has specific policies for assessing itself with a continuous reassessment of quality assurance and accreditation practices and for the development of the professional expertise of the agency in the field of quality assurance, also needs to be understood in the international context. In general, QAAs have been assessing themselves as they evolve their procedures but many of them might not have subjected themselves to assessment by an external body. Similarly, with field experience they might be growing in professional expertise but policy specifications on professional development may need to be firmed up. If WQR recommends an external review and policy on professional development, the QAAs may have to evolve appropriate policies and procedures. The surety about the internal and external consequences of a QAA's actions and decisions for institutions accredited, which is seen as an evidence of a sound EQA mechanism by WQR, is also still a developing area in many countries. QAAs, especially in developing countries where there is tension between increasing access to higher education and quality education, have to work on establishing the definiteness of the consequences of the accreditation outcomes.

While the WQR framework has a regulatory flavour, CHEA proposes an international confederation as another alternative.

CHEA and the Quality Confederation

The Quality Confederation proposed by CHEA would be composed of national quality assurance agencies and would address higher education and quality review in an international setting. It would explore shared values, establish useful and authoritative sources of information and develop quality review agreements where needed. The Quality Confederation would not require regulatory international standards; an individual country's obligation and prerogative of defining its concept of quality would remain intact. Decisions about comparability of curricula, degrees, and academic standards would be made at a national level.

In a paper outlining the international confederation, the President of CHEA, Dr. Judith Eaton (2002) lists that this "Quality Confederation" would provide Service, Communication and Information and elaborates them as follows:

Service: QC would assist nations to maintain themselves as primary sources of responsibility for higher education quality in their countries. At the same time, the confederation would be a vehicle to establish working relationships among countries to expand higher education and improve quality.

Communication: QC would work with other organisations and provide an ongoing forum for exchange of ideas especially about the core value issues that confront higher education and higher education quality worldwide. This might include the difficult questions of the intellectual foundation on which to base the development and enhancement of higher education in various countries, general education and the liberal arts, and higher education in the service of the public good. This forum would address fundamental principles of higher education quality as well as sound practices in quality review.

Information: QC would work with interested quality review organisations to establish and maintain an accurate international database of quality courses, programmes, institutions and degrees as well as other information needed by individual countries to function effectively in an international environment.

The Quality Confederation cannot be the answer to all the issues of quality assurance that need an international approach. Whether QC will result in a large number of individual bilateral national agreements about higher education quality and the confusions it might create need to be explored. There is also the danger of sidestepping the issue of international quality standards that may be needed in a global world. The ability of QC to protect against dubious providers of higher education ("diploma mills") and dubious providers of higher education quality review ("accreditation mills") is also not clear. It is also not clear as to how it is distinctly different from the WQR and the related efforts of other international bodies like INQAAHE.

In sum, there is a growing need internationally to seek more information about issues and concerns regarding quality assurance. Conferences and seminars are held for exchange of information about quality assurance practices and challenges in different parts of the world. There is a general awareness of the need to have a system of international recognition of quality agencies and options for cooperation across national boundaries are being explored. There is a need to work together, to be more international in viewing these issues, and to work for mutually acceptable standards with increased cooperative relationships. The Global Forum, the World Quality Register and Quality Confederation are certainly the right steps forward to realise these objectives.

13. Asia-Pacific Regional Co-operation and Lessons from the Bologna Process

The need for better co-operation in the Asia-Pacific region, more so in the sector of higher education, is felt more now. As in many other sectors, the European region has taken a lead through the Bologna declaration and the related 'Bologna Processes' to develop European higher education that is comparable and compatible with that of the rest of the world. The main objectives of such an initiative is not only to have a competitive edge in all the socio-economic activities of a new order in the knowledge era but also to restore its past glory of being the leader in organised and institutionalised mass education. This effort to harmonise higher education within a geographical region of contiguous countries in line with the global trends is worthy of emulation by other regions that have similar aspirations. However, to concretise the dreams into reality the regional context has to be analysed with care. This chapter is an attempt to look at the regional context of the Asia-Pacific and the lessons from the Bologna process that are applicable to the region.

With the accelerating pace of globalisation and internationalisation of Higher Education, interest in regional co-operation through conventions is growing. According to UNESCO data, more than 130 countries have ratified one or more of the regional conventions initiated by UNESCO on the single issue of mutual recognition of studies, diplomas and degrees in higher education. These conventions serve as important legal instruments for the international community in mutual recognition of qualifications for mobility across national boundaries.

Asia-Pacific Region

The Asia-Pacific region is as heterogeneous and diverse as the European region. Diversities can be seen in the size of the population, per capita income, language, ethnic culture and tradition. There is also diversity in the status of development of higher education. Countries like Australia, New Zealand and Japan, have well developed education systems. While the Indian and the Chinese higher education systems are huge and fairly stabilised following one or the other European Model, there are countries that are still engaged in restructuring their system. Australia has become one of the major providers of education to other countries. New Zealand and Japan have proved that they are also capable of functioning as providers of education to others while the rest remain at the receiving end. Many governments in the region are still struggling to cope with the problem of enhancing the access and ensuring equity with limited resources and therefore investing resources on major changes in the higher education structure may not be a priority for them. Integrating these diverse systems is a major challenge and UNESCO has played a pro-active role in this regard.

The regional convention for recognition of studies, diplomas and degrees in higher education in Asia and the Pacific was adopted at the conference of member states in Bangkok in 1983 in which 33 countries participated. The major mandate of the Regional Committee is to promote the application of the convention, examine periodic reports from member states on progress and difficulties in applying the convention and building partnership with stakeholders for its implementation. Twenty countries have already adopted the convention including India. India became the 20th country to ratify the convention in August 2000. In Philippines, the ratification proposal has been submitted by the Philippine Government to the Philippine Senate for its consideration in October 1999. The outcome of all these developments is expected to encourage other countries, mainly ASEAN members such as Thailand, Lao PDR, Cambodia and Vietnam, to follow suit. This gains significance in view of the fact that ASEAN countries will be declared as a free-trade zone by 2003 with a policy for free flow of labours and materials. Mutual Recognition of qualifications will definitely be a priority and a practical challenge, once the free trade zone idea is in operation.

As of now, mutual recognition of qualifications may not appear to be a pressing problem in the Asia-Pacific region unlike the case with the European region since the integration of economic activities in Asia-Pacific is still on. But if we are to take a clue from the experience of Europe, where the pressure to work towards academic mobility followed after the policy of economic integration and related changes in the region, and resulted in consequent hardships, Asia-Pacific region stands to gain in focusing on academic mobility along with other integration efforts. The regional convention of UNESCO has been a facilitating factor in this regard but it has to be taken forward in letter and spirit.

Experience elsewhere would also indicate that the general agreement arrived through such conventions would only promote a congenial atmosphere for further initiatives, but a lot more has to be done by the participating countries. Active collaboration between the state parties, sound partnership between all stakeholders at the national, regional and international levels are essential. It is here that the

Bologna process has many valuable lessons of experience for the Asia-Pacific Region.

European Region and the Bologna Process

The countries of the European union have been the pioneers in developing the institutionalised mass education system like universities and colleges right from about 10th century AD The higher education system in most countries of the world is patterned after the medieval European universities and consequently share a common structure and governance, besides a broadly comparable qualification framework and awards, largely as a legacy of the erstwhile colonial rulers. Consequently, the education system world over also shares the common concerns about the quality and relevance of education in the changing context. Therefore, any attempt to improve the higher education system in Europe would have a far reaching influence on the rest of the world, particularly the third world.

The Bologna Declaration signed by 29 European countries aims to establish European higher education of a new order. The declaration has led to a set of well-deliberated and accepted action plans to achieve the main objective. The Bologna declaration is not a simple declaration of intent but a document with a clearly defined common goal, a set of specified objectives, a realistic deadline, a feasible action plan, an organised follow-up and a well structured implementation process. The factors that contributed to its acceptance by all the signatories are: 1. Sentimentally appealing goals and objectives such as to restore the past preeminent position as leaders in the higher education sector, 2. Evolving a set of reformative measures that are not in conflict with the ongoing development oriented measures and thus ensuring that the processes do not appear as intrusive, but as a way forward, 3. Focusing mostly on structural changes and 4. Interfacing the implementation strategy with the other developmental initiatives already underway.

Likewise, the set of well-defined quality targets towards which the higher education system was expected to work, such as Mobility, Employability and Competitiveness/ attractiveness of education, also contributed to its acceptance by both politicians and academia. The focused line of action for convergence such as Easily readable and comparable degrees, Organisation of the qualifications into two main cycles, Modularisation of the curricula on European Credit Transfer System (ECTS) lines into credits with a system that permits credit accumulation and credit transfer and a commonly useable Quality Assurance mechanism have contributed to the ready acceptance. The issues identified, remedial measures conceived and the acceptable modalities suggested are relevant to all the regions of the world so far as higher education is concerned and therefore the Bologna process constitutes a worthy model to emulate while shaping the Asia-Pacific regional co-operation.

Lessons from the Bologna Process

It has been well understood in the Asia-Pacific countries, that regional co-operation is imperative to facilitate the mobility of students and workers at the global level. As mentioned earlier, thanks to the initiatives of UNESCO and other regional organisations, initiatives are underway to establish and promote such regional co-operation. Discussion on the Bologna process is yet another right step forward in this direction. A brief outline of a few selective issues that can be adopted from the Bologna experience for the Asia-Pacific region is given in the following pages.

a) Core Objectives of regional cooperation

The adoption of the core objectives of the Bologna declaration in evolving a system of sharable higher education programmes with suitable modifications, if necessary to meet the regional context can be considered favourably. There can be no two opinions on Mobility, Employability and Competitiveness/attractiveness being the main goals of the regional effort in enhancing and improving the quality of higher education of the region.

b) Tools of the convergence process

Except perhaps for making their awards 'easily readable and comparable', the Asia-Pacific region is no stranger to the tools adopted in the Bologna process to achieve convergence amidst diversity such as 1. Providing easily readable and comparable degrees and other awards, 2. Organising the higher education awards mainly into two cycles, namely, undergraduate and postgraduate phases, 3. Introduction of the Credit system that will facilitate credit accrual and transfer of course credits and 4. Establishing National Quality Assurance mechanisms and their network at the regional level. The major challenge will be to implement all the four tools throughout the region, applying them to all the educational institutions in each one of the member countries. The relevance of the major tools used to bring in convergence by the Bologna process to the Asia-Pacific region is discussed briefly below.

(i) Easily readable and comparable degrees and awards

Traditionally, education, particularly higher education was designed as discipline- or subject-based conventions, by and large by the teachers. In common parlance, it could be construed that education was like a seller's market in a broad sense of the term, when there were a few takers. But in an era of mass education consequent to the increased access, it has become a buyer's market. The stakeholders—society, employers, parents and students—now want to know what the graduates learn and how it will suit their purposes. All the academic programmes of studies need to have a descriptor with reference to the aims and purpose of the programme, how it is designed to impart knowledge, skills and competencies and at what level along with the curricular content, in order to make them easily readable and comparable with similar offerings elsewhere.

The Bologna process gives in detail as to how it can be brought into practice. All the new programmes introduced afresh should provide the descriptor in a precise form to enlighten students, parents and employers. For the existing ones, such details can be prepared as diploma supplements and made available for current as well as past students. The adoption of a similar method to enhance the readability of various academic programmes in other regions of the world would enhance the marketability of education offered both locally and regionally. In fact, it would also increase the awareness among the academic community as to what they should do beyond classroom teaching to fulfill the claims in the descriptors.

(ii) Adoption of a system essentially based on two main cycles

Most Asia-Pacific countries have inherited their system of higher education from their erstwhile colonial rulers and basically have the Anglo-Saxon model. Hence attempting a convergence in this regard may not be a serious problem. Presently, the undergraduate programmes are designed as a terminal degree for the majority of students with necessary components to ensure substantial subject-based knowledge, subject-related skills and other general and cognitive competencies. This is due to the fact that nearly 90 per cent of the undergraduate students do not pursue postgraduate education but enter the job market. A set of postgraduate programmes of studies mostly with advanced levels of subject-based knowledge content designed for a two-year study after the undergraduate degrees caters to the small fraction who would like to pursue their intellectual interest and research. This two-tier programme structure, if supplemented with a variety of career oriented diploma courses of varying duration, would make the awards meaningful and readable for the employers which is the key factor in determining academic mobility. Hence, it is feasible to strengthen the existing two-tier system of learning at the higher education level in the Asia-Pacific countries with advantage. However, the suitability of the two tier system proposed by the Bologna process to the professional areas is still being debated in Europe and will continue to be a debatable issue for the Asia-Pacific region as well.

(iii) Adoption of credit-based academic courses

Modular credit-based academic programmes are not entirely new to many of the Asia Pacific countries. They are already in vogue in many institutions of higher learning in some countries. Making it universal in all the institutions in all the countries of the region may not be a formidable task but would take considerable time in view of the disparity in the development of the higher education system in the region. There would also be some difficulties in interfacing the credits earned from the new and vocational forms of education.

The credit system in the formal sector itself is a process that needs to be stabilised in many Asia-Pacific countries. The problem gets compounded with the credits accrued through other modes of life-long learning. For example, the Community College concept is an emerging concept in the region which is yet to gain due respectability among the academia, at least in India. What will be the acceptability of the credits earned through community colleges if students wish to transfer them to the traditional formal universities and colleges is an issue that has to be sorted out. The non-higher education sector offers need-based non-degree programmes and the credits earned from those institutions will also pose challenges in credit accrual and credit transfer. With more and more transnational providers offering programmes online, the credits earned through those providers who need not have a base in the Asia-Pacific region, is also emerging as a challenge.

Nonetheless, the credit system provides the best option to promote academic flexibility and we are yet to find a better alternative to it. Until the Asia-Pacific region develops its own credit-related criteria and standards, adoption of ECTS compatible or a similar form of credit system may be worthwhile.

(iv) Promotion of National Quality Assurance systems and regional co-operation

One of the important instruments envisaged in the Bologna process is the effective use of an External Quality Assurance (EQA) mechanism that is credible and acceptable for all the countries of the region. The EQA system should safeguard acceptable quality and standards without neglecting the interest of the local context. While the development of comprehensive national quality assurance systems is taking place in almost all the countries, there appears to be some confusion even in European countries about using the terms 'Assessment' and 'Accreditation'. If one uses the operational definition generally accepted by the EQA agencies the world over, there can be no confusion. It is generally accepted that Accreditation denotes the certification of a minimal threshold level of quality and the term Assessment would indicate the relative standing of the institutions in the quality continuum beyond that threshold level. If these definitions are well understood, there can be no doubt in adopting 'quality assurance' as an instrument of choice. Any lead established by the Bologna process in establishing the standards for national quality assurance units would be useful and applicable to the Asia-Pacific region as well. However, as mentioned earlier, there are areas where the Asia-Pacific region calls for a different approach and one of them relates to the partnership among quality assurance agencies.

Assessment or Accreditation of an institution or a programme is meant to lead ultimately to the Mutual Recognition (MR) of the qualifications gained from any country by the others in the region. European Union countries have a long tradition of using national Equivalence/ Recognition/acceptance units for formally recognising the award. The network of such national recognition units with all the infrastructure and databases like NARIC and EUNIC are considered as a point of reference for MR. While this may work in Europe because of the long tradition and well endowed infrastructure, it may be difficult for other regions, particularly Asia-Pacific, to adopt the system and develop national recognition centers as well in each country. One should realise that the route to MR can be achieved either the NARIC/EUNIC way or through the mutual recognition of national Quality Assurance systems. In an era of mass higher education and large scale mobility of knowledge seekers and workers, collecting information about all the institutions of higher learning and their programmes of studies will be a stupendous task and may require enormous effort and resources which can be best used for other quality enhancement activities particularly in the developing world. Mutual recognition of quality assurance agencies as the route to mutual recognition of qualifications appears to be the best option with appropriate regulatory mechanisms. The Washington Accord outlines the protocols for mutual recognition of quality assurance agencies specialising in engineering education and INQAAHE is evolving similar protocols for the agencies that quality assure general higher education.

c) Other general aspects that underpin the success of the Bologna Process

Learning from the experiences of other systems is always useful to broaden the discussions and helps in analysis and evaluation. However, the experiences of one region may not offer a perfect solution to the problems of another region, since any strategy has to necessarily take cognizance of the contextual conditions. The Bologna process should be viewed with this understanding and the regional dimension of the Asia-Pacific needs to be considered with care. Some of the issues that need in-depth reflection are outlined below.

(i) Mapping the system of higher education and its trends

The European countries have put in concerted efforts to map the areas of convergence and the trends in higher education in their region before initiating the Bologna processes. Such a comprehensive effort is yet to be made in the Asia-Pacific region. UNESCO has brought out valuable publications on the higher education systems of the region and case studies. There are a few other studies that analyse the trends in the region. But with the view to understanding the similarities and strengths in the higher education space and ways to build on those strengths, a comprehensive study on the current position needs to be undertaken.

(ii) Balancing Ministerial Participation and Academic consultations

A valuable lesson that can be usefully learnt from the Bologna declaration and the subsequent progression towards the implementation is the way the ministerial level commitment has been brought in right from the beginning as the process rests on intergovernmental cooperation. Although it is the higher education system—the academic institutions and the faculty and others – who will ultimately have to implement the action plan through hard work and steer the system towards the success of the process, involving the ministers of the States provides the political and social 'Will' without which not much can be achieved in the democratic social structure. Ministerial level participation comes along with the power and resources to launch such multinational co-operation as well as to accept a common system of education. When the ministers commit themselves and engage their countries, they can introduce the necessary fundamental changes in their system. Fortunately, the Ministers of Education themselves recognised the important role to be played by the institutions and all sections of academia as competent, active and constructive partners in shaping the European higher education area and they have made this clear during their meeting at Prague in May 2001. This explicit recognition of the role of the institutions and the academia had sorted out most of the internal apprehensions among the academic community. But following a similar line of action in Asia-Pacific will be a stupendous task, given the political underpinnings in the region. The process may have to evolve from the academia. The Bologna declaration would have had no impact had it not fallen on prepared ground. This is true for any process in international quality improvement. The national quality assurance systems have a pivotal role in this context.

(iii) Ensuring Wider Participation

Another avoidable mistake relates to the possible impression that a few countries of the region would dominate and ignore the interests of the relatively smaller ones. The initial confusion related to the Sorbonne declaration and the Bologna declaration need a mention here in this connection. It is a fact that the Sorbonne initiative had been taken by the large European Union (EU) member states and was not well received by smaller states. It resulted in initial resistance by smaller countries, which thought that they had not been consulted beforehand. Consequently, the process encountered some resistance and led to numerous discussions at all possible levels. This emphasises the need to make a highly participative beginning in the Asia-Pacific region as it is even more heterogeneous than Europe.

(iv) Bridging the Gaps

Yet another factor that needs attention is the perception of the member countries about the possible role they may have to play. Australia and New Zealand may look at this as exporters of higher education service and Hong Kong and Malaysia may look at this as ways to facilitate import of education while safeguarding the interest of their people. Cambodia and Laos PDR are at the stage of stabilising their higher education systems. The divide between the countries has to be bridged and every country has to be democratically facilitated to move towards convergence as has been done in the European region.

(v) Appropriate Forum and Resources

The efforts mentioned above require not only the commitment of the leaders of the countries but also a strong forum to formulate the initiatives and mobilise the resources to support them.

The major implication for facilitating cooperation in the Asia-Pacific Quality Network (APQN) is on Mutual recognition. The rationale behind this argument needs a little more elaboration.

Mutual Recognition of Quality Assurance Agencies in Asia-Pacific

In practice, recognition of qualifications depends very much on the confidence the institutions have in each other's process and quality of their offerings. A well-planned mechanism that can ensure and maintain this confidence is needed to facilitate academic mobility. Partnership building and mutual recognition between national agencies based on "quality" is seen as a viable mechanism to instill this confidence.

Mutual recognition between quality assurance agencies has existed in North America for a number of years and the regional accrediting agencies in the USA have been the forerunner of mutual recognition models. Between the USA and Canada, a number of accrediting agencies have mutual recognition agreements. These agreements mean that the award/qualification is recognised in both countries and the field of practice in both countries is open to the graduates of accredited institutions. Such agreements between the USA and Canada came into being long before the Washington Accord introduced it in Engineering.

Mutual recognition has become prominent due to the necessity to assess the equivalency of professional qualifications and is linked with professional mobility. Because of this link with professional qualifications, mutual recognition has developed between agencies of similar specialisation – among engineering groups, medicine groups, etc., and has been the affair of specialised agencies with similar educational systems and languages. For example, countries participating in the Washington Accord are all English speaking. With increasing demand for non-professional service personnel areas in the global market, we need to explore the strategy for mobility that will include general education as well. This strategy should also be capable of handling the large volume of migration across national borders for which a shift from programme level to institutional level may do well. In other words, what we need to explore now at the Asia-Pacific level, is the possibility of extending the existing professional studies programme level recognition of some countries to the general education institution level strategy of the region.

The best way to achieve it is by bringing the national quality assurance agencies together. The complexity of the system of higher education within the country is so much that only the recognised national agency(ies) can be relied on for any dependable information that would decide the recognition. Further, quality becomes the baseline for international mobility, which calls for the involvement of quality assurance agencies that can assure the quality of the institutions, through a third party/external assessment.

Even if one assumes that the outcomes of quality assessment would indicate only the relative standing of the qualifications, and not be absolutely comparable with those of the other countries, their assurance about quality will definitely form the first level of recognition. Instead of bearing the burden of basic sifting and separating the legitimate from the fraudulent, institutions can deal with ones where that sifting has already occurred. Institutions/ programmes accredited by a reliable agency would mean that the institution has undergone external review by an agency with acceptable procedures and has stood the test of external review against standards of quality. In the context of expansion of higher education and global market with greater demand for student mobility, that is enough information to have.

The bi-phase strategy—the declaration and the processes—bring out how many of the problems of harmonising the higher education system among the participating communities can be resolved through transparent and flexible approaches and consultations on such sensitive issues. Convergence through an acceptable qualification framework, accommodating the divergence within the overall framework and evolving effective External Quality Assurance (EQA) mechanisms are some of the other key elements worthy of emulation. Their experience also highlights the importance of ministerial level involvement and their commitment to the process right from the beginning to bring about regional co-operation.

The Bologna process is leading to fundamental changes in the European higher education sector. By the year 2010 it is expected that there would be some kind of convergence between the different national systems of Europe. The two-year pilot project "Tuning Educational Structures in Europe", launched with the support of the European Commission, is investigating this development through five samples of university studies and methodologies in the fields of Mathematics, Geology, History, Business and Educational Sciences. The results of the pilot are expected to be introduced soon. The "Tuning" project aims at bringing about a

European-wide convergence in higher education in the above-mentioned subject areas by introducing commonly accepted learning outcomes. Contextualising the lessons of experience of the EU and suitably adapting them to the Asia-Pacific region requires careful reflection and in-depth discussions.

Appendix

Criterion Statements and Key Aspects

Criterion – I: Curricular Aspects

1.1 The programmes of teaching and learning are consistent with the goals and objectives of the institution.

1.2 Feedback from academic peers and employers is used in the initiation, review and redesign of programmes.

Key aspects:

- Compatibility of the programmes with goals and objectives
- Initiation, review and redesign of programmes
- Feedback on programmes and interaction with academic peers and employers
- Programme options

Criterion – II: Teaching-learning and Evaluation

2.1 The programmes of teaching and learning cater to individual differences among learners and offer academic flexibility.

2.2 The institution facilitates the effective running of the teaching-learning programmes.

2.3 The evaluation procedures in the educational programmes are rigorous and fair.

2.4 The regularity and the confidentiality of examinations

are maintained.

2.5 The institution has an efficient mechanism to recruit qualified and adequate faculty.

2.6 The institution has an open and participative mechanism for evaluation of teaching, research and work satisfaction of the faculty.

2.7 The faculties have opportunity for continued academic progress and professional advancement.

2.8 The institution has a transparent admission process.

Key aspects

- Judging students' knowledge & bridge/remedial courses
- Teaching-learning process & use of new technology in teaching
- Co-curricular activities
- Examination process & innovative evaluation methods
- Recruitment of faculty & faculty development programmes
- Evaluation of teaching, research and work satisfaction of faculty & monitoring and rewarding successful teaching innovation
- Access to national and/or international linkages

Criterion – III: Research, Consultancy and Extension

3.1 The institution promotes research culture among faculty and students.

3.2 The institution has a vigorous and well scrutinized publication programme and actively encourages faculty and students to publish in academic forum.

3.3 The institution promotes faculty participation in

consultancy work.

3.4 The institution is responsive to community needs and conducts relevant extension and awareness programmes.

Key aspects

- Promotion and sustenance of research culture and research output
- Freedom to publish in academic forum and publication
- Benefits of Consultancy to the institution and society
- Faculty participation in extension programmes and the extension activities conducted so far
- Resources to conduct extension activities and service provided in the area of expertise

Criterion – IV: Infrastructure and Learning Resources

4.1 The institution has adequate library and computer facilities with easy access to all its constituencies.

4.2 The institution has adequate physical facilities to run the educational programmes and administrative functions efficiently.

4.3 The growth of the infrastructure keeps pace with the academic growth of the institution.

4.4 The institution has effective mechanisms for maintenance and optimal use of infrastructure.

Key aspects

- Physical facilities
- Maintenance
- Optimal use of infrastructure
- Library

- Computer facilities
- Laboratories
- Health services & sports and physical education
- Hostel, Canteen, Guest House
- Others

Criterion - V: Student Support and Progression

5.1 The institution has sufficient and well-run support services to ensure the physical and intellectual health of all its constituencies.

5.2 The institution has an effective mechanism to use student feedback for the quality enhancement.

5.3 The prospectus of the institution gives clear guidance to students about admission and completion requirements for all programmes, the fee-structure and refund policies, financial aid and student support services.

5.4 Financial aid to students is fairly distributed.

5.5 The institution offers competent academic counseling and placement services to its students.

Key aspects

- Progression to employment and further study
- Pass and dropout rate and student achievement
- Alumni association, its activities and Alumni Profile
- Financial aid to students
- Personnel and Academic counselling
- Placement services

Criterion - VI: Organisation and Management

6.1 The offices and departments of the institution are governed on the principles of participation and transparency.

6.2 Academic and administrative planning in the institution move hand in hand.

6.3 Management techniques and technologies, to the extent possible, are used by the institution for efficient running of every administrative and academic decision-making.

6.4 The institution practices relevant welfare schemes for all its constituencies.

6.5 There are fair and expeditious grievance redressal mechanisms at all levels of the institution's functioning.

6.6 The finances of the institution are judiciously allocated and effectively utilized to make its programmes and functioning cost-effective.

6.7 The institution has imaginative and effective resource mobilization and management strategies.

6.8 Budgeting and auditing procedures are regular and standardized.

Key aspects

- Organisation structure & functions and powers of functionaries
- Human power requirement & recruitment of staff
- Performance appraisal & new technologies in communication
- Welfare schemes & grievance redressal mechanism
- Budgeting and auditing procedures
- Resource mobilisation and effective utilisation

Criterion - VII: Healthy Practices

The goals and objectives of the institution are clearly stated, periodically reviewed, and communicated systematically to all its constituencies.

Key aspects

- Complementary System like self-financing courses, need-based courses
- National/International linkages for teaching and research
- Industry linkage
- Educational Innovations such as credit system, examination reforms and modular curriculum
- Working with specific mission and goals
- Awards won by the faculty
- Others

Source: Institutional Accreditation: Mannual for self-study, www.naac-india.com

Bibliography

Adam, S. (2001) *Transnational Education Report*, CEURC, Brussels.

Altbach, P.G. (2001) *Higher Education and the WTO: Globalization Run Amok, University News*, 39(37), pp.1-4.

Altbach, P.G. (2002) *Asia: Trends and Developments in Private Higher Education, International Higher Education*, The Boston College Center for International Higher Education, Number 29 Fall 2002.

American Council on Education (ACE) (1996) *Guiding Principles for Distance Learning in a Learning Society*, ACE, Washington DC.

Association of Indian Universities (AIU) (1995) *Policies of Higher Education*, AIU, New Delhi.

Association of Indian Universities (AIU) (2000) *Universities Handbook* - 28th edition, AIU, New Delhi.

Barblan, A. (2001) *International Quality Assurance*, CHEA Annual Conference, January 2001, New Orleans.

Bhalla, V. (2002) *International Students in India*, In K.B.Powar (Ed), *Internationalization of Higher Education*, Association of Indian Universities, New Delhi, pp. 85-94.

Blight, D. and West, L. (2000) *Demand for Transnational Education in the Asia Pacific*, National Center for Higher Education, Washington DC.

Bloom, D.E. and Rosovsky, H. (2001) *Higher Education and International Development, Current Science*, 81(3), pp.252-256.

Brender, A. (2001) *Japan will allow universities to Grant Credit for Online Courses, The Chronicle of Higher Education*, April 13, 2001.

Brennan, J. and Shah, T. (2000) *Managing Quality in Higher Education: An International Perspective on Institutional Assessment and Change*, OECD, SRHE and Open University Press, USA.

Campbell, C. and Van der Wende, M. (2000) *International Initiatives and Trends in Quality Assurance for European Higher Education*, European Network for Quality Assurance, Helsinki.

Carr, S. and Foster, A.L. (2001) *States Struggle to Regulate Online Colleges that Lack Accreditation, The Chronicle of Higher Education*, March 23, 2001.

Castillo, D.D. (2001) *Greece Shuns Private Colleges, The Chronicle of Higher Education*, September 21, 2001.

Centro Interuniversitario De Desarrollo (CINDA) and Quality Assurance International (QAI) (2002), *Standards and Procedures Manual*, International Institute for Quality (IIQ), Washington DC.

Chaffee, E.E. and Sherr, L.A. (1993) *Quality: Transforming Post-secondary Education*, ASHE-ERIC Higher Education Report Series, Washington DC.

Chon-Hong, K. (2001) *Asia-Pacific Regional Overview* presented in the Expert Meeting on The Impact of Globalisation on Quality Assurance, Accreditation and the Recognition of Qualifications in Higher Education, 10-11 September, 2001, Paris.

Commission on Evaluation of Colleges (CEEC) (1994a) *Evaluating Institutional Policies on Program Evaluation*, CEEC, Quebec.

Commission on Evaluation of Colleges (CEEC) (1994b) *Evaluating Institutional Policies on the Evaluation of Student Achievement*, CEEC, Quebec.

Commission on Evaluation of Colleges (CEEC) (1994c) *The Commission d'evaluation de l' enseignement collegial: Its Mission and Orientations*, CEEC, Quebec.

Commission on Evaluation of Colleges (CEEC) (1997) *Specific Guide to the Evaluation of Program of Studies leading to a Diploma of College Studies in the Business Administration Technology and Cooperation Sectors*, CEEC, Quebec.

Council for Higher Education Accreditation (CHEA) (2000) *Distance Learning in Higher Education*, CHEA Update No.3, online www.chea.org.

Council of Vice-chancellors and College Principals (CVCP) and Higher Education Funding Council of England (HEFCE) (2000) *The Business of Borderless Education: UK Perspectives*, CVCP, London.

Craft, A. (1992) *Quality Assurance in Higher Education*, Proceedings of the International Conference held at Hong Kong in 1991, The Falmer Press, Bristol.

Craft, A. (1994) *International Developments in Assuring Quality in Higher Education*, Proceedings of the International Conference held at Montreal in 1993, The Falmer Press, Bristol.

Crow, S.D. (1988) *International Education and Institutional Accreditation, NCA Quarterly*, Commission on Institutions of Higher Education, North Central Association for Colleges and Schools, Chicago, 63(2), pp.379-387.

Crow, S.D. (1994 & 1995) *Distance Learning: Challenges for Institutional Accreditation, NCA Quarterly*, Commission on Institutions of Higher Education, North Central Association for Colleges and Schools, Chicago, 69(2&3), pp.354-358.

De Wit, H. (1999) *Changing Rationales for Internationalization of Higher Education, International Higher Education*, 15, pp. 2-3.

Department of Education, Training and Youth Affairs (DETYA) (2000), *The Australian Higher Education Quality Assurance Framework*, DETYA, Canberra.

Desai, A.S. (1999) *Community Colleges*, Inaugural Address at the Seminar on Community Colleges, Avinashilingam Institute for Home Science and Higher Education for Women (AIHSHEW), Coimbatore.

Dill, D.D., Massey, W.F., William, P.R. and Cook, C.M. (1996) *Accreditation and Academic Assurance: Can we get there from here? Change*, 28 (5), pp.16-24.

Distance Education and Training Council (DETC) (1998) *Distance Education Survey*, DETC, Washington DC.

Distance Education and Training Council (DETC) (2001a) *Accreditation Handbook: Policies, Procedures, and Standards of the Accrediting Commission of the DETC*, DETC, Washington DC.

Distance Education and Training Council (DETC) (2001b) *DETC Accreditation: Overview*, DETC, Washington DC.

Draft Position Paper on World Quality Register, Discussion Paper by the Board of INQAAHE, unpublished, 2003.

Draft Principles of Good Practice for an EQA Agency, Discussion Paper by the INQAAHE Working Group, unpublished, 2003.

Eaton, J.S. (1999) *Letter from the President*, CHEA Newsletter dated 16th July 1999, online www.chea.org.

Eaton, J.S. (2001a) *Core Academic Values, Quality, and Regional Accreditation: The Challenge of Distance Learning*, Council for Higher Education Accreditation, Washington DC.

Eaton, J.S. (2001b) *Distance Learning: Academic and Political Challenges for Higher Education Accreditation*, CHEA Monograph Series No.1, Council for Higher Education Accreditation, Washington DC.

Eaton, J.S. (2001c) *Taking a Look at Ourselves: Accreditation*, Fifth CHEA Conference on Enhancing Usefulness, online www.chea.org.

Eaton, J.S. (2002) *Do We Need an International Confederation for Quality Review of Higher Education*, Paper presented in the UNESCO meet held at Lisbon, April 2002.

Ewell, P.T. (1998) *Examining a Brave New World: How Accreditation Might be Different*, National Center for Higher Education Management Systems (NCHEMS), Washington DC.

Frazer, M. (1996) *Recognition: The Role of Quality Assessment Agencies, Higher Education in Europe*, 30(4).

Glidden, R. (1996) *Policy Issues for the 21st Century: Accreditation at a Crossroads, Educational Record*, Fall, pp.22-24.

Glidden, R. (1998) *The Contemporary Context of Accreditation: Challenges in a Changing Environment*, Keynote address for the CHEA Usefulness Conference, online www.chea.org.

Global Alliance for Transnational Education (GATE) (1999) *Certification Manual: Assuring the Quality of Education and Training which cross National Borders*, GATE, Washington DC.

Gnanam, A. (1999) *Quality Assurance*, Discussion Paper, South Zone Vice-Chancellors' Meet, Pondicherry.

Gnanam, A. and Stella, A. (1998) *Relevance of National Assessment and Accreditation Council in the Indian Context, University News*, Association of Indian Universities, New Delhi, 36(51), pp.1-10.

Gnanam, A. and Stella, A. (1999), *Emerging Trends in Higher Education and Their Implications for Future, Journal of Educational Planning and Administration*, National Institute for Educational Planning and Administration, New Delhi, 13(2), pp.187-197.

Gordon, G. (1993) *Quality Assurance in Higher Education: Progress Achieved and Issues to be Addressed, Quality Assurance in Education,* 1(3), pp.15-20.

Government of India (GoI) (1986) *National Policy on Education - 1986,* GoI, New Delhi.

Government of India (GoI) (1992a) *National Policy on Education* (with modifications undertaken in 1992), Ministry of Human Resource Development, GoI, New Delhi.

Government of India (GoI) (1992b) *Programme of Action - 1986,* GoI, New Delhi.

Government of India (GoI) (1995) *Budgetary Resources for Education (1951-52 - 1993-94),* MHRD, GoI, New Delhi.

Green, D. (Ed.) (1993) *What is Quality in Higher Education?* Open University Press, London.

Hamalaonen, K. et.al. (2001) *Institutional Evaluations in Europe,* Workshop Report of European Network for Quality Assurance in Higher Education (ENQA), Helsinki.

Harman, G. (1998) *The Management of Quality Assurance: A Review of International Practice, Higher Education Quarterly,* 52 (4), pp.345-364.

Harvey, L. (1997) *Quality Monitoring and Transformative Learning: Changing International Trends and Future Directions,* Paper presented in the INQAAHE-1997 conference held at South Africa, 24-28 May, 1997.

Higher Education Funding Council of England (HEFCE) (1998) *About the HEFCE: An Introduction to the Work of the Higher Education Funding Council for England,* HEFCE, UK.

Higher Education Quality Council (HEQC) (1996) *Code of Practice for Overseas Collaborative Provision in Higher Education,* HEQC, London.

Hirsch, D. (2001) *E-learning in Post-secondary Education,* Report of the OECD Seminar on E-learning, Japan.

Horton, B.J. (1999) *Confidentiality Vs Public Disclosure of Information, ASPA News,* July 1999 issue, online *www.aspa-usa.org.*

Imrie, B. (1998) *Professional Development is Quality Assurance: Now and Zen, Quality in Higher Education,* 4(3).

Institute for Higher Education Policy (IHEP) (1999) *What's the Difference? A Review of Contemporary Research on the Effectiveness of Distance Learning in Higher Education*, IHEP, Washington DC.

Institute for Higher Education Policy (IHEP) (2000) *Quality On-the-Line: Benchmarks for Success in Internet-based Distance Education*, IHEP, Washington DC.

Jones, D.R. and Pritchard, A.L. (2000) *The Distance Education Debate: The Australian View, Change*, Nov-Dec 2000, pp.32-33.

Joshi, M.M. (1998) *Higher Education in India: Vision and Action*, UNESCO World Conference on Higher Education in the 21st Century, 5-9 October 1998, Paris, *www.education.nic.in/htmlweb/unhighedu.htm*.

Kells, K.R. (1996) *Self-study Process*, American Council on Education and MacMillan Publishing Company, USA.

Khan, A.W. (1999) *Quality Assurance in Distance Education*, In *Quality Assurance in Distance Education*, Powar K B and Bhalla V (Eds.) (1999), Association of Indian Universities, New Delhi.

Knight, J. (2002) *Trade in Higher Education Services: The Implications of GATS*, The Observatory on Borderless Higher Education, London.

Knight, J. and Hans de Wit (1999) *An Introduction to the IQRP Project and Process*, In *Quality and Internationalization in Higher Education*, Imhe Publication.

Lemaitre, M. J. and Raczynski, D. (2001) *Stakeholders in Higher Education: How to Deal with Complexity?* Paper presented in the INQAAHE-2001 conference on Quality, Standards and Recognition, March 21st-24th, 2002, India.

Lenn, M.P. (1996) *The Globalisation of the Professions and Higher Education: Trade Agreements, New Technologies and the Quality Imperative, Higher Education in Europe*, 21 (4), pp.89-96.

Lenn, M.P. (2000) *A Guide to Accreditation and Higher Education*, World Bank and Center for Quality Assurance in International Education (CQAIE), Washington DC.

Lenn, M.P. (2002) *The Right Way to Export Higher Education, The Chronicle of Higher Education*, March 1, 2002.

Lenn, M.P. (Ed.) (1988) *Site Visitors in the Accreditation Process: A Guide to Issues and Practical Concerns*, Council on Post-secondary Accreditation, Washington DC.

Lenn, M.P. (Ed.) (1990) *Law, Lawyers and Accreditation: A Bewildering Relationship*, Council on Post Secondary Accreditation, Washington DC.

Lenn, M.P. (Ed.) (1991a) *Conflicts of Interest and the Accreditation Process*, Professional Development Series, Council on Post Secondary Accreditation, Washington DC.

Lenn, M.P. (Ed.) (1991b) *Distance Learning and Accreditation*, Professional Development Series, Council on Post Secondary Accreditation, Washington DC.

Lenn, M.P. and Lenn J (1990) *Ethics and Educational Assessment* in *Ethics and Higher Education* edited by Massey F William, Macmillan Publishing Company, USA.

Lim, D. (2001) *Quality Assurance in Higher Education: A Study of Developing Countries*

Liston, C. (1999) *Managing Quality and Standards*, Oxford University Press, London.

Mallea, J. (1998), *International Trade in Professional and Educational Services: Implications for the Professions and Higher Education* , OECD-CERI Paris, [http://www.oecd.org/els/papers/papers.htm].

Massaro, V. (1996) *Institutional Responses to Quality Assessment: Developing Diversity, Journal of Higher Education Policy and Management*, 18(1).

Meade, P. and Woodhouse, D. (2000) *Evaluating the Effectiveness of the New Zealand Academic Audit Unit: Review and Outcomes, Quality in Higher Education*, 6(1).

Middle States Association of Colleges and Schools (MSACS) (1995) *What is Accreditation?* MSACS, Philadelphia.

Middle States Association of Colleges and Schools (MSACS) (1997) *Guidelines for Distance Learning Programs*, MSACS, Philadelphia.

Middle States Association of Colleges and Schools (MSACS) (2001) *Substantive Changes Get Speedier Review, CHE Letter*, Fall 2001, MSACS, Philadelphia.

Middle States Commission on Higher Education (MSCHE) (2000) *Characteristics of Excellence in Higher Education*, MSCHE, Philadelphia.

Ministry of Human Resource Development (MHRD) (1999) Discussion Paper on *Internationalization of Education*, Department of Education, MHRD, Government of India, New Delhi.

Nair, S. (1990) *Action Plan cum Project Report for Setting up the National Accreditation Board for Higher Education (NABHE)*, Project document submitted to University Grants Commission, New Delhi.

National Assessment and Accreditation Council (NAAC) (2000) *Memorandum of Association and Rules of NAAC*, NAAC, Bangalore.

National Assessment and Accreditation Council (NAAC) and Distance Education Council (DEC) (2001) *Institutional Accreditation: Manual for Self Study for Distance Education Units*, NAAC, Bangalore.

National Assessment and Accreditation Council (NAAC) (2001) *Frequently Asked Questions and Answers on Assessment and Accreditation*, NAAC, Bangalore.

National Assessment and Accreditation Council (NAAC) (2002a) *Institutional Accreditation: Manual for Self Study for Universities*, NAAC, Bangalore.

National Assessment and Accreditation Council (NAAC) (2002b) *Institutional Accreditation: Manual for Self Study for Affiliated/ Constituent Colleges*, NAAC, Bangalore.

National Assessment and Accreditation Council (NAAC) (2002c) *Institutional Accreditation: Manual for Self Study for Autonomous Colleges*, NAAC, Bangalore.

National Assessment and Accreditation Council (NAAC) and National Council of Teacher Education (NCTE) (2002d) *Institutional Accreditation: Manual for Self Study for Teacher Education Institutions*, NAAC, Bangalore.

National Assessment and Accreditation Council (NAAC) (2003) *A Profile*, NAAC, Bangalore.

National Informatics Centre (2001) *Educational Statistics*, online *www.education.nic.in*.

National Policy Board on Higher Education Institutional Accreditation (1994) *Independence, Accreditation, and the Public interest*, Special report on accreditation, Washington DC.

New England Association of Schools and Colleges (1996) *Evaluation Manual*, Commission on Institutions of Higher Education, Bedford, USA.

Nigavekar, A.S. (1996) *Quest for Quality*, National Assessment and Accreditation Council, Bangalore.

Nigavekar, A.S. (2001) *GATS and Higher Education: What is at Stake for India*, Paper circulated at a National Level Meeting on 'Trade in Education Services under WTO Regime', NIEPA, New Delhi (unpublished).

Nilsson, K.A. and Wahlen, S. (2000) *Institutional Response to the Swedish Model of Quality Assurance, Quality in Higher Education*, 6(1).

North Central Association of Colleges and Schools (NCACS) (1995) *Accreditation of Higher Education Institutions: An Overview*, NCACS, Chicago.

Oblinger, D.G., Barone, A.A. and Hawkins, B.L. (2001) *Distributed Education and its Challenges: An Overview*, American Council on Education, Washington DC.

OECD-IMHE (1999) *Quality and Internationalisation in Higher Education*, OECD, Paris.

O'Neil, M. and Pennington, G. (1994) *Enhancing the Quality of Teaching and Learning in Higher Education, Quality Assurance in Education*, 2(3), pp.13-18.

Ontario Council on Graduate Studies (OCGS) (1996) *The Appraisals Process in Ontario*, OCGS, Toronto.

Papers presented in the INQAAHE-1999 Conference on *Framework for Quality: Evaluating Evaluation*, Santiago, Chile, 1999.

Petersen, J. (1999) *Internationalizing Quality Assurance in Higher Education*, Council for Higher Education Accreditation (CHEA), Washington DC.

Phipps, R. (1999) *What's the Difference? A Review of Contemporary Research on the Effectiveness of Distance Learning in Higher Education*, The Institute for Higher Education Policy, Washington DC.

Phipps, R.A., Wellman, J.V. and Merisotis, J.P. (1998) *Assuring Quality in Distance Learning: A Preliminary Review*, Council for Higher Education Accreditation and The Institute for Higher Education

Policy, Washington DC.

Powar, K.B. (1996) *Accreditation in Higher Education: An Indian Perspective*, Viva Books Private Limited, New Delhi.

Powar, K.B. (2000) *Reforms and Innovations in India: The Relevance and Role of Research*, Occasional Paper 2000/1, Association of Indian Universities, New Delhi.

Powar, K.B. (2001) *Addressing the Issues of Access and Equity in Indian Higher Education through Distance Education*, Association of Indian Universities, Occasional Paper 2001/3, Association of Indian Universities, New Delhi.

Powar, K.B. (2002) *WTO, GATS and Higher Education: An Indian Perspective*, Occasional Paper 2002/1, Association of Indian Universities, New Delhi.

Powar, K.B. and Bhalla, V. (2000) *International Students in Indian Universities*, Status Report, 2000/2, Association of Indian Universities, New Delhi.

Powar, K.B. (2001) (Ed.) *Higher Education for Human Development in the 21st Century*, Association of Indian Universities, New Delhi.

Powar, K.B. (2002) (Ed.) *Internationalization of Higher Education*, Association of Indian Universities, New Delhi.

Powar, K.B. and Bhalla, V. (1999) (Eds.) *Quality Assurance in Distance Education*, Association of Indian Universities, New Delhi.

Powar, K.B. et al (Eds.) (2000) *Performance Indicators in Distance Higher Education*, Aravali Books International Private Ltd, New Delhi.

Quality Assurance Agency (QAA) (1999) *Code of Practice in Collaborative Provision*, QAA, UK.

Quality Assurance Agency (QAA) (1998) *Quality Audit Reports*, QAA, UK.

Report of the CABE Committee on Policy (1992) Ministry of Human Resource Development, Government of India, New Delhi.

Report of the Committee on Review of National Policy on Education 1986 (1990) Ministry of Human Resource Development, Government of India, New Delhi.

Report of the Workshop on National Qualifications Framework (2000) National Institute of Educational Planning and Administration, New Delhi, 25-26 July 2000.

Report of the UGC Committee on NAAC's Policies and Procedures (2001) Unpublished.

Salmi, J. (2000) *Tertiary Education in the Twenty First Century: Challenges and Opportunities*, World Bank, Washington DC.

Scott, P. (Ed). (1998) *The Globalisation of Higher Education*, Open University Press and Society for Research in Higher Education, Buckingham.

Sharma, G.D. (2000) *Trade in Education Service Under WTO Regime-An Indian Response*, Paper Circulated at a National Meeting on 'Trade in Education Services under WTO Regime', National Institute for Educational Planning and Administration (NIEPA), New Delhi (unpublished).

Singh, M. (2002) *International Quality Assurance, Ethics and the Market: A View from a Developing Country*, Paper presented in the CHEA International Seminar III, January 24 2002, San Francisco.

Southern Association of Colleges and Schools (SACS) (1996) *Resource Manual on Institutional Effectiveness*, The Commission on Colleges of the SACS, USA.

Stella, A. (1999a) *A Strategy for Internal Quality Enhancement, University News*, 37(30), pp.1-4.

Stella, A. (1999b) *Performance Indicators in Quality Assessment: Where do we Draw the Line? University News*, 37(38), pp.1-4.

Stella, A. (1999c) *Quality Assurance in Higher Education: Long Term Strategy or One-Shot Change? College News*, Association of Indian College Principals, December issue, pp.10-12.

Stella, A. (2000) *Ensuring Objectivity in Assessment, University News*, 38(6), pp.77-81.

Stella, A. (2001a) *Impact of Assessment and Accreditation on Institutions of Higher Education, University News*, 39(15), pp.1-4.

Stella, A. (2001b) *Quality Assessment in Indian Higher Education: Issues of Impact and Future Perspectives*, Allied Publishers, Bangalore.

Stella, A. and Gnanam, A. (2001a) *Institutional Response to Quality Assessment: From Rejection to Appreciation, QA*, January issue, pp.6-9.

Stella, A. and Gnanam, A. (2001b) *Resistance to External Quality Assessment: An Analysis, University News*, 39(19), pp.1-4.

Stella, A. and Gnanam, A. (2001c) *Institutional Accreditation by NAAC: Scores and Stars, University News*, 39(36), pp.50 – 59.

Stella, A. and Gnanam, A. (2001d) *Assessment and Accreditation in Indian Higher Education: Issues of Policy and Prospects*, Books Plus, New Delhi.

Stella, A. (2002a) *Challenging Post-accreditation Complacency, University News*, 40(27), pp.5-11.

Stella, A. (2002b) *Exploring the Advisory Role of NAAC: Analysis of Assessment Reports to Advise the Stakeholders, Experiments in Education*, October 2002, pp.184-190.

Stella, A. and Gnanam, A. (2002a) *Renewal of Accreditation: Next Cycle of Assessment or Re accreditation? University News*, 40(42), pp.1-6.

Stella, A. and Gnanam, A. (2002b) *Assuring Quality and Standards in Higher Education: The Contemporary Context and Concerns*, Allied Publishers, Bangalore.

Stella, A. (2003a) *Research on Institutional Effectiveness: An Agenda for the Internal Quality Assurance Cell (IQAC), University News*, 40(52), pp.1-5.

The European Network for Quality Assurance in Higher Education, *Newsletter*, No.7 April 2002.

Theme paper on NAAC, All India Vice-chancellor's Conference, Pune, 1994.

Thompson, H. L. (1993) *Re-charting the Future of Accreditation, Educational Record*, 74 (4), pp.39-42.

Thompson, L. M. (1998) *New Challenges for Accreditation, Planning for Higher Education*, 27(Fall), pp.58-63.

Thune, C. (2000) *Evaluation of European Higher Education: A Status Report*, Occasional paper of European Network for Quality Assurance in Higher Education (ENQA), Helsinki.

Tilak, J. (1994) *Education for Development in Asia*, Sage Publications, New Delhi.

Tilak, J. (1995) *Privatisation of Higher Education in India: The Capitation Fee Colleges* in *Higher Education in India*, in *In Search of Quality* (Ed) Powar, K.B. and Panda, S. K., Association of Indian Universities, New Delhi.

Twigg, C. A. (2001) *Quality Assurance for Whom? Providers and Consumers in Today's Distributed Learning Environment*, Center for Academic Transformation, New York.

UNESCO (1995) *UNESCO Policy Paper for Change and Development in Higher Education*, UNESCO, Paris.

UNESCO (1996) *Learning: The Treasure Within*, Report of the International Commission on Education for the Twenty First Century (Delors Report), UNESCO, Paris.

UNESCO (1998) *Higher Education in the Twenty-first Century: Vision and Action – Final Report*, UNESCO, Paris.

University Grants Commission (UGC) (1987) *Concept Paper for Discussion: Report of the Committee on Accreditation and Assessment Council*, UGC, New Delhi.

University Grants Commission (UGC) (1990) *Report of the UGC Committee Towards New Educational Management*, UGC, New Delhi.

University Grants Commission (UGC) (1996) *Policy Frame and Programmes of the UGC: Proposals for the Development of Higher Education in the IX Five Year Plan*, submitted by the Working group on Higher Education, Planning Commission, UGC, New Delhi.

University Grants Commission (UGC) (1999) *Annual Report of the University Grants Commission 1998-99*, UGC, New Delhi.

University Grants Commission Act 1956 (as modified up to the 20th December 1985) and Rules and Regulations under the Act (1994) University Grants Commission, New Delhi.

Uvalic-Trumbic, S. (2001) *Introductory Remarks in the Expert Meeting on The Impact of Globalisation on Quality Assurance, Accreditation and the Recognition of Qualifications in Higher Education*, 10-11 September, 2001, Paris.

Van Damme, D. (2000) *Accreditation in Global Higher Education: The Need for International Information and Co-operation*, Memo for the Commission on Global Accreditation of the International Association of University Presidents.

Van Damme, D. (2001a) *Higher Education in the Age of Globalization*, Introductory paper presented at the UNESCO Expert Meeting, On the Impact of Globalization on Quality Assurance,

Accreditation and the Recognition of Qualifications in Higher Education, Paris.

Van Damme, D. (2001b) *Quality Issues in the Internationalisation of Higher Education, Higher Education*, 41, pp.415-441.

Van Damme, D. (2002) *Quality Assurance in an International Environment: National and International Interests and Tensions*, Paper presented in the CHEA International Seminar III, January 24, 2002, San Francisco.

Vlasceanu, L. and Wilson, L. (2000) *Transnational Education and Recognition of Qualifications*, UNESCO/CEPES, Bucharest.

Vroeijenstijn, A.I. (1999) *Towards a Quality Hallmark for Higher Education and Towards Mutual Recognition of Quality Assessment Agencies*, Proceedings of the INQAAHE conference held at Santiago.

Weening, L.R. (1994) *An Assessment of the Effectiveness of Regional Accreditation*, New England Association of Schools and Colleges, Commission on Institutions of Higher Education, Bedford.

Westerheijden, D.F. and Vught, F.A. van (1994) *Towards a General Model of Quality Assessment in Higher Education, Journal of Higher Education*, 28(3), pp.355-371.

Woodhouse, D. (1998) *Quality Assurance in Higher Education: The Next 25 years, Quality in Higher Education*, 4(3), pp.257-273.

Woodhouse, D. (1999) *Quality and Quality Assurance*, In *Quality and Internationalization in Higher Education*, imhe Publication.

Woodhouse, D. (2001) *Quality Assurance in Higher Education in the 21st Century*, Address at the Higher Education Quality Committee Inauguration, South Africa.

World Bank (1994) *Higher Education: The Lessons of Experience*, World Bank, Washington DC.

World Bank (2000) *Higher Education in Developing Countries: Peril and Promise*, World Bank, Washington DC.

www.aicte.ernet.in

www.aiuweb.org

www.aspa-usa.org

www.auqa.edu.au

www.chea.org

www.ed.gov

www.education.nic.in

www.enqa.net

www.gatsindiaeducation.org

www.hefce.ac.uk

www.hkcaa.edu.hk

www.ilt.org

www.inqaahe.nl

www.itsm.ac.uk

www.naac-india.com

www.nba-aicte.org

www.niepaonlines.org

www.oecd.org

www.qaa.ac.uk

www.relint.deusto.es/TUNINGProject/index.htm

www.tradeineducation.org

www.ugc.ac.in

www.unesco.org

www.worldbank.org

Yorke, M. (1993) *Quality Assurance for Education Franchising, Journal of Higher Education*, 26(2), pp.167-182.

Yorke, M. (1994) *Enhancement-led Higher Education? Quality Assurance in Education*, 2(3), pp.6-12.

Young, K.E., Chambers, C.M. and Kells, H.R. (Ed.) (1983) *Understanding Accreditation*, Jossey-Bass, San Francisco.

Index